LINEAR REGRESSION

THE SAGE QUANTITATIVE RESEARCH KIT

Beginning Quantitative Research by Malcolm Williams, Richard D. Wiggins, and the late W. Paul Vogt is the first volume in *The SAGE Quantitative Research Kit*. This book can be used together with the other titles in the *Kit* as a comprehensive guide to the process of doing quantitative research, but it is equally valuable on its own as a practical introduction to completing quantitative research.

Editors of The SAGE Quantitative Research Kit:

Malcolm Williams – *Cardiff University, UK*

Richard D. Wiggins – *UCL Social Research Institute, UK*

D. Betsy McCoach – *University of Connecticut, USA*

Founding editor:

The late W. Paul Vogt – *Illinois State University, USA*

LINEAR REGRESSION:
AN INTRODUCTION TO STATISTICAL MODELS

PETER MARTIN

$SAGE

Los Angeles | London | New Delhi
Singapore | Washington DC | Melbourne

THE SAGE QUANTITATIVE RESEARCH KIT

SAGE

Los Angeles | London | New Delhi
Singapore | Washington DC | Melbourne

SAGE Publications Ltd
1 Oliver's Yard
55 City Road
London EC1Y 1SP

SAGE Publications Inc.
2455 Teller Road
Thousand Oaks, California 91320

SAGE Publications India Pvt Ltd
B 1/I 1 Mohan Cooperative Industrial Area
Mathura Road
New Delhi 110 044

SAGE Publications Asia-Pacific Pte Ltd
3 Church Street
#10-04 Samsung Hub
Singapore 049483

Editor: Jai Seaman
Assistant editor: Charlotte Bush
Production editor: Manmeet Kaur Tura
Copyeditor: QuADS Prepress Pvt Ltd
Proofreader: Elaine Leek
Indexer: Cathryn Pritchard
Marketing manager: Susheel Gokarakonda
Cover design: Shaun Mercier
Typeset by: C&M Digitals (P) Ltd, Chennai, India
Printed in the UK

© Peter Martin 2021

This volume published as part of *The SAGE Quantitative Research Kit* (2021), edited by Malcolm Williams, Richard D. Wiggins and D. Betsy McCoach.

Apart from any fair dealing for the purposes of research, private study, or criticism or review, as permitted under the Copyright, Designs and Patents Act, 1988, this publication may not be reproduced, stored or transmitted in any form, or by any means, without the prior permission in writing of the publisher, or in the case of reprographic reproduction, in accordance with the terms of licences issued by the Copyright Licensing Agency. Enquiries concerning reproduction outside those terms should be sent to the publisher.

Library of Congress Control Number: 2020949998

British Library Cataloguing in Publication data

A catalogue record for this book is available from the British Library

ISBN 978-1-5264-2417-4

At SAGE we take sustainability seriously. Most of our products are printed in the UK using responsibly sourced papers and boards. When we print overseas we ensure sustainable papers are used as measured by the PREPS grading system. We undertake an annual audit to monitor our sustainability.

CONTENTS

List of Figures, Tables and Boxes	ix
About the Author	xv
Acknowledgements	xvii
Preface	xix

1 What Is a Statistical Model? — 1

    Kinds of Models: Visual, Deterministic and Statistical — 2
    Why Social Scientists Use Models — 3
    Linear and Non-Linear Relationships: Two Examples — 4
    First Approach to Models: The *t*-Test as a Comparison of Two Statistical Models — 6
        The Sceptic's Model (Null Hypothesis of the t-Test) — 8
        The Power Pose Model: Alternative Hypothesis of the t-Test — 9
        Using Data to Compare Two Models — 10
    The Signal and the Noise — 14

2 Simple Linear Regression — 17

    Origins of Regression: Francis Galton and the Inheritance of Height — 18
    The Regression Line — 21
    Regression Coefficients: Intercept and Slope — 23
    Errors of Prediction and Random Variation — 24
    The True and the Estimated Regression Line — 25
    Residuals — 26
    How to Estimate a Regression Line — 27
    How Well Does Our Model Explain the Data? The R^2 Statistic — 29
        Sums of Squares: Total, Regression and Residual — 29
        R^2 as a Measure of the Proportion of Variance Explained — 31
        R^2 as a Measure of the Proportional Reduction of Error — 31
        Interpreting R^2 — 32
        Final Remarks on the R^2 Statistic — 32
    Residual Standard Error — 33
    Interpreting Galton's Data and the Origin of 'Regression' — 33
    Inference: Confidence Intervals and Hypothesis Tests — 35

	Confidence Range for a Regression Line	39
	Prediction and Prediction Intervals	42
	Regression in Practice: Things That Can Go Wrong	44
	Influential Observations	45
	Selecting the Right Group	46
	The Dangers of Extrapolation	47
3	**Assumptions and Transformations**	**51**
	The Assumptions of Linear Regression	52
	Investigating Assumptions: Regression Diagnostics	54
	Errors and Residuals	54
	Standardised Residuals	55
	Regression Diagnostics: Application With Examples	56
	Normality	56
	Homoscedasticity and Linearity: The Spread-Level Plot	61
	Outliers and Influential Observations	64
	Independence of Errors	70
	What if Assumptions Do Not Hold? An Example	71
	A Non-Linear Relationship	71
	Model Diagnostics for the Linear Regression of Life Expectancy on GDP	73
	Transforming a Variable: Logarithmic Transformation of GDP	73
	Regression Diagnostics for the Linear Regression With Predictor Transformation	79
	Types of Transformations, and When to Use Them	79
	Common Transformations	80
	Techniques for Choosing an Appropriate Transformation	83
4	**Multiple Linear Regression: A Model for Multivariate Relationships**	**87**
	Confounders and Suppressors	88
	Spurious Relationships and Confounding Variables	88
	Masked Relationships and Suppressor Variables	91
	Multivariate Relationships: A Simple Example With Two Predictors	93
	Multiple Regression: General Definition	96
	Simple Examples of Multiple Regression Models	97
	Example 1: One Numeric Predictor, One Dichotomous Predictor	98
	Example 2: Multiple Regression With Two Numeric Predictors	107
	Research Example: Neighbourhood Cohesion and Mental Wellbeing	113

Dummy Variables for Representing Categorical Predictors		117
What Are Dummy Variables?		118
Research Example: Highest Qualification Coded Into Dummy Variables		118
Choice of Reference Category for Dummy Variables		122

5 Multiple Linear Regression: Inference, Assumptions and Standardisation — 125

Inference About Coefficients	126
Standard Errors of Coefficient Estimates	126
Confidence Interval for a Coefficient	128
Hypothesis Test for a Single Coefficient	128
Example Application of the t-Test for a Single Coefficient	129
Do We Need to Conduct a Hypothesis Test for Every Coefficient?	130
The Analysis of Variance Table and the *F*-Test of Model Fit	131
F-Test of Model Fit	132
Model Building and Model Comparison	135
Nested and Non-Nested Models	135
Comparing Nested Models: F-Test of Difference in Fit	137
Adjusted R^2 Statistic	139
Application of Adjusted R^2	140
Assumptions and Estimation Problems	141
Collinearity and Multicollinearity	141
Diagnosing Collinearity	142
Regression Diagnostics	144
Standardisation	148
Standardisation and Dummy Predictors	151
Standardisation and Interactions	151
Comparing Coefficients of Different Predictors	152
Some Final Comments on Standardisation	152

6 Where to Go From Here — 155

Regression Models for Non-Normal Error Distributions	156
Factorial Design Experiments: Analysis of Variance	157
Beyond Modelling the Mean: Quantile Regression	158
Identifying an Appropriate Transformation: Fractional Polynomials	158
Extreme Non-Linearity: Generalised Additive Models	159
Dependency in Data: Multilevel Models (Mixed Effects Models, Hierarchical Models)	159

Missing Values: Multiple Imputation and Other Methods	159
Bayesian Statistical Models	160
Causality	160
Measurement Models: Factor Analysis and Structural Equations	161
Glossary	163
References	171
Index	175

LIST OF FIGURES, TABLES AND BOXES

List of figures

1.1	Child wellbeing and income inequality in 25 countries	4
1.2	Gross domestic product (GDP) per capita and life expectancy in 134 countries (2007)	6
1.3	Hypothetical data from a power pose experiment	8
1.4	Illustrating two statistical models for the power pose experiment	8
1.5	Partition of a statistical model into a systematic and a random part	15
2.1	Scatter plot of parents' and children's heights	19
2.2	Galton's data with superimposed regression line	22
2.3	An illustration of the regression line, its intercept and slope	23
2.4	Illustration of residuals	27
2.5	Partition of the total outcome variation into explained and residual variation	30
2.6	Illustration of R^2 as a measure of model fit	31
2.7	Galton's regression line compared to the line of equal heights	34
2.8	Regression line with 95% confidence range for mean prediction	40
2.9	Regression line with 95% prediction intervals	43
2.10	Misleading regression lines resulting from influential observations	45
2.11	The relationship between GDP per capita and life expectancy, in two different selections from the same data set	46
2.12	Linear regression of life expectancy on GDP per capita in the 12 Asian countries with highest GDP, with extrapolation beyond the data range	48
2.13	Checking the extrapolation from Figure 2.12 by including the points for the 12 Asian countries with the lowest GDP per capita	48
3.1	Illustration of the assumptions of normality and homoscedasticity in Galton's regression	54
3.2	An illustration of the normal distribution	57
3.3	Histogram of standardised residuals from Galton's regression, with a superimposed normal curve	58
3.4	Histograms of standardised residuals illustrating six distribution shapes	59

3.5	Normal q–q plot of standardised residuals from Galton's regression	60
3.6	Normal q–q plots of standardised residuals for six distribution shapes	61
3.7	Spread-level plot: standardised residuals and regression predicted values from Galton's regression	62
3.8	Spread-level plots and scatter plots for four simulated data sets	63
3.9	Illustration of a standard normal distribution, with conventional critical values	65
3.10	Observations with the largest Cook's distances from Galton's regression	68
3.11	Galton's regression data with four hypothetical influential observations	69
3.12	Life expectancy by GDP per capita in 88 countries	71
3.13	Diagnostic plots for the linear regression of life expectancy on GDP per capita	73
3.14	Life expectancy and GDP per capita – illustrating a linear regression on the logarithmic scale	76
3.15	The curvilinear relationship between life expectancy and GDP per capita	78
3.16	Diagnostic plots for the linear regression of life expectancy on $\log_2(GDP)$	79
3.17	The shape of the relationship between Y and X in three common transformations, with positive slope coefficient (top row) and negative slope coefficient (bottom row)	81
4.1	A hypothetical scatter plot of two apparently correlated variables	89
4.2	Illustration of a confounder causing a spurious association between X and Y	90
4.3	A hypothetical scatter plot of two apparently unrelated variables	91
4.4	Illustration of a suppressor variable masking the true relationship between X and Y	91
4.5	Five hypothetical data sets illustrating possible models for Mental Wellbeing predicted by Social Participation and Limiting Illness	94
4.6	The distributions of Mental Wellbeing, Social Participation and Limiting Illness	98
4.7	Scatter plot of Mental Wellbeing by Social Participation, grouped by Limiting Illness	100
4.8	Mental Wellbeing, Social Participation and Limiting Illness: an illustration of five possible models for the National Child Development Study data	101
4.9	Distributions of Neighbourhood Cohesion and Social Support scales	108

4.10	Three-dimensional representation of the relationship between Mental Wellbeing, Neighbourhood Cohesion and Social Support	110
4.11	Three regression lines for the prediction of Mental Wellbeing by Neighbourhood Cohesion, for different values of Social Support	111
4.12	Three regression lines for the prediction of Mental Wellbeing by Neighbourhood Cohesion, Social Support and their interaction	113
4.13	Comparing predictions of Mental Wellbeing from the unadjusted and adjusted models (Models 4.1 and 4.2)	116
4.14	Distribution of 'Highest Qualification'	119
5.1	Fisher distribution with $df_1 = 5$ and $df_2 = 7597$, with critical region	133
5.2	Normal q–q plot for standardised residuals from Model 5.3	145
5.3	Spread-level plot of standardised residuals against predicted values from Model 5.3	145

List of tables

1.1	Testosterone change from a power pose experiment (hypothetical data)	11
2.1	Extract from Galton's data on heights in 928 families	19
2.2	A typical regression results table (based on Galton's data)	38
3.1	The largest positive and negative standardised residuals from Galton's regression	66
3.2	Estimates from a simple linear regression of life expectancy on GDP per capita	72
3.3	Logarithms for bases 2, 10 and Euler's number e	75
3.4	Calculating the base-2 logarithm for a selection of GDP per capita values	75
3.5	Raw and log-transformed GDP per capita values for six countries	76
3.6	Estimates from a simple linear regression of life expectancy on $\log_2(GDP)$	77
4.1	Coefficient estimates for five models predicting Mental Wellbeing	101
4.2	Coefficient estimates from a regression of Mental Wellbeing on Neighbourhood Cohesion and Social Support	109
4.3	Coefficient estimates for the prediction of Mental Wellbeing by Neighbourhood Cohesion, Social Support and their interaction	112

4.4	Coefficient estimates, standard errors and confidence intervals for two regression models predicting Mental Wellbeing	115
4.5	A scheme for coding a categorical variable with three categories into two dummy variables	118
4.6	A scheme to represent Highest Qualification by five dummy variables	120
4.7	Hypothetical data set with five dummy variables representing the categorical variable Highest Qualification	120
4.8	Estimates from a linear regression predicting Mental Wellbeing, with dummy variables representing Highest Qualification (Model 4.3)	122
5.1	Coefficient estimates, standard errors and confidence intervals for a multiple regression predicting Mental Wellbeing (Model 5.1)	127
5.2	Estimated coefficients for a regression of Mental Wellbeing on four predictors and two interactions (Model 5.2)	130
5.3	Analysis of variance table for linear regression	132
5.4	Analysis of variance table for a multiple regression predicting Mental Wellbeing (Model 5.1)	134
5.5	Model comparison of Models 5.1 and 5.3	138
5.6	Analysis of variance table for Models 5.1 and 5.3	140
5.7	Multicollinearity diagnostics for Model 5.3	143
5.8	The largest standardised residuals from Model 5.3	146
5.9	Estimates from a linear regression predicting Mental Wellbeing (Model 5.3)	149
5.10	Unstandardised and standardised coefficient estimates from Model 5.3	151

List of boxes

2.1	Types of Variables	18
2.2	Galton and Eugenics	20
2.3	Various Names for the Variables Involved in a Regression Model	21
2.4	Finding the Slope and the Intercept for a Regression Line	28
2.5	How to Calculate a Confidence Range Around the Regression Line	40
2.6	How to Calculate a Prediction Interval	43
3.1	The Normal Distribution and the Standard Normal Distribution	56
3.2	Regression Diagnostics and Uncertainty	59
3.3	Further Properties of the Normal Distribution	64
3.4	Logarithms	74

4.1	Variables From the National Child Development Study Used in Example 1	99
4.2	Interactions in Regression Models	104
4.3	Measurement of Neighbourhood Cohesion and Social Support in the NCDS	108
5.1	Nested and Non-Nested Models	136

ABOUT THE AUTHOR

Peter Martin is Lecturer in Applied Statistics at University College London. He has taught statistics to students of sociology, psychology, epidemiology and other disciplines since 2003. One of the joys of being a statistician is that it opens doors to research collaborations with many people in diverse fields. Dr Martin has been involved in investigations in life course research, survey methodology and the analysis of racism. In recent years, his research has focused on health inequalities, psychotherapy and the evaluation of healthcare services. He has a particular interest in topics around mental health care.

ACKNOWLEDGEMENTS

Thanks to Richard D. Wiggins, Malcolm Williams and D. Betsy McCoach for inviting me to write this book. To Amy Macdougall, Andy Ross, D. Betsy McCoach, Kalia Cleridou, Praveetha Patalay and Richard D. Wiggins for generously providing feedback on draft chapters. To the team at Sage for editorial support. To Brian Castellani for suggesting a vital phrase. To my colleagues for giving me time. To the staff of several East London cafés for space and warmth. To everyone I ever taught statistics for helping me learn. To Richard D. Wiggins for generous advice and encouragement over many years. To Pippa Hembry for being there.

Thanks also to

- The UNICEF MICS team for permission to use data from their archive (https://mics.unicef.org).
- The Gapminder Foundation for making available data on life expectancy and GDP from around the world.
- The UK Data Archive for permission to use data from the National Child Development Study.

The data analyses reported in this book were conducted using the R Software for Statistical Computing (R Core Team, 2019) with the RStudio environment (RStudio Team, 2016). All graphs were made in R, in most cases using the package ggplot2. Other R packages used in the making of this book are catspec, gapminder, ggrepel, grid, knitr, MASS, plyr, psych, reshape2, scales, scatterplot3d, tidyverse.

PREFACE

This is a book about statistical models as they are used in the social sciences. It gives a first course in the type of models commonly referred to as linear regression models. At the same time, it introduces many general principles of statistical modelling, which are important for understanding more advanced methods.

Statistical models are useful when we have, or aim to collect, data about social phenomena and wish to understand how different phenomena relate to one another. Examples in this book are based on real social science research studies that have investigated questions about:

- *Sociology of community:* Do neighbourhoods with a more cohesive community spirit foster mental wellbeing for local people?
- *Demography and economics:* Is it necessary for a country to get richer and richer to increase the health of its population?
- *Inequality and wellbeing:* Is a country's income inequality related to the wellbeing of its children?
- *Psychology:* Can some people increase their feelings of confidence by assuming certain 'power poses'?

This book won't give conclusive answers to these questions. But it does introduce some of the analytical methods that have been used to address them, and other questions like them. Specifically, this book looks at linear regression, which is a method for analysing continuous variables, such as a person's height, a child's score on a measure of self-rated depression or a country's average life expectancy. Other types of outcome variables, such as categorical and count variables, are covered in *The SAGE Quantitative Research Kit*, Volume 8.

Realistic data sets

The examples in this book are based on published social science studies, and most analyses shown use the original data on which these source studies were conducted, or subsets thereof. Since the statistical analysis uses realistic data, the results reported are sometimes ambiguous, which is to say: what conclusions we should draw from the analysis may remain debatable. This highlights an important point about statistical models: in themselves, statistical models do not give you the answers to your research questions. What statistical analysis does provide is a principled way to derive evidence from data. This evidence is important, and you can use it in your argument for or against a certain conclusion. But all statistical results need to be interpreted to be meaningful.

Prior knowledge useful for understanding this book

This book is intended for those who have a thorough grounding in descriptive statistics, as well as in the fundamentals of inferential statistics. I assume throughout that you understand what I mean when I speak of means, standard deviations, percentiles, histograms, and scatter plots, and that you know the basic ideas underlying a t-test, a z-test and a confidence interval. Finally, I assume that you are familiar with some of the ways social science data are collected or obtained – surveys, experiments, administrative data sources, and so forth – and that you understand that all these methods have strengths and weaknesses that affect the conclusions we can draw from any analysis of the data. An excellent way to acquire the knowledge required to benefit from this book is to study Volumes 1 to 6 of *The SAGE Quantitative Research Kit*.

Mathematics: equations, calculations, Greek symbols

This book is intended for social scientists and students of social science who wish to understand statistical modelling from a practical perspective. Statistical models are based on elaborate and advanced mathematical methods, but knowledge of advanced mathematics is not needed to understand this book.

Nonetheless, this book does require you, and possibly challenges you, to learn to recognise the essential equations that define statistical models, and to gain an intuitive understanding of how they work. I believe that this is a valuable skill to have. For example, it's important to recognise the difference between the sort of equation that defines a straight line and another sort that defines a curve. As you will see, this is essential for the ability to choose an appropriate model for a given research question and data set. Attempts at using statistical models without *any* mathematical understanding carry a high risk of producing nonsensical and misleading results.

So there will be equations. There will be Greek symbols. But there will be careful explanations of them all, along with graphs and illustrations to illuminate the maths. Think of the maths as a language that it's useful to get a working understanding of. Suppose you decide to live in a foreign country for a while, and that you don't yet know the main language spoken in this country. Suppose further that enough people in that country understand and speak your own language, so that most of the time you can get by using a language you are familiar with. Nonetheless, you will understand more about the country if you learn a little bit of its language. Even if you don't aspire to ever speak it fluently, or write poetry in it, you may learn enough of it to enable you to understand a newspaper headline, read the menu in a restaurant and have a good guess what the native speakers at the next table are talking about. In a similar way, you don't need to become an expert mathematician to understand a little bit of the mathematical aspect of statistical modelling, and to use this understanding to your advantage. So what's needed to benefit from this book is not so much mathematical skill, but rather an openness to considering the language of mathematics as an aid to understanding the underlying logic of statistical modelling.

Software

This book is software-neutral. It can be read and understood without using any statistical software. On the other hand, what you learn here can be applied using any statistical software that can estimate regression models. In writing this book, I used the free open-source software R (R Core Team, 2019). Other statistical packages often used by social scientists for linear regression models are Stata, SPSS and SAS.

Web support pages with worked examples

It is generally a good idea to learn statistics by doing it – that is, to work with data sets and statistical software and play around with fitting statistical models to the data. To help with this, the support website for this book supplies data sets for most of the examples used in this book and gives worked examples of the analyses.

The support website is written in the R software. R has the advantage that it can be downloaded free of charge, and that it has a growing community of users who write new add-on packages to extend its capability, publish tutorials, and exchange tips and tricks online. However, if you prefer to use a different software, or if you are required to learn a different software for a course you are attending, you can download the data sets from the support website and read them into your software of choice. Instructions for this, as well as instructions on how to download R for free, are given on the support website. Head to: *https://study.sagepub.com/quantitativekit*

References

R Core Team. (n.d.). *R: A language and environment for statistical computing*. R Foundation for Statistical Computing. www.R-project.org

RStudio Team. (2016). *RStudio: Integrated development for R*. RStudio. www.rstudio.com

1
WHAT IS A STATISTICAL MODEL?

Chapter Overview

Kinds of models: visual, deterministic and statistical 2
Why social scientists use models 3
Linear and non-linear relationships: two examples 4
First approach to models: the *t*-test as a comparison of two
statistical models 6
The signal and the noise 14

What is a statistical model? This chapter gives a first introduction. We start by considering the concept of a 'model' in areas other than statistics. I then give some examples of how statistical models are applied in the social sciences. Finally, we see how a simple parametric statistical hypothesis test, the *t*-test for independent samples, can be understood as a systematic comparison of two statistical models. An important aim of this chapter is to convey the notion that statistical models can be used to investigate how well a theory fits the data. In other words, statistical models help us to systematically evaluate the evidence for or against certain hypotheses we might have about the social world.

Kinds of models: visual, deterministic and statistical

Models are simplified representations of systems, objects or theories that allow us to understand things better. An architect builds a model house to help herself and her clients imagine how the real house will look once it is built. The Paris metro map is a model that helps passengers understand where they can catch a train, where they can travel to and where they can change trains.

Some models come in the form of mathematical equations. For example, consider an engineer who wants to design a submarine. The deeper the submarine dives, the higher the water pressure is going to be. The engineer needs to account for this lest the walls of his submarine crack and get crushed. As you may know, pressure is measured in a unit called bar, and the air pressure at sea level is equal to 1 bar. A mathematical model of the pressure experienced by a submarine under the surface of the sea is as follows:

$$\text{Pressure} = 1\,\text{bar} + 0.1\,\text{bar} \times \text{depth}$$

where depth is measured in metres. This equation expresses the insight that, with every metre that the submarine dives deeper, the water pressure increases by 0.1 bar. Using this model, we can calculate that the pressure at 100 m depth will be

$$\text{Pressure} = 1\,\text{bar} + 0.1\,\text{bar} \times 100 = 11\,\text{bar}$$

Thus, if your job is to build a submarine that can dive to 100 m, you know you need to build it so that its walls can withstand 11 bars of pressure (i.e. 11 times the pressure at sea level).

Statistical models also are expressed in the form of equations. As you will see, a simple statistical model looks very similar to the mathematical model we just considered. The difference between the two is how they deal with the differences between what the model predicts about reality and observations from reality itself. The engineer who uses the mathematical model of pressure might be happy to ignore small differences between the model and reality. The pressure at 100 m is taken to be 11 bar. If it is really 10.997 bar or 11.029 bar, so what? The approximation is good enough for the engineer's purposes. Such a model is called *deterministic*, because according to the model, the depth determines the pressure precisely.

In contrast, statistical models are used in situations where there is considerable *uncertainty* about how accurate the model predictions are. This is almost always the case in social science, because humans, and the societies they build, are complex, complicated, and not predictable as precisely as some natural phenomena, such as the relationship between depth and water pressure.

All models are simplifications of reality. The architect's model house lacks many details. The Paris metro map does not accurately represent the distances between the stations. Our (simplistic) mathematical model of underwater pressure ignores that pressure at the same depth will not be the same everywhere the submarine goes (e.g. because the waters of different oceans vary in salinity). Whether these imprecisions matter depends on the purpose of the model. The Paris metro map is useful for travellers but not detailed enough for an engineer who wishes to extend the existing tunnels to accommodate a new metro line. In the same way, a statistical model may be good for one purpose but useless for another.

Why social scientists use models

Social scientists use statistical models to investigate relationships between social phenomena, such as:

- *Diet and longevity:* Is what you eat associated with how long you can expect to live?
- *Unemployment and health:* Is unemployment associated with poorer health?
- *Inequality and crime:* Do countries with a wide income gap between the highest and the lowest earners have higher crime rates than more equal countries?

Of course, descriptive statistics provide important evidence for social research. Tables and graphs, means and standard deviations, correlation coefficients and comparisons of groups – all these are important tools of analysis. But statistical models go beyond description in important ways:

- Models can serve as formalisations of theories about the social world. By comparing how well two models fit a given set of data, we can rigorously assess which of two competing theories is more consistent with empirical observations.
- Statistical models provide rigorous procedures for telling the signal from the noise: for deciding whether a pattern we see in a table or a graph can be considered evidence for a real **effect**, relationship, or regularity in the social world.

- We can also use statistical models to develop specific predictions that we can test in a new data set.
- Finally, statistical models allow us to investigate the influences of several variables on one or several others simultaneously.

Linear and non-linear relationships: two examples

So what sort of things do we use statistical models for? Have a look at Figure 1.1, which shows data on income inequality and child wellbeing in 25 of the richest countries of the world. Income inequality is measured by the Gini coefficient; a higher Gini coefficient indicates more unequal incomes. Child wellbeing is measured by the UNICEF (United Nations Children's Fund) index; a higher number means better child wellbeing across the domains health, education, housing and environment, and behaviours.

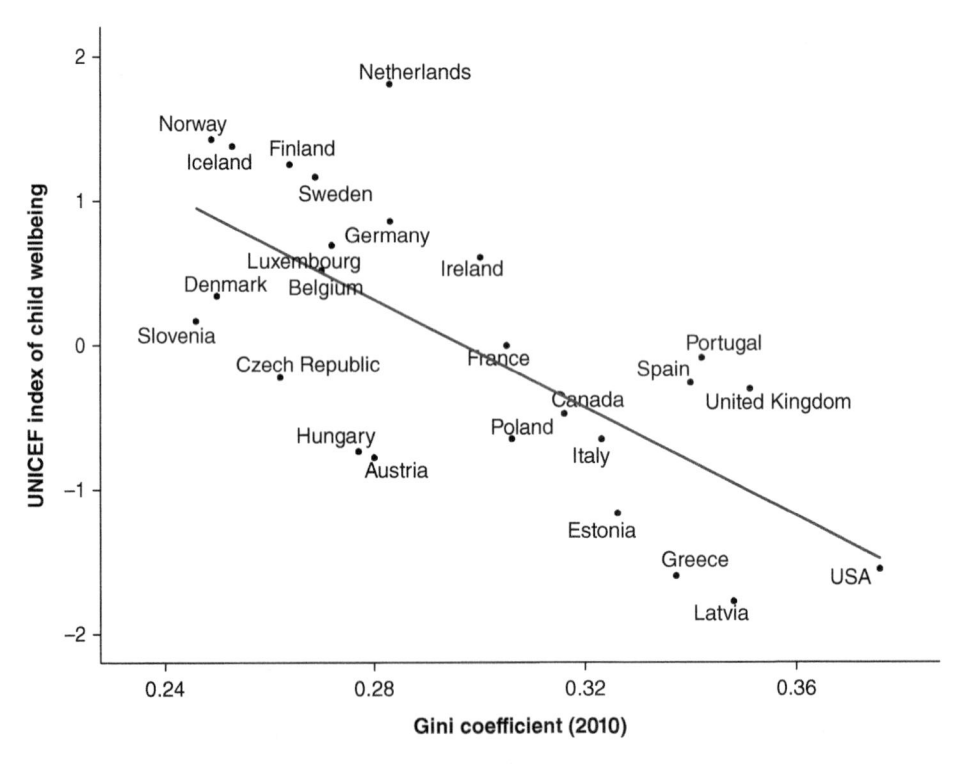

Figure 1.1 Child wellbeing and income inequality in 25 countries

Note. Gini coefficient: a higher coefficient indicates more income inequality. UNICEF index of child wellbeing: a higher number indicates better child wellbeing averaged over four dimensions: health, education, housing and environment, and behaviours. Data for Gini coefficient: Organisation for Economic Co-operation and Development (www.oecd.org/social/income-distribution-database.htm) and child wellbeing: Martorano et al. (2014, Table 15). This graph is inspired by Figure 1 in Pickett and Wilkinson (2007) but is based on more recent data. UNICEF = United Nations Children's Fund.

One way to describe these data is to draw attention to the positions of individual countries. For example, the Netherlands, Norway and Iceland are rated the highest on UNICEF's index of child wellbeing, while Latvia, the USA and Greece are rated the lowest. The three countries with the highest income inequality are the USA, Latvia and the UK. The most egalitarian countries in terms of income are Slovenia, Norway and Denmark.

Figure 1.1 also demonstrates a general pattern. The distribution of countries suggests that the more inequality there is in a country, the poorer the wellbeing of the children. As you may remember from *The SAGE Quantitative Research Kit*, Volume 2, this is called a negative relationship (as one variable goes up, the other tends to go down), and it can be represented by a correlation coefficient, Pearson's r. The observed **correlation** between inequality and child wellbeing in Figure 1.1 is $r = -0.70$.

We might also want to illustrate the relationship by drawing a line, as I have done in Figure 1.1. This line summarises the negative relationship we have just described. The line describes how the wellbeing of children in a country depends on the degree of a country's economic inequality. The points don't fall on the line exactly, but we may argue that the line represents a fair summary of the general tendency observed in this data set. This line is called a regression line, and it is a simple illustration of linear regression, a type of statistical model that we will discuss in Chapter 2.

Every statistical model is based on assumptions. For example, by drawing the straight line in Figure 1.1, we are assuming that there is a *linear relationship* between inequality and child health. The word *linear* in the context of statistical models refers to a *straight* line. Curved lines are not considered 'linear'. Judging from Figure 1.1, the assumption of linearity might seem reasonable in this case, but more generally many things are related in non-linear ways. Consider, for example, Figure 1.2, which shows the relationship between GDP (gross domestic product) per capita and life expectancy in 134 countries.

The graph suggests that there is a strong relationship between GDP and life expectancy. But this relationship is not linear; it is not well represented by a straight line. Among the poorest countries, even relatively small differences in GDP tend to make a big difference in life expectancy. For the richer countries, even relatively large differences in GDP appear to affect life expectancy only a little, or maybe not at all. We may try to represent this relationship by drawing a curved line, as shown in Figure 1.2. This is a simple illustration of a non-linear model, representing a non-linear relationship. Like the line in Figure 1.1, the line in Figure 1.2 does not represent the relationship between GDP and life expectancy perfectly. For example, there are at least six African countries whose life expectancy is much lower than the line predicts based on these countries' GDP. We will see later in the book how cases that don't appear to fit our model can help us to improve our analysis.

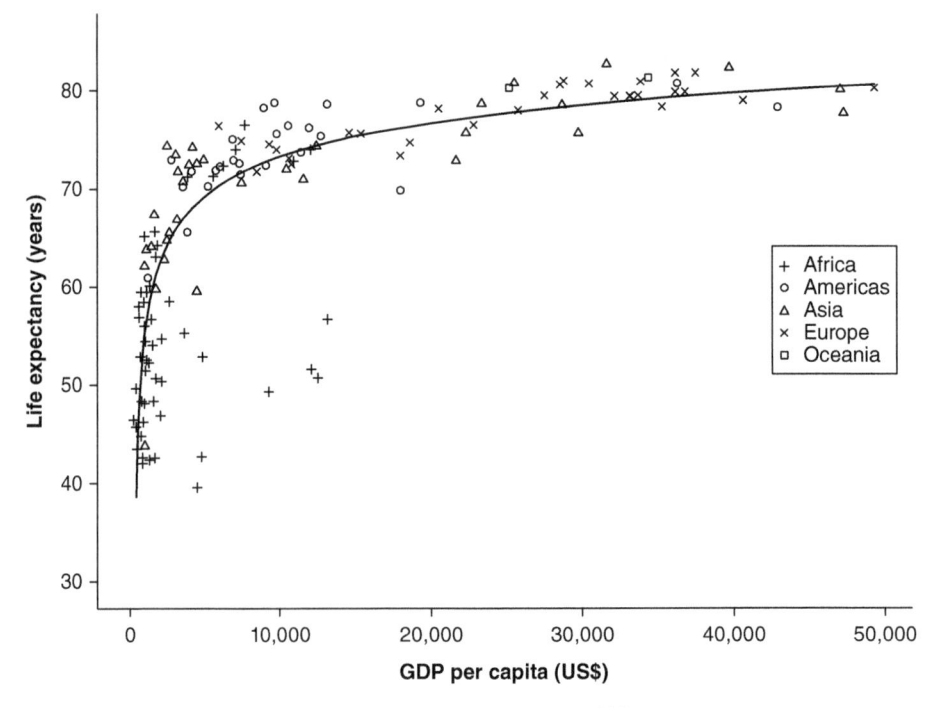

Figure 1.2 Gross domestic product (GDP) per capita and life expectancy in 134 countries (2007)

Note. Data from the Gapminder Foundation (Bryan, 2017). See www.gapminder.org

First approach to models: the *t*-test as a comparison of two statistical models

The practice of modelling often involves investigating which of a set of models gives the best account of the data. In this way, we might compare a linear model with a non-linear one, a simpler model with a more complex one, or a model corresponding to one theory with a model corresponding to another. As a first introduction to how this works, I will show you how an elementary hypothesis test, the *t*-test for independent samples, can be understood as a systematic comparison of two statistical models. The example will also introduce you to some simple mathematical notation that will be useful in understanding subsequent chapters.

The example concerns psychological aspects of the mind–body problem. Most of us have experienced that the way we hold our body can reflect the state of mind that we are in: when we are anxious our body is tense, when we are happy our body is relaxed, and so forth. But does this relationship work the other way around? Can we change our state of mind by assuming a certain posture? Carney et al. (2010) published an experimental study about what they called *power poses*. An example of a power pose is to sit on a chair with your legs stretched out and your feet resting on your desk, your arms comfortably crossed behind your neck. Let's call this the 'boss pose'. Carney et al. (2010) reported that participants who were instructed to hold a power pose felt more powerful subjectively, assumed a more risk-taking attitude and even had higher levels of testosterone in their bodies compared to other participants, who were instructed to hold a 'submissive pose' instead. The study was small, involving 42 participants, but it was covered widely in the media and became the basis of a popular TED talk by one of the co-authors.

A sceptic may have doubts about the study's results. From a theoretical point of view, one might propose that the mind–body connection is a bit more complicated than the study appears to imply. Methodologically speaking, we may also note that with such a small sample ($n = 42$), there is a lot of uncertainty in any estimates derived from the data. Could it be that the authors are mistaking a chance finding for a signal of scientific value?

A scientific way to settle such questions is to conduct a replication study. For the sake of example, let's focus on one question only: does assuming a power pose increase testosterone levels in participants, compared to assuming a different kind of pose?

To test this, let's imagine we conduct a replication of Carney et al.'s (2010) experiment. We will randomise respondents to one of two conditions: The experimental group are instructed to assume a power pose, such as the 'boss pose' described above. In contrast, the control group are asked to hold a submissive pose – the opposite of a power pose – such as sitting hunched, looking downwards, with hands folded between the thighs. Before assuming their pose, the participants have their testosterone levels measured. They then hold their assigned pose for 2 minutes, after which time testosterone is measured again. The outcome variable is the difference in testosterone after holding the pose minus testosterone before holding the pose. A positive value on this variable means that testosterone was higher after posing than before. A negative number means the opposite. Zero indicates no change.

Before we conduct the study, we might visualise what the the data will look like. Figure 1.3 shows hypothetical distributions of testosterone difference for the two groups, the power pose group and the control group.

Let's begin by turning the two competing theories about power poses – either power poses can change testosterone levels or they cannot – into two different models that aim to account for these hypothetical data.

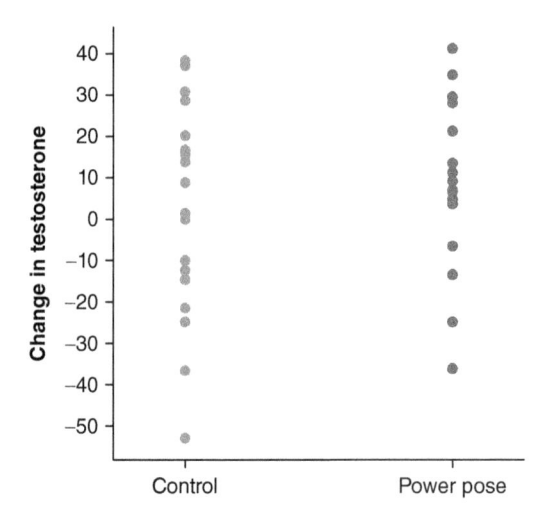

Figure 1.3 Hypothetical data from a power pose experiment

The sceptic's model (null hypothesis of the *t*-test)

The sceptic doesn't believe that power poses influence testosterone levels. So she predicts that, on average, the two groups have the same testosterone change. This is symbolised by the line on the left panel of Figure 1.4: the means for the two groups are predicted to be the same. The sceptic also recognises that not everyone may react to the experiment in the same way, however, and so she expects individual variation around the mean testosterone change. In brief, the sceptic says, 'All we need to say about testosterone change in this experiment is that there is random variation around the overall mean. Nothing else to see here.'

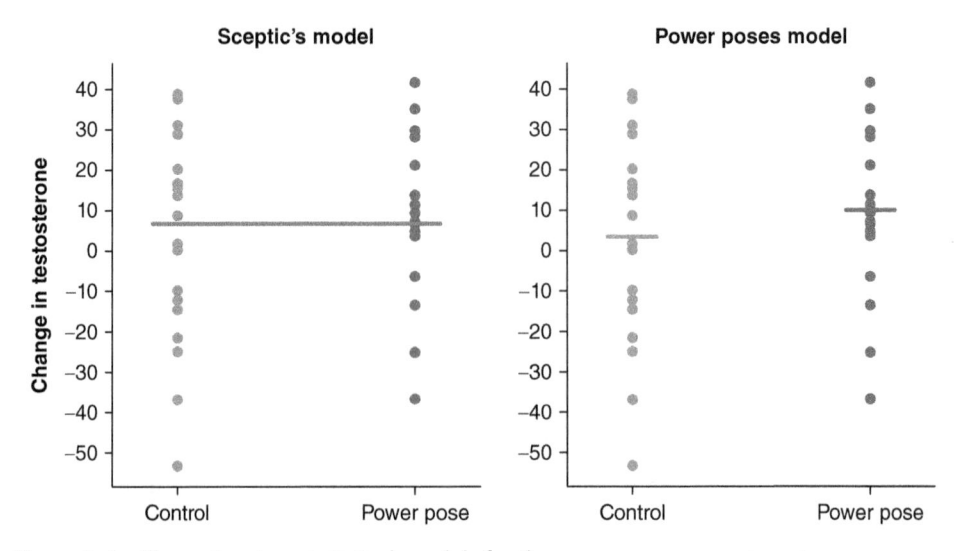

Figure 1.4 Illustrating two statistical models for the power pose experiment

Let's now look at how we can formalise this model using mathematical notation. The sceptic's model can be written as follows:

Individual's testosterone change = mean testosterone change + individual variation

In mathematical symbols, we might write the same equation as:

$$Y_i = \mu + \varepsilon_i$$

where

- Y_i refers to the *testosterone change* of the *i*th individual:
    - for example, Y_1 is the *testosterone change* of the first person, Y_5 is the testosterone change of the fifth person, and so on.
- μ is the population mean of *testosterone change*. This is denoted by the Greek letter μ ('mu').
- ε_i is the difference between the *i*th individual's testosterone change and the mean μ. For example, ε_1 is the difference between Y_1 and the mean μ. This is denoted by the Greek letter ε ('epsilon').

The equation thus represents each participant's testosterone change (Y_i) as a combination of two components: the population mean μ and the participant's individual deviation from that mean, ε_i.

The ε_i are called the **errors**. This might be considered a confusing name, as the term *error* seems to imply that something has gone wrong. But this is not meant to be implied here. If we rearrange the sceptic's model equation, we can see that the errors are simply the individual differences from the population mean:

$$\varepsilon_i = Y_i - \mu$$

The power pose model: alternative hypothesis of the t-test

Now let's contrast the sceptic's model with the power pose model. If you thought that holding a power pose can increase testosterone, you would predict that the mean change in testosterone is higher in the power pose group than in the control group. This is illustrated by the lines in the right panel of Figure 1.4: the means for the two groups are predicted to be different.

In mathematical notation, we can write this model as follows:

$$Y_i = \alpha + \beta X_i + \varepsilon_i$$

where

- Y_i is, once again, the change in testosterone level for individual i.
- X_i is a variable that indicates the group membership of individual i; this variable can either be 0 or 1, where
    - $X = 0$ indicates the control group and
    - $X = 1$ indicates the power pose group.
- α is a **coefficient**, which in this case represents the mean of the control group.
- β is a coefficient that represents the difference in average testosterone change between the power pose group and the control group.
- ε_i represents individual variation in testosterone change around the group mean.

In this type of model, we call X the predictor variable, and Y the outcome variable. X is used to predict Y. In our example, the power pose model proposes that knowledge of an individual's experimental group membership – did they adopt a power pose or not? – can help us predict that individual's testosterone levels. (In other publications, you may find other names for X and Y: X may also be called the independent variable, the exposure or the explanatory variable; Y may be called the dependent variable or the response.)

To understand how the model works, consider how the equation looks for the control group, where $X = 0$. We have

$$Y_i = \alpha + \beta \times 0 + \varepsilon_i$$
$$= \alpha + \varepsilon_i$$

(Since the term $\beta \times 0$ is always zero, it can be left out.)

So for the control group, the model equation reduces to $Y_i = \alpha + \varepsilon_i$. The coefficient α thus represents the mean of the control group.

For the power pose group, where $X = 1$, the model looks like this:

$$Y_i = \alpha + \beta \times 1 + \varepsilon_i$$
$$= \alpha + \beta + \varepsilon_i$$

So the power pose model predicts that the mean of the power pose group is different from α by an amount β. Note that if $\beta = 0$, then there is no difference between the means of the power pose group and the control group. In other words, if $\beta = 0$, then the power pose model becomes the sceptic's model (with $\alpha = \mu$). The power pose hypothesis of course implies that the power pose group mean is higher than the control group mean, which implies that $\beta > 0$.

Using data to compare two models

So we have two competing models: the sceptic's model and the power pose model. The sceptic's model corresponds to the null hypothesis of a statistical hypothesis test; the power pose model corresponds to the alternative hypothesis.

WHAT IS A STATISTICAL MODEL? | 11

If we have conducted a study and observed data, we can estimate the coefficients of each model. We will use the hypothetical data displayed in Figure 1.3. Table 1.1 shows them as raw data with some descriptive statistics.

Table 1.1 Testosterone change from a power pose experiment (hypothetical data)

	Control	Power Poses
	8.9	27.9
	15.7	13.0
	−52.8	7.6
	16.9	6.7
	−24.9	−24.9
	−12.4	21.3
	14.0	11.8
	−9.9	41.2
	38.2	34.9
	−14.6	9.1
	30.7	13.5
	1.3	35.0
	15.7	29.4
	20.1	10.8
	37.1	4.7
	−21.5	−13.3
	−36.5	3.7
	28.6	−6.5
	16.0	6.5
	0.2	−36.0
Mean	3.54	9.81
Standard deviation	24.84	19.63
Overall mean	6.68	
Overall standard deviation	22.33	
Pooled standard deviation	22.39	

We will now use these data to estimate the unknown coefficients in the power pose model. We denote estimates of coefficients by putting a hat (^) on the coefficient symbols. Thus, we use $\hat{\alpha}$ (read 'alpha-hat') to denote an estimate of α, and $\hat{\beta}$ ('beta-hat') to denote an estimate of β.

Recall that the power pose model is as follows:

$$Y_i = \alpha + \beta X_i + \varepsilon_i$$

I said above that the coefficient α represents the population mean testosterone change of the control group in the power pose model. How best to estimate this coefficient? Intuitively, it makes sense to estimate the population mean by the sample mean we observe in our data. In this case,

$$\hat{\alpha} = \bar{Y}_{Control}$$

where $\bar{Y}_{Control}$ is the observed mean testosterone change in the control group.

Similarly, I said above that the coefficient β represents the difference between the mean testosterone change in the power pose group and the mean change in the control group. As the estimate of this, we are going to use the difference between the sample means of our two groups:

$$\hat{\beta} = \bar{Y}_{Power\ pose} - \bar{Y}_{Control}$$

From the descriptive statistics given in Table 1.1, we can calculate these estimates:

$$\hat{\alpha} = \bar{Y}_{Control} = 3.54$$

$$\hat{\beta} = \bar{Y}_{Power\ pose} - \bar{Y}_{Control} = 9.81 - 3.54 = 6.27$$

So the control group mean is estimated to be 3.54, and the difference between the experimental and the control group is estimated to be 6.27. Recall, however, that these estimates are based on the assumption that the power pose model is correct.

The sceptic, who disagrees with the power pose model, would argue that a simpler model is sufficient to account for the data. Recall that the sceptic's model is as follows:

$$Y_i = \mu + \varepsilon_i$$

According to this model, there is no difference between the group means in the population. All we need to estimate is the overall group mean μ. Again, to denote an estimate of μ, we furnish it with a hat. And we will use the overall sample mean as the estimator:

$$\hat{\mu} = \bar{Y}_{all}$$

From Table 1.1, we have

$$\hat{\mu} = 6.68$$

Under the assumption of the sceptic's model, then, we estimate that, on average, holding some pose for 2 minutes raises people's testosterone levels by 6.68 (and it doesn't matter what kind of pose they are holding).

The power pose model and the sceptic's model estimate different coefficients, and the two models are contradictory: they cannot both be correct. Either power poses make a difference to testosterone change compared to submissive poses, or they do not. How do we decide which model is better?

We will use the data to test the two models against each other. The logic goes like this:

- We write down the model equation of the more complex model. In our case, this is the power pose model, and it is written as $Y_i = \alpha + \beta X_i + \varepsilon_i$.
- We hypothesise that the simpler model is true. The simpler model is the sceptic's, in our case. If the sceptic is right, this would imply that the coefficient β in the model equation is equal to zero. So we wish to conduct a test of the hypothesis $\beta = 0$.
- We then make assumptions about the data and the distribution of the outcome variable. These are the usual assumptions of the *t*-test for independent samples (see *The SAGE Quantitative Research Kit*, Volume 3):
    - *Randomisation:* Allocation to groups has been random.
    - *Independence of observations:* There is no relationship between the individuals.
    - *Normality:* In each group, the sampling distribution of the mean testosterone change is a normal distribution.
    - *Equality of variances:* The population variance is the same in both groups.
- If the null model is true and all assumptions hold, the statistic

$$t = \frac{\hat{\beta}}{s_{\hat{\beta}}}$$

   - has a central *t*-distribution with mean zero and degrees of freedom $df = n_0 + n_1 - 2$. With $s_{\hat{\beta}}$, I denote the estimated standard error of $\hat{\beta}$.
- We calculate the observed *t*-statistic from the data. Then, we compare the result to the *t*-distribution under the null model. This allows us to calculate a *p*-value, which is the probability of obtaining our observed *t*-statistic, or one further away from zero, if the null hypothesis model is true.

I have already shown how to calculate $\hat{\beta}$ from the data; in the previous section, we found that $\hat{\beta} = 6.27$. But I haven't shown how to calculate the estimated standard error of $\hat{\beta}$, which we denote by the symbol $s_{\hat{\beta}}$. This standard error is a measure of the variability of $\hat{\beta}$. We can estimate this standard error from our data. In Chapter 2, I will show you how this is done. For now, I will ask you to accept that this is possible to do and to believe me when I say that $s_{\hat{\beta}} = 7.08$ for our data. Approximately, this means that if we conducted an infinite number of power pose experiments, each with exactly the same design and sample size $n = 42$, our estimate $\hat{\beta}$ would differ from the true value β by 7.08 on average (approximately). The smaller the standard error, the more precise our estimates. So a small standard error is desirable.

But now to conduct the test. Using our estimates of $\hat{\beta}$ and $s_{\hat{\beta}}$, we have

$$t = \frac{\hat{\beta}}{s_{\hat{\beta}}} = \frac{6.27}{7.08} = 0.89$$

So $t = 0.89$. With 38 degrees of freedom, this yields a two-sided p-value of 0.38 (or a one-sided p-value of 0.19). Since the p-value is quite large, we would conclude that there is little evidence, if any, for the power pose model from these data. Although in our sample there is a small difference in testosterone change between the power pose group and the control group, this is well within the range of random variability that we would expect to see in an experiment of this size. In the logic of the t-test for independent samples, we say that we have little evidence against the null hypothesis. In the logic of statistical modelling, we might say that the sceptic's simple model seems to be sufficient to account for the data.

In the original experiment, Carney et al. (2010) did find evidence for an effect of power poses on testosterone (i.e. their p-value was quite small). In the language of model comparison, their conclusion was that β is larger than zero. I made up the data used in this chapter, so these pages are not a contribution to the scientific literature on power poses. I do want to mention, however, that other research teams have tried to replicate the power pose effect. For example, Ranehill et al. (2015) used a sample of 200 participants to test the power pose hypothesis and found no evidence for an effect of power poses on either risk taking, stress or testosterone, although they did find evidence that power poses, on average, increase participants' *self-reported* feeling of power.

Further research may shift the weight of the overall evidence either way. These future researchers may employ statistical hypothesis tests, such as a t-test, without specifically casting their report in the language of statistical models. But underlying the research will be the effort to try to establish which of two models explains better how the world works: the power pose model, where striking a power pose can raise your testosterone, or the sceptic's model, according to which testosterone levels may be governed by many things but where striking a power pose is not one of them.

The signal and the noise

Statistics is the science of reasoning about data. The central problem that statistics tackles is uncertainty about the data generating process: we don't know why the data are the way they are. If there is regularity in the way the world works, then research may generate data that make this regularity visible. For example, if it is the case that children in countries with more equal income distributions fare better than children in unequal countries, we would expect to see a relationship between a measure of income (in)equality and a measure of child wellbeing.

But there are many other processes that influence how the data turn out. Measurement errors may cause the data to be inaccurate. Also, random processes may introduce variations. Examples of such random processes are random sampling or small variations over time, such as year-on-year variations in a country's GDP, that are not related to the research problem at hand. Finally, other variables may interfere and hide the true relationship between child wellbeing and income inequality. Or they may interfere in the opposite way and bring about the appearance of a relationship, when really there is none.

Let's make a distinction between the signal and the noise (Silver, 2012). The signal is the thing we are interested in, such as, say, the relationship between GDP and life expectancy. The noise is what we are less interested in but what is nonetheless present in the data: measurement errors, random fluctuations in GDP or life expectancy, and influences of other variables whose importance we either don't know about or which we were unable to measure.

In fancier words, we call the signal the systematic part of the model and the noise the random part of the model. Recall the model we considered for the power poses, which is shown in Figure 1.5.

$$Y_i = \underbrace{\alpha + \beta X_i}_{\text{Systematic part}} + \underbrace{\varepsilon_i}_{\text{Random part}}$$

Figure 1.5 Partition of a statistical model into a systematic and a random part

The systematic part of the model is $\alpha + \beta X_i$. This specifies the relationship between the predictor and the outcome. The random part, ε_i, collects individual variation in the outcome that is not related to the predictor. It is this random part which distinguishes a statistical model from a deterministic one (e.g. the model of depth and water pressure we considered in the section 'Kinds of Models'). When using statistical models, we aim to detect and describe the signal, but we also pay attention to the noise and what influence it might have on what we can say about the signal.

2
SIMPLE LINEAR REGRESSION

Chapter Overview

Origins of regression: Francis Galton and the inheritance of height 18
The regression line 21
Regression coefficients: intercept and slope 23
Errors of prediction and random variation 24
The true and the estimated regression line 25
Residuals 26
How to estimate a regression line 27
How well does our model explain the data? The R^2 statistic 29
Residual standard error 33
Interpreting Galton's data and the origin of 'regression' 33
Inference: confidence intervals and hypothesis tests 35
Confidence range for a regression line 39
Prediction and prediction intervals 42
Regression in practice: things that can go wrong 44
Further Reading 50

Linear regression is a statistical model that represents the relationship between two variables as a straight line. In doing so, a distinction is made between the outcome variable and the predictor variable, as we did in Chapter 1. Linear regression is appropriate for outcome variables that are continuous and that are measured on an interval or ratio scale. Box 2.1 gives an overview of the different kinds of variables that can feature in a statistical model. For measurement levels (nominal, ordinal, interval and ratio), see *The SAGE Quantitative Research Kit*, Volume 2.

Box 2.1

Types of Variables

In statistics, variables are distinguished in various ways, according to their properties. An important distinction is made between **numeric variables** and **categorical variables**. Numeric variables have values that are numbers (1, 68.2, −15, 0.9, and so forth). Height is one such numeric variable. The values of categorical variables are categories. Country of birth is categorical, with values 'Afghanistan', 'Albania', 'Algeria' and so forth. Categorical variables are sometimes represented by numbers in data sets (where, say, '1' means Afghanistan, '2' means Albania, and so forth), but in that case, the number just acts as a label for a category and doesn't mean that the variable is truly numeric.

Numeric variables, in their turn, are divided into continuous and discrete variables. A **continuous variable** can take any value within its possible range. For example, age is a continuous variable: a person can be 28 years old, 28.4 years old or even 28.397853 years old. Age changes every day, every minute, every second, so our measurement of age is limited only by how precise we can or wish to be. Another example of a continuous variable is human height.

In contrast, a **discrete variable** only takes particular numeric values. For example, number of children is a discrete variable: you can have zero children, one child or seven children, but not 1.5 children.

The outcome variable of a linear regression should be continuous. In practice, our measurement of continuous variables may make them appear discrete – for example, when we record height only to the nearest inch. This does not necessarily harm the estimation of our regression model, as long as the discrete measurement is not too coarse.

The predictor in a linear regression should be numeric and may be discrete or continuous. In Chapter 4, we will see how we can turn categorical predictors into numeric 'dummy variables' to enable us to include them in a regression model.

This chapter considers simple linear regression, which is a linear regression with exactly one predictor variable. In Chapters 4 and 5, we will look at linear regression with more than one predictor.

Origins of regression: Francis Galton and the inheritance of height

The first regression in history was carried out in the late 19th century by Francis Galton, a half-cousin of Charles Darwin. One interest of Galton's was the study of biological inheritance: how parents pass on their individual characteristics to their children.

Among other things, he studied the relationship between the heights of parents and their children (once the children had grown up). To this end, he collected data from 928 families. An extract of the data is shown in Table 2.1, and Figure 2.1 illustrates the data.[1]

Table 2.1 Extract from Galton's data on heights in 928 families

Family Number (i)	Height of Parents (Average)	Height of Adult Child
1	66.5	66.2
2	69.5	67.2
3	68.5	64.2
4	68.5	68.2
5	70.5	71.2
6	68.5	67.2
⋮	⋮	⋮
926	69.5	66.2
927	69.5	71.2
928	68.5	69.2
Mean	68.30	68.08
Standard deviation	1.81	2.54
Variance	3.29	6.44

Note. The means, standard deviations and variances deviate slightly from Galton's original results, because I have added a small random jiggle to the data to make illustration and explanation easier.

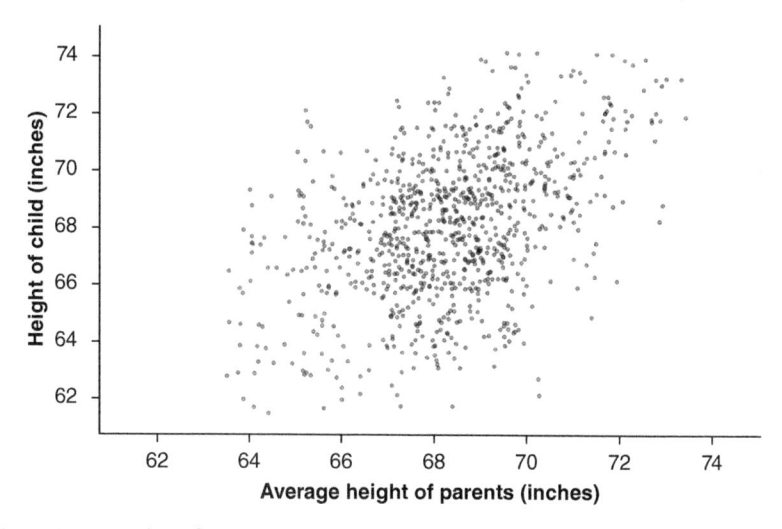

Figure 2.1 Scatter plot of parents' and children's heights

Note. Data are taken from Galton (1886) via the 'psych' package for R (Revelle, 2020). Data points have been jiggled randomly to avoid overlap.

---

[1] I use Galton's original data, as documented in Revelle (2020), but I have added a slight modification. Galton recorded the heights in categories of 1-inch steps. Thus, most combinations of parents' and child's height occur more than once, which makes for an unattractive overlap of points in a scatter plot, and would generally have made the analysis difficult to explain. I have therefore added a small random jiggle to all data points. All my analyses are done on the jiggled data, not Galton's original data. Therefore, for example, the means and standard deviations shown in Table 2.1 differ slightly from those in Galton's original data. I have done this purely for didactic purposes.

> **Box 2.2**
>
> **Galton and Eugenics**
>
> Francis Galton's interest in heredity was linked to his interest in eugenics: the belief that human populations can and should be 'improved' by excluding certain groups from having children, based on the idea that people with certain heritable characteristics are less worthy of existence than others. Galton was a leading eugenicist of his time. In fact, it was he who coined the term *eugenics*. Eugenicist ideas were widespread in the Western world in the early 20th century and in many countries inspired discriminatory policies such as forced sterilisation and marriage prohibition for people labelled 'unfit to reproduce', which included people with mental or physical disabilities. Historically, the eugenics movement had close ideological links with racism (Todorov, 1993), and pursued the aim of 'purifying' a population by reducing its diversity. Eugenicist ideas and practices were most strongly and ruthlessly adopted by the Nazi regime in Germany, 1933–1945. Like many Europeans of his time, Galton also held strong racist views about the supposed superiority of some 'races' over others. Galton thus leaves a complicated legacy: he was a great scientist (his scientific achievements reach far beyond regression), but he promoted ideas that were rooted in racist ideology and that helped to promote racism and discrimination. For further information about Galton, and how contemporary statisticians grapple with his legacy, see Langkjær-Bain (2019).

The scatter plot, Figure 2.1, provides a first look at the relationship between the parents' and the children's heights. Each dot represents one pair of measurements: the average height of the parents[2] and the height of the adult child.[3] The scatter plot suggests that there is a positive, moderately strong relationship between parents' and children's heights. In general, taller parents tend to have taller children. Nonetheless, for any given parental height, there is much variation among the children.

One way of describing the relationship between parents' and children's heights is to calculate a correlation coefficient. If the relationship is linear, Pearson's product moment correlation coefficient provides a suitable description of the strength and direction of the relationship. (You may remember this from *The SAGE Quantitative Research Kit*, Volume 2.)

From Figure 2.1, it looks as though there is a linear relationship between the heights of parents and their children. Thus we are justified in calculating Pearson's r for Galton's data. Doing so, we obtain a Pearson correlation of $r = 0.456$. This confirms the impression gained from the scatter plot: this is a linear positive relationship of moderate strength.

---

[2]From now on, I shall refer to the average of the parents' height simply as 'parents' height'. Galton himself used the term *height of the mid-parents*.

[3]To make male and female heights comparable, Galton multiplied the heights of females in his sample by 1.08.

The regression line

Now let's consider how to develop a statistical model. This goes beyond the correlation coefficient, as we now make a distinction between the **outcome** variable, and the **predictor** variable. The outcome is the variable that we wish to explain or predict. The predictor is the variable we use to do so. Different books and texts use different names for the outcome and the predictor variables. Box 2.3 gives an explanation.

In making this distinction between the predictor and the outcome, we do not necessarily imply a causal relationship. Whether it is plausible to deduce a causal relationship from an observed correlation depends on many things, including knowledge about the research design and data collection process, as well as evidence from other studies and theoretical knowledge about the variables involved in the analysis. In our example, Galton wished to understand why people have different heights (the outcome) and thought he could find an explanation by considering the heights of people's parents (the predictor). Our current scientific knowledge suggests that parent's and children's heights are indeed related due to common causes, including the genes shared by parents with their children as well as environmental and social factors such as nutrition, which tend to be more similar within families than between different families.

Box 2.3

Various Names for the Variables Involved in a Regression Model

The outcome of a regression model is also known as the *dependent variable* (DV), or the *response*. The predictor is also sometimes called an *independent variable* (IV), an *exposure* or an *explanatory variable*. The terminological fashion varies somewhat between disciplines. For example, psychology prefers the terms *DV* and *IV*, while in epidemiology, *outcome* and *exposure* are more commonly used. In this book, I shall use the terms *outcome* and *predictor* consistently.

Because we have concluded that the relationship between parents' and children's heights is approximately linear, we propose a linear model: we will draw a straight line to represent the relationship in Galton's data. Such a line is shown in Figure 2.2.

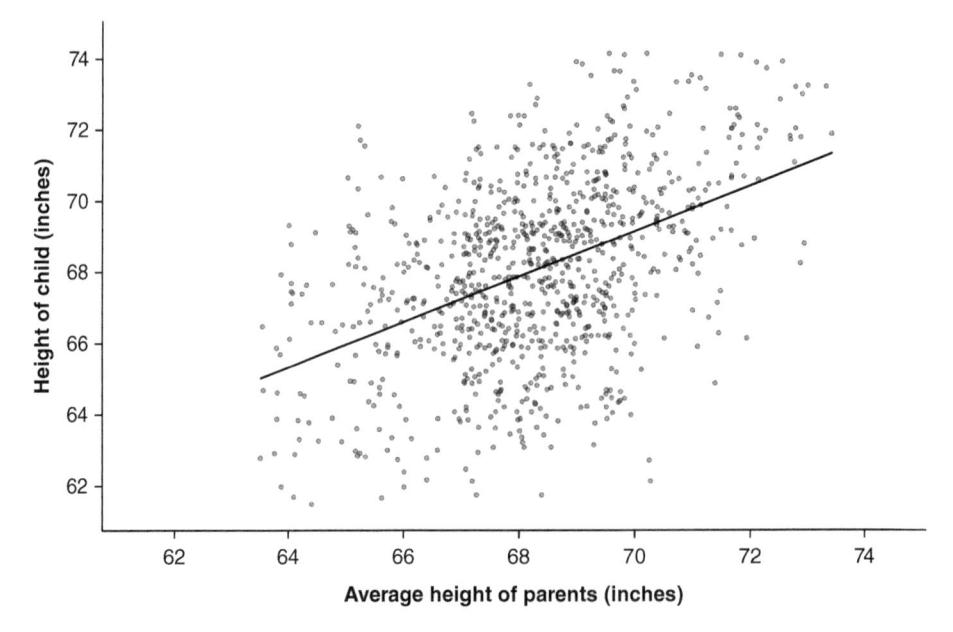

Figure 2.2 Galton's data with superimposed regression line

The regression line is a representation of the relationship we observe between a predictor variable (here, parents' height) and an outcome variable (here, the height of the adult child). By convention, we call the predictor X and the outcome Y. The algebraic expression of a regression line is an equation of the form

$$\hat{Y}_i = \alpha + \beta X_i$$

where

- $\hat{Y}_i$ is the **predicted value** of the outcome Y for the ith person – in our case, the predicted height of the child of the ith family (read $\hat{Y}$ as 'Y-hat', the hat indicates that this is a prediction).
- X_i is the value of the predictor variable for the ith person – here, the parents' height in family i.
- α is called the **intercept** of the regression line; this is the value of $\hat{Y}$ when $X = 0$.
- β is called the **slope** of the regression line; this is the predicted difference in Y for a 1-unit difference in X – in our case, the predicted height difference between two children whose parents' heights differ by 1 inch.

To understand how the regression equation works, let's look at the equation for the line in Figure 2.2. This is:

$$\hat{Y}_i = 24.526 + 0.638 X_i$$

If it helps, you may write this equation as follows:

Predicted child's height = 24.526 + 0.638 × Parents' height

We can use this equation to derive a predicted height for a child, if we are given the parents' height. For example, take a child whose parents' height is 64.5 inches. Plugging that number into the regression equation, we get:

$$\hat{Y} = 24.526 + 0.638 \times 64.5$$
$$= 65.7$$

A child of parents with height 64.5 inches is predicted to be 65.7 inches tall. In the equation above, the 'hat' over Y indicates that this result is a prediction, not the actual height of the child. This is important because the prediction is not perfect: not every child is going to have exactly the height predicted by the regression equation. The aim of the regression equation is to be right *on average*, not necessarily for every individual case.

Regression coefficients: intercept and slope

Let us have a closer look at the intercept (α) and the slope (β) of the regression equation. Jointly, they are referred to as the coefficients. The coefficients are unknown but can be estimated from the data. This is analogous to using a sample mean to estimate a population mean, or estimating a correlation from a sample data set. Figure 2.3 provides an illustration of how the coefficients define a regression line.

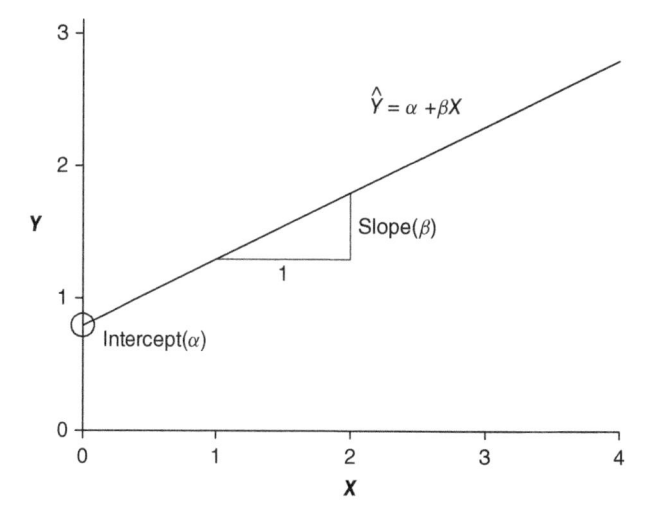

Figure 2.3 An illustration of the regression line, its intercept and slope

Note. Intercept: the value of Y when X is zero. Slope: the predicted difference in Y for a 1-unit difference in X.

The intercept is the predicted value of Y at the point when X is zero. In our example, the intercept is equal to 24.526. Formally, this means that the predicted height of a person whose parents have zero height is 24.526 inches. As a prediction, this obviously does not make sense, because parents of zero height don't exist. The intercept is of scientific interest only when $X = 0$ is a meaningful data point.

The slope determines by how much the line rises in the Y-direction for a 1-unit step in the X-direction. In our example, the slope is equal to 0.638. This means that a 1-inch difference in parents' height is associated with a 0.638-inch difference in the height of the children. For example, if the Joneses are 1 inch taller than the Smiths, the Joneses' children are predicted to be taller than the Smiths' children by 0.638 inches on average. In general, a positive slope indicates a positive relationship, and a negative slope indicates a negative relationship. If the slope is zero, there is no relationship between X and Y.

Errors of prediction and random variation

The regression line allows us to predict the value of an outcome, given information about a predictor variable. But the regression line is not yet a full statistical model. If we had only the regression line, our prediction of the outcome would be deterministic, rather than statistical. A deterministic model would be appropriate if we believed that the height of a child was precisely determined by the height of their parents. But we know that is not true: if it was, all children born to the same parents would end up having the same height as adults. In Galton's data, we see that most children do not have exactly the height predicted by the regression line. There is variation around the prediction. That is why we need a statistical model, not a deterministic one.

As we saw in Chapter 1, a full statistical model includes two parts: a systematic part that relates Y to X and a random part that represents the variation in Y unrelated to X. The linear regression model looks like this:

$$Y_i = \alpha + \beta X_i + \varepsilon_i$$

where

- Y_i is the Y value of the ith individual.
- X_i is the X value of the ith individual.
- α and β are the intercept and the slope as before.
- $\alpha + \beta X_i$ is the systematic part of the model; in our example, this represents the part of a child's height that is determined by their parents' heights.
- ε_i is called the error (of the ith individual): it is the difference between the observed value (Y_i) and the predicted value ($\hat{Y}_i$). The errors represent the random part of our model: this is the part of a child's height that is determined by things other than their parents' heights.

Note that this regression equation looks just the same as the equation of the power pose model in Chapter 1. But there is one difference. In Chapter 1, X was a **dichotomous variable** – that is, a variable that could assume one of two values: 0 (for the control group) or 1 (for the experimental group). In the model for Galton's data, however, X is a continuous variable, which, in our data, takes values between 63.5 inches and 73.5 inches.

The systematic part of our model, $\alpha + \beta X_i$, describes the part of the outcome that is related to the predictor. In our example, we might say that the systematic part of Galton's regression represents the part of a child's height that is inherited from the parents. Galton did not know about genes, but today we might assume that a child might inherit their height from their parents through two kinds of processes: nature (genes) and nurture (experiences – e.g. nutrition and other living conditions during the growth period, which might have been similar for the parents and their children – e.g. because they each grew up in the same social class).

The error term, ε_i, represents the variation in Y that is not related to X. In our example, such variation might be due to things such as:

- Differences between living conditions in the parents' and the children's growth periods (e.g. due to changes in society and culture, historical events such as famines, or changes in family fortune)
- The vagaries of genetic inheritance (different children inherit different genes from the same parents)
- Other influences, some of which we either do not understand or that might be genuinely random (governed by a probabilistic natural process, rather than a deterministic one)

Importantly, the errors are the differences between the observed values Y_i and the predicted values $\hat{Y}_i$. That is, the errors tell you by how much the regression prediction is off for a particular case. To see this mathematically, rearrange the regression equation as follows:

$$\varepsilon_i = Y_i - (\alpha + \beta X_i)$$
$$= Y_i - \hat{Y}_i$$

We will later see that the full specification of the statistical model will require us to make certain assumptions about the errors. These assumptions are the topic of Chapter 3.

The true and the estimated regression line

When we conceptualise a model in the abstract, the coefficients and errors are conceptualised as properties of the 'true' regression model, which is valid for the population. In practice, however, we will only ever have information from a sample, and we use that sample to **estimate** the coefficients. This is called **fitting a model** to a data set, or (equivalently) **estimating a model** on a data set. Our model, $Y_i = \alpha + \beta X_i + \varepsilon_i$, specifies the sort of relationship between X and Y that we propose, or wish to investigate. When we fit this model to a data set, we obtain estimates of the model **parameters** α and β. The predictive equation that contains these estimates, $\hat{Y}_i = 24.526 + 0.638 X_i$, is called the fitted model, or the estimated model.

So just as we distinguish between the population mean μ and the sample mean $\bar{x}$, and between the population standard deviation σ and its sample estimate s, we also need to distinguish between the parameters α and β in the true (population) model and the estimates of these parameters, which we will call $\hat{\alpha}$ and $\hat{\beta}$ (read these as 'alpha-hat' and 'beta-hat', respectively). We also need to distinguish between the errors (the departures from the true regression line) and the estimates of the errors. This is because a regression line fitted to a sample of data is just an estimate of the 'true' regression line proposed by our model. For this reason, we never directly observe the errors. We must make do with the departures from our estimated regression line. We call these departures the **residuals**.

Residuals

The residuals are the differences between the observed values of Y and the predicted values of Y from an estimated regression equation. Let's return to Galton's data. The regression line predicts a child's height, given the height of the parents, using the equation

$$\hat{Y}_i = 24.526 + 0.638 X_i$$

As we have noted, the prediction is not perfect: although a few dots are exactly on the regression line, most are not.

Have a look at Figure 2.4. I have given names to two of the children in Galton's data: Francis and Florence. Let's consider Francis first. His parents are 64.5 inches tall. Given this information, the regression equation predicts Francis's height to be 65.7 inches, as we saw above in the section 'The Regression Line'. But Francis actually measures in at 63.3 inches, a bit shorter than the model predicts. Between Francis's actual height and the prediction, there is a difference of 2.4 inches. We call this difference a residual.

Formally, a residual is defined as the difference between the observed value and the predicted value of the dependent variable, where the prediction comes from a regression line estimated from a sample. We can express this definition in algebraic symbols:

$$e_i = Y_i - \hat{Y}_i$$

SIMPLE LINEAR REGRESSION

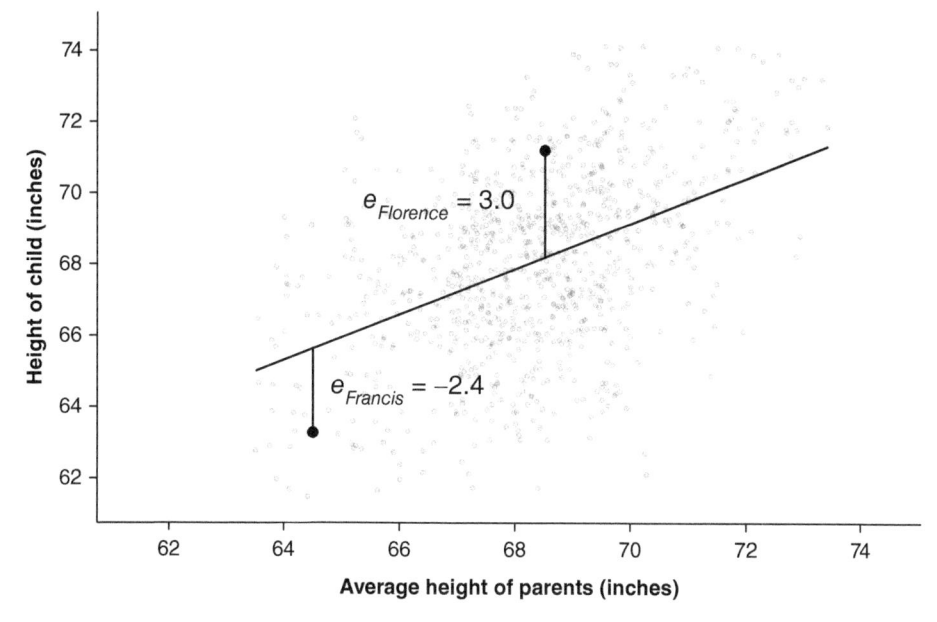

Figure 2.4 Illustration of residuals

It is customary to represent residuals with the letter *e*, to distinguish them from the errors ε. We write e_i if we want to refer to any particular residual (the residual of person *i*). In Francis's case, the calculation would go as follows:

$$e_{Francis} = Y_{Francis} - \hat{Y}_{Francis}$$
$$= 63.3 \text{ inches} - 65.7 \text{ inches}$$
$$= -2.4 \text{ inches}$$

Francis's residual is a negative number, because Francis is shorter than our model predicts.

Now consider Florence. Her parents' height is 68.5 inches. From this, we can calculate that her predicted height is 68.2 inches. But Florence is in fact 71.2 inches tall. Because she is taller than predicted, her residual is a positive number:

$$e_{Florence} = Y_{Florence} - \hat{Y}_{Florence}$$
$$= 71.2 \text{ inches} - 68.2 \text{ inches}$$
$$= 3.0 \text{ inches}$$

This residual tells us that Florence is 3.0 inches taller than the model predicts.

How to estimate a regression line

Now that we understand residuals, we can consider how the estimates of coefficients are found. A residual represents how wrong the regression prediction is for a given individual.

The regression line, the line of best fit, can be thought of as the line whose predictions are 'least wrong' overall. A mathematical measure of 'least wrong' is implemented by defining the line of best fit as the line that minimises the squared residuals.[4] What does this mean?

Take our regression line. It has been fitted to 928 dots representing the heights of parents and children. Each of these 928 dots has a residual. Consider now that we can square each residual. For example,

$$e^2_{Francis} = (-2.4)^2 = 5.76$$

and

$$e^2_{Florence} = 3.0^2 = 9.00$$

When you add all the 928 squared residuals together, you get the *sum of squared residuals*, which we denote by $SS_{Residual}$:

$$SS_{Residual} = \sum_{i=1}^{n}(Y_i - \hat{Y}_i)^2 = \sum_{i=1}^{n} e_i^2$$

This notation uses the Greek letter Σ (capital Sigma) to indicate a sum. The term $\sum_{i=1}^{n} e_i^2$ means that we sum the residuals of all individuals from the first ($i = 1$) to the last ($i = n$, where in this case $n = 928$).

The regression line is that line which leads to the smallest $SS_{Residual}$, for a given set of dots. Because of this, it is often called the ordinary least squares regression line – or OLS regression line for short. Given any set of dots,[5] there is a unique line that, by the criterion of **least squares**, fits the data best, and this determines the estimates of the coefficients. Box 2.4 gives a bit more detail.

Box 2.4

Finding the Slope and the Intercept for a Regression Line

The regression line is found by minimising the sum of the squared residuals. Of all possible lines we could draw through a set of points, the regression line is the one that has the smallest sum of squared residuals. It can be shown mathematically that there is always a unique line that fits the points best. In the simple linear regression model,

$$Y_i = \alpha + \beta X_i + \varepsilon_i$$

---

[4] Squaring the residuals ensures that the procedure finds a unique line of best fit for any possible data set. This can be shown mathematically, but I won't show the proof here. The mathematical reason for defining the line of best fit in this way is given by the so-called Gauss–Markov theorem, which proves that minimising the squared residuals leads to the most precise estimates of the regression coefficients (given certain assumptions and conditions).
[5] To be precise, I should say 'for any set of at least two dots'. If there is only one dot, an infinite number of lines can be drawn that 'fit the dot best' – namely, all possible lines that pass through the dot.

the slope estimate can be found from the data with the equation:

$$\hat{\beta} = \frac{r_{x,y} s_y}{s_x}$$

where $r_{x,y}$ is the sample Pearson correlation between X and Y, s_y is the standard deviation of Y, and s_x is the standard deviation of X. This equation shows that the slope is influenced by the size of the correlation between the predictor and the outcome: the larger the correlation, the steeper the slope, everything else being equal.

However, the slope is also influenced by the scales on which predictor and outcome are measured. Changing the scale of either the predictor or the outcome changes the respective standard deviation, s_x or s_y, and hence the slope. In Galton's data, both parents' and children's heights are measured in inches, which was a natural choice for Galton, and makes the slope readily interpretable. However, in other situations, the choice of scale for each variable may not be obvious, and it is worth choosing your measurement scales wisely so as to make interpretation of the slope as easy as possible.

Once the estimate of the slope has been found, the estimate of the intercept can be calculated as follows:

$$\hat{\alpha} = \bar{Y} - \hat{\beta}\bar{X}$$

How well does our model explain the data? The R^2 statistic

One indication of a good model is that it fits the data well. An intuitive definition of 'fitting well' is that most data points are pretty close to the regression line. This section will introduce one formal method to assess model fit, also called **goodness of fit**. It will introduce the R^2 statistic (read, '**R-squared**'), which measures the proportion of the total variation of the outcome that is accounted for by the predictor variable. To understand this, we need to consider how we can partition the total variation of our outcome variable into two parts: one part accounted for by the predictor and another part unrelated to the predictor.

Sums of squares: total, regression and residual

First, consider the total variation of the outcome variable (children's heights, in our example). We can measure this as the sum of squared deviations from the overall mean, which is calculated as follows:

$$SS_{Total} = \sum_{i=1}^{n}(Y_i - \bar{Y})^2$$

This is called the *total sum of squares* (SS_{Total} for short).[6] Think of SS_{Total} as an estimate of the errors you make in predicting Y in the absence of information about anything that predicts Y (i.e. without knowing X).

Next, consider the variation of the residuals around the regression line. This is represented by the *residual sum of squares* ($SS_{Residual}$), as we saw in the previous section:

$$SS_{Residual} = \sum_{i=1}^{n}\left(Y_i - \hat{Y}_i\right)^2 = \sum_{i=1}^{n} e_i^2$$

Think of $SS_{Residual}$ as an estimate of the errors you make in predicting Y once you have taken account of X. $SS_{Residual}$ is usually[7] smaller than SS_{Total}: the variance of the residuals is smaller than the variance of Y itself. This is because our predictor, X, accounts for (or 'explains') some of the variance of Y.

Finally, we can also measure the variation of the outcome that is accounted for by the predictor (the height of the parents, in our example). This measure is called the *regression sum of squares*, $SS_{Regression}$, and it is equal to the sum of the squared deviations of the predicted values around the sample mean:

$$SS_{Regression} = \sum_{i=1}^{n}\left(\hat{Y}_i - \bar{Y}\right)^2$$

The regression sum of squares represents the variation of the outcome that is explained by the predictor.

In general, the following equation holds true:

$$SS_{Total} = SS_{Regression} + SS_{Residual}$$

That is, we can partition the total variation of Y into two parts: (1) the variation accounted for by the predictor variable and (2) the residual variation. This is analogous to the partition of the right-hand side of our model equation into a systematic and a random part, as shown in Figure 2.5.

$$SS_{Total} = SS_{Regression} + SS_{Residual}$$

| Total variation of Y | Variation explained by the systematic part of the model | Unexplained variation: the random part of the model |

Figure 2.5 Partition of the total outcome variation into explained and residual variation

---

[6] You may recognise the right side of the equation as part of the formula for calculating the variance of a sample (see *The SAGE Quantitative Research Kit*, Volume 2). The equation works like this: we calculate the mean height of the children, $\bar{Y}$. For each child in the sample, we take their height Y_i and subtract the mean from that. This gives us the deviation of the child's height from the mean. Then we square each deviation, and sum these squared deviations for all children (from 1 to n).
[7] There is only one case in which $SS_{Residual}$ is equal to SS_{Total}: when there is no linear relationship (zero correlation) between X and Y. In all other cases, $SS_{Residual} < SS_{Total}$.

R^2 as a measure of the proportion of variance explained

The R^2 statistic measures the proportion of the outcome variation that is explained by the predictor. It is calculated as follows:

$$R^2 = \frac{SS_{Regression}}{SS_{Total}}$$

For a linear regression on any set of data, R^2 is a number between 0 and 1. $R^2 = 0$ indicates that the predictor variable is not correlated with the outcome variable, and so the predictor cannot account for any variation in the outcome. $R^2 = 1$ indicates a perfect fit: the predictor allows errorless prediction of the outcome (all residuals are zero). Figure 2.6 illustrates four different values of R^2 with scatter plots of hypothetical data sets. The R^2 is also known as the *coefficient of determination*.

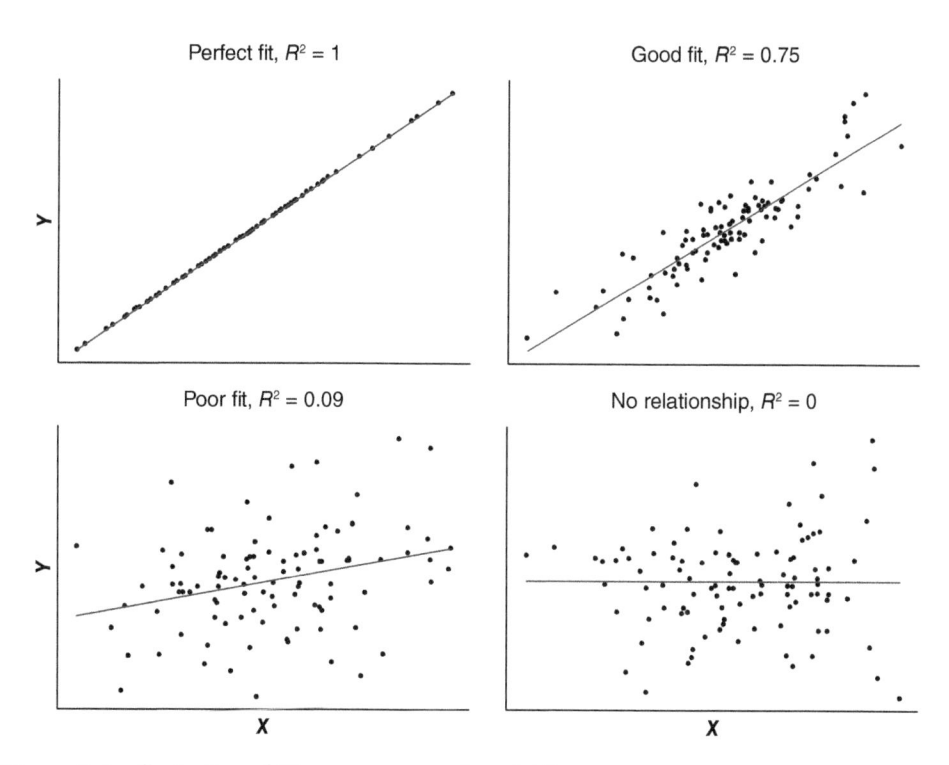

Figure 2.6 Illustration of R^2 as a measure of model fit

R^2 as a measure of the proportional reduction of error

Another way to understand R^2 is as a measure of the *proportional reduction of error*. Once again, think of the total variation of Y as a representation of the error we would make in predicting Y if we didn't have information about any predictors. Then, once we take into account the relationship between our predictor X and our outcome Y, we can improve our prediction, thereby reducing the prediction errors. R^2 can be understood as a measure of the proportion of the total error that the predictor is able to remove.

Let's consider the role of R^2 as a measure of the proportional reduction of error in a mathematical way. To do this, we can rearrange the equation I have given above:

$$R^2 = \frac{SS_{Regression}}{SS_{Total}}$$

$$= \frac{SS_{Total} - SS_{Residual}}{SS_{Total}}$$

$$= 1 - \frac{SS_{Residual}}{SS_{Total}}$$

This illustrates mathematically that the smaller the residual variation relative to the total variation, the closer R^2 will be to 1. The equation $R^2 = 1 - \frac{SS_{Residual}}{SS_{Total}}$ is the most popular mathematical definition of R^2.

Interpreting R^2

To see how we might interpret R^2 in practice, let's calculate it for Galton's data. In this book, I won't illustrate how to calculate SS_{Total} and $SS_{Residual}$ from the data. The equations for doing so are given above, but in practice the calculations are done routinely by software packages that can perform linear regression. For the present, let's not focus on these calculations but simply accept the numbers. For Galton's data, we have $SS_{Total} = 5972.43$ and $SS_{Residual} = 4731.11$. This gives the following calculation of R^2:

$$R^2 = 1 - \frac{SS_{Residual}}{SS_{Total}}$$

$$= 1 - \frac{4731.11}{5972.43}$$

$$= 0.21$$

The proportional reduction of error is 0.21. This can be interpreted thus: the regression model reduces the error of prediction, relative to having no predictors, by 21%. Alternatively, we might express this in either of the following ways: 'the model accounts for 21% of the variation of the outcome variable' or 'the model explains 21% of the variation of the outcome'. So in our case, we might say that 21% of the overall variation in child's height can be accounted for by parents' height.

Final remarks on the R^2 statistic

Like all statistics calculated from a sample, R^2 is an estimate of a 'true' population parameter. If you drew a new sample of parents and children, with different individuals, you would likely obtain a different value for R^2, even if the sample was drawn randomly from the same population as Galton's data. The population R^2 is usually unknown, but the larger the sample, the better in general our estimate of R^2 (provided that the sample is a random sample from the population).

The R^2 of a simple linear regression is also equal to the square of the Pearson correlation between the predictor and the outcome. Not surprisingly, there is a correspondence between how strongly two variables are correlated and how well a model based on one variable can predict the other variable. The stronger the correlation, the better the model prediction; the weaker the correlation, the poorer the model prediction. In Chapters 4 and 5, we will see that R^2 has a slightly different meaning in regression models that have more than one predictor variable.

Residual standard error

It is useful to have a measure of the average error made by the regression prediction of the outcome. This is called the *residual standard error* (also sometimes called *standard error of the estimate*), which I will denote by the symbol s_e. Given a set of data, we can calculate the residual standard error as follows:

$$s_e = \sqrt{\frac{SS_{Residual}}{N-2}}$$

The resulting number gives us an estimate of how wrong we are on average when using regression to predict the outcome. For our data,

$$\begin{aligned} s_e &= \sqrt{\frac{SS_{Residual}}{N-2}} \\ &= \sqrt{\frac{4731.11}{926}} \\ &= 2.26 \end{aligned}$$

This means that, on average, our prediction of the children's heights in our sample data is wrong by 2.26 inches. The residual standard error gives an intuitive measure of the precision of our prediction. For example, we might ask ourselves how much it matters for our purposes if a prediction is wrong by 2.26 inches, and this might influence how we judge our model.

Interpreting Galton's data and the origin of 'regression'

In general, how we interpret the results from a statistical model will depend on why we did the modelling in the first place. Throughout this book, we will encounter data from a variety of research situations, and these will serve as examples of different purposes and interpretations of models. For now, let's take the regression line estimated on Galton's data and try to make sense of it.

Obviously, the regression line demonstrates that people's height is related to the height of their parents. Short parents tend to have short children, and tall parents tend to have tall children. But there is a more interesting result lurking in Galton's data. We will see this in a moment. Before we do, let's see what we might have hypothesised about the relationship between parents' and children's heights, had we not seen any data.

A natural hypothesis might be that parents have children who on average are the same height as them.[8] Figure 2.7 illustrates this hypothesis by adding the *line of equal heights* to Galton's data: dots that lie on this line represent children who are the same height as their parents. Dots above the line represent children taller than their parents, and dots below the line represent children shorter than their parents. But as we know, the line of equality is not the best fit to the data – the regression line is. So the hypothesis of equal heights is not correct. Something else is going on. In Galton's own words, 'When the [parents] are taller than average, their Children tend to be shorter than they', and when parents 'are shorter than average, their Children tend to be taller than they' (Galton, 1886, plate IX). If you compare the regression line to the line of equal heights, you can see this for yourself.

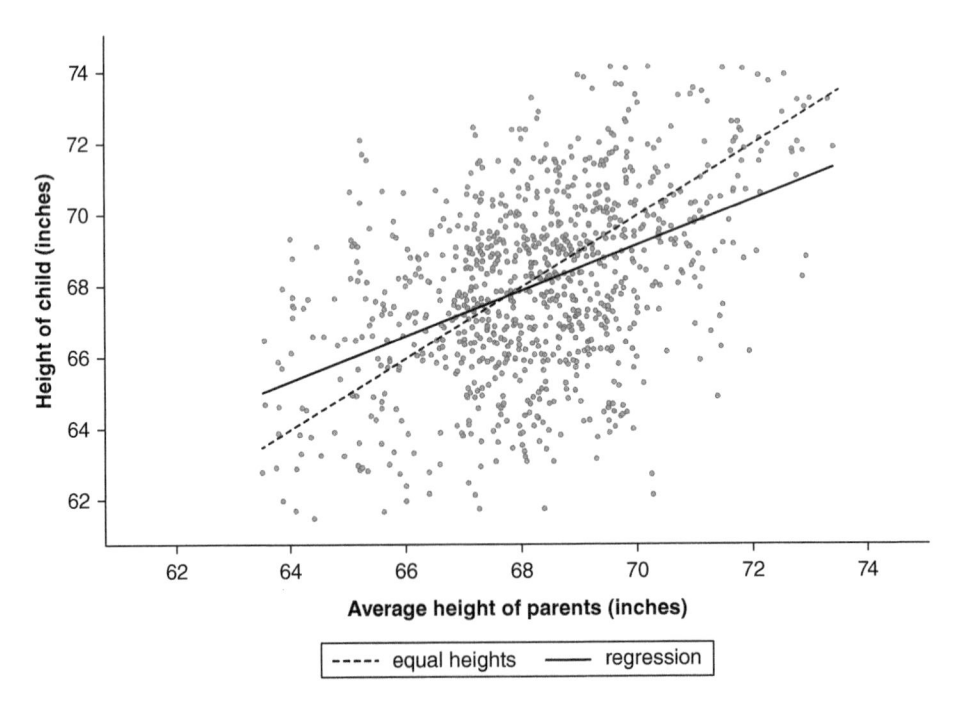

Figure 2.7 Galton's regression line compared to the line of equal heights

---

[8]We assume that we adjust for the difference in mean heights between men and women, as Galton did. Also, we ignore any trend for subsequent generations to grow taller than their parents. Galton was not concerned with such a trend.

This is Galton's famous finding. The children of parents with non-average height tend to have heights that move some way toward the average height of the population, relative to their parents' height. Galton called this 'filial regression to mediocrity' (Galton, 1886, p. 246). He uses the word *regress* in the sense of 'return towards': his idea is that a child of parents whose heights deviate from the population mean has a tendency to 'return' some way towards that population mean. Today, we call this phenomenon *regression to the mean*. The word *regression* itself has since become the name for a class of statistical models, which includes linear regression as well as many others (including those introduced in *The SAGE Quantitative Research Kit*, Volume 8).

Inference: confidence intervals and hypothesis tests

So far, we have considered the regression line simply as a summary of the observed relationship between two variables. We haven't performed any hypothesis tests, and neither have we calculated confidence intervals. In other words, we have looked at regression as a descriptive technique only and haven't concerned ourselves with statistical **inference**. If we want to generalise from our data set to make a statement about the population from which the sample was drawn, we will need to think about inference. We are usually most interested in making inferences about the slope coefficient, because it is the slope that tells us the strength and the direction of the relationship between the predictor and the outcome.

To test hypotheses about the slope, and to construct a confidence interval around it, we need to make certain assumptions about the data. I will remain silent about those assumptions in this chapter but deal with them in Chapter 3. For now, let's assume that Galton's data meet all necessary assumptions. (They do, as it happens.)

Remember what inference is about. We use sample data to estimate properties of a population. Specifically, we calculate sample statistics to estimate population parameters. The slope estimate, $\hat{\beta}$, which we obtain from fitting a linear regression model to a sample, is a statistic. The true slope, β, which is the parameter we are trying to estimate, doesn't change. But our estimate of it, $\hat{\beta}$, is likely to be different with every new sample we take. So there is variation in our estimates. In order to test hypotheses about β, then, we need to know how variable our estimates are. As you may remember from *The SAGE Quantitative Research Kit*, Volume 3, a statistic to measure the variability of estimates is the standard error.

Let's give the estimated standard error of $\hat{\beta}$ a name and call it $s_{\hat{\beta}}$, as we did in Chapter 1. Now, it can be shown that if the regression assumptions hold, then $\hat{\beta}$ will have a normal sampling distribution with a standard error estimated by

$$s_{\hat{\beta}} = \frac{s_e}{s_x \sqrt{n-1}}$$

where s_x is the standard deviation of X, n is the sample size, and s_e is the residual standard error (see section 'Residual Standard Error'). This equation implies that the larger the sample size, the smaller the standard error of $\hat{\beta}$, and therefore the more precise our slope estimate. This makes sense: the larger our sample, the better our estimate of the slope will be (all other things being equal).

For our data, the standard deviation of X, s_x, was given in Table 2.1 as $s_x = 1.81$. The residual standard error is $s_e = 2.26$, as we saw in the Section 'Residual Standard Error'. Our sample size is $n = 928$. Putting these values into the equation, we can calculate the estimated standard error of $\hat{\beta}$ for Galton's regression:

$$s_{\hat{\beta}} = \frac{s_e}{s_x \sqrt{N-2}}$$

$$= \frac{2.26}{1.81 \times \sqrt{928-2}}$$

$$= 0.041$$

We can then use a *t*-test to test hypotheses about the slope and use a *t*-distribution to construct a confidence interval for it.[9] To take one example, let's suppose that our research hypothesis was as follows:

Hypothesis: 'On average, children have the same height as their parents.'

How would we turn this conceptual hypothesis into a specific prediction about the regression coefficients? Consider what the hypothesis implies about the slope. For parents who are 63 inches tall, the average of their children's height should also be 63 inches. For parents with height 64 inches, the average of their children should be 64 inches. Whatever the parents' height, the predicted height of the children should be the same value. So for 1-inch difference in parents' height, we would expect a 1-inch difference in children's height. In other words, if the hypothesis of equal heights was true, we would expect the slope to be equal to 1. You can see this illustrated in Figure 2.7 above: the line of equal heights has a slope of 1 exactly.

---

[9]The reason we use a *t*-test, and a *t*-distribution for confidence intervals, is the same as the reason that motivates the *t*-tests for single, matched and independent samples and confidence intervals for a mean or a mean difference explained in *The SAGE Quantitative Research Kit*, Volume 3: because we don't know the standard error of the slope estimate, we need to estimate this standard error, so that test statistics and limits of confidence intervals follow a *t*-distribution rather than a normal distribution.

Let's put this hypothesis to the test. Are the data consistent with the hypothesis that the true slope is equal to 1? To construct a t-test of $H_0: \beta = 1$, we calculate the t-statistic[10]:

$$t = \frac{\hat{\beta} - \beta_0}{s_{\hat{\beta}}}$$

$$= \frac{0.638 - 1}{0.041}$$

$$= -8.86$$

The t-statistic is evaluated against a t-distribution with degrees of freedom $df = n - 2$.[11] Since $n = 928$, we have $df = 928 - 2 = 926$. A table or a computer program will tell you that the p-value for $t = -8.86$ with $df = 926$ is vanishingly small ($p = 0.000000000...$). So Galton's data provide strong evidence against the idea of equal heights. The estimated slope coefficient (0.638) is consistent with Galton's idea of regression to the mean.

I made the case that the hypothesis $H_0: \beta = 1$ is a reasonable hypothesis to test about Galton's data. However, in the context of modelling practice in social science, this is an unusual hypothesis to test. Typically, researchers test the hypothesis $H_0: \beta = 0$. As we said above, a slope coefficient of 0 implies that there is no relationship between the predictor and the outcome. So the test of $H_0: \beta = 0$ amounts to testing the null hypothesis of no relationship.

This test of 'no relationship' is obviously interesting in many situations. If the result of our test suggests that we don't have evidence for a relationship between the predictor and the outcome, we can save ourselves the work of interpreting the estimated slope coefficient. Another reason that the test of $H_0: \beta = 0$ is so popular is that it is easily available in statistical software programs, which usually include this test in their output by default, whether the user explicitly requests it or not.

However, in some situations the test of 'no relationship' is not very interesting. Take Galton's study: if Galton had collected the data only to show that there is a relationship between the heights of parents and their children, he might have been

---

[10] If you check the calculation that follows, you will notice that the result (−8.86) does not exactly match what you'd get from a hand calculation using the numbers shown. $\frac{0.638 - 1}{0.041} = -8.83$, not −8.86. This slight difference is due to rounding error. To calculate the result, I have used more precise numbers for $\hat{\beta} = 0.6376784$ and $s_{\hat{\beta}} = 0.04091067$.

[11] Why are the degrees of freedom here equal to $n - 2$? An intuitive explanation is that from the total degrees of freedom in the data (which is equal to the sample size n), our regression analysis has used up 2 df by estimating two quantities: the intercept and the slope of the regression equation. Chapter 4 provides more detail on degrees of freedom in regression analysis.

accused of wasting his time. Who would doubt that children's height is influenced by parents' height to some extent? On the other hand, the rejection of the 'equal average heights' hypothesis and the conclusion that there is 'regression to the mean' was a surprising result in Galton's days, and it still surprises people today when they come across it for the first time.

Nonetheless, the routine reporting of model estimation results in statistical software usually includes a test of the null hypothesis $H_0: \beta = 0$. Table 2.2 shows a typical display of a regression equation with **inferential statistics**. Here you see the estimated coefficients and their standard errors, as well as a confidence interval of the slope and a test of $H_0: \beta = 0$.

Table 2.2 A typical regression results table (based on Galton's data)

	Coefficient Estimate	Standard Error	95% Confidence Interval for the Coefficient		t-Test of $H_0: \beta = 0$		
			Lower Bound	Upper Bound	t	df	p
Intercept	24.526	2.795					
Parents' height	0.638	0.041	0.557	0.718	15.587	926	0.000

Note. The results differ slightly from Galton's original analysis, because I have added a small random jiggle to the data, to avoid overlap of points in scatter plots. df = degrees of freedom.

The test of $H_0: \beta = 0$ is conducted as follows[12]:

$$t = \frac{\hat{\beta} - \beta_0}{s_{\hat{\beta}}}$$

$$= \frac{0.638 - 0}{0.041}$$

$$= 15.59$$

As before, using a t-distribution with 926 df, we find a very small p-value, as displayed in Table 2.2.

Next, let's have a look at the confidence interval. The 95% confidence interval for the slope of parents' height is 0.540 to 0.752. Informally, we might interpret this to mean that we are 95% confident that this interval contains the true slope parameter.[13] Thus, the confidence interval gives us a likely plausible range of slope values which are compatible with the data.

---

[12] A slight difference between the result displayed and the result you would get by hand calculation is due to rounding error.
[13] A technically more precise interpretation of a 95% confidence interval is: 'if I construct 95% confidence intervals around parameter estimates on each of an infinite number of random samples from the same population, and all model assumptions hold in each case, then 95% of these intervals will contain the true parameter'.

The confidence interval can be derived as follows: if regression assumptions hold, the sampling distribution of $\hat{\beta}$ is a t-distribution with mean β and $n - 2$ df. The formula for the confidence interval is then as follows:

$$CI = \hat{\beta} \pm t_{crit} \times s_{\hat{\beta}}$$

To calculate the 95% confidence interval, we need to determine t_{crit} as the point in the t-distribution (with $n - 2$ df) that cuts off 2.5% in one tail of the distribution (since $2 \times 2.5\% = 5\%$, which is the error probability for a 95% confidence interval – see *The SAGE Quantitative Research Kit*, Volume 3). This value is usually denoted by $t_{926, 0.975}$ and can be found from a table of critical t-values, or calculated using statistical software. In our case, $t_{crit} = t_{926, 0.975} = 1.963$. The 95% confidence interval is then calculated thus[14]:

$$\begin{aligned}CI_{0.95} &= 0.638 \pm 1.963 \times 0.041 \\ &= 0.638 \pm 0.080 \\ &= [0.557, 0.718]\end{aligned}$$

This is the confidence interval displayed in Table 2.2. If we had wanted to give the 99% confidence interval instead, we would have needed to use as t_{crit} the value that cuts off 0.5% of the t-distribution with $df = 926$ in one tail. (This turns out to be $t_{926, 0.995} = 2.581$). The 99% confidence interval would be wider than the 95% confidence interval, of course.

Confidence range for a regression line

It can be useful to visualise the uncertainty around a regression line. We can extend inference to the regression line as a whole, by displaying the uncertainty in the estimated regression line as a confidence range. This can be done by calculating a confidence interval around the predicted outcome value for every value of the predictor variable. For those who are interested in the details, the calculation is shown in Box 2.5. Figure 2.8 shows the confidence range for Galton's regression line.

Notice that the confidence range for the regression line is narrowest near the mean of X and fans out to the left and to the right. This indicates that our prediction of Y is more reliable close to the mean of X than further away from the mean. The following is an intuitive way to understand why this should be the case. Imagine pivoting the line on its centre point, thereby changing the slope. A given amount of change in the slope would make a relatively small difference to the predicted values in the region

---

[14] A slight difference between the hand calculation and the result displayed is due to rounding error in the hand calculation.

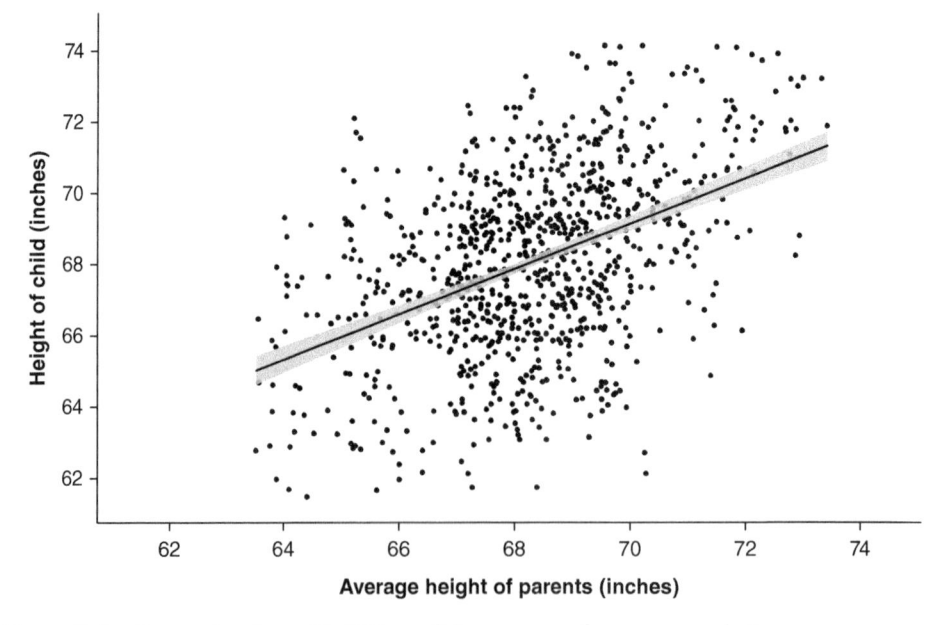

Figure 2.8 Regression line with 95% confidence range for mean prediction

near the pivot point, but a relatively bigger difference at either end. So uncertainty about the true slope coefficient effects predictions near the mean of X less than predictions at either end of the range of X.

Box 2.5

How to Calculate a Confidence Range Around the Regression Line

The confidence range around the regression line is estimated by calculating a separate confidence interval for each predicted mean outcome, $\hat{Y}$. This predicted mean outcome of course depends on the value of X. It can be shown mathematically that the standard error of $\hat{Y}$ as a predictor of the mean of Y for a given X value can be estimated by the following equation:

$$\hat{SE}(\hat{Y}) = s_e \sqrt{\frac{1}{n} + \frac{(X-\bar{X})^2}{(n-1)s_x^2}}$$

where s_e is the residual standard error and s_x^2 is the variance of X. If you look at the equation carefully, you may notice that $\hat{SE}(\hat{Y})$ is influenced by four quantities:

- The larger the residual standard error, s_e, the larger is $\hat{SE}(\hat{Y})$.
- The smaller the sample size, n, the larger is $\hat{SE}(\hat{Y})$.

- The smaller the variance of X, s_x^2, the larger is $\hat{SE}(\hat{Y})$.
- The further X is away from the mean $\bar{X}$, the larger is $\hat{SE}(\hat{Y})$; this results in the 'fanning-out' of the confidence range that we see in Figure 2.8.

A 95% confidence interval of the mean prediction is then given by:

$$CI_{0.95} = \hat{Y} \pm t_{n-2, 0.975} \times \hat{SE}(\hat{Y})$$

where $t_{n-2, 0.975}$ is the value that cuts off 2.5% of values in the tail of a t-distribution with $df = n - 2$. For example, let's calculate a 95% confidence interval for the mean height of children whose parents' height is 72 inches. We have:

$X = 72$

$n = 928$

$\bar{X} = 68.30$ (from Table 2.1)

$s_x^2 = 3.29$ (from Table 2.1)

$s_e = 2.26$ (from the section 'Residual Standard Error')

$t_{926, 0.975} = 1.963$

$\hat{Y} = 70.44$ (the child's predicted height if the parents are 72 inches tall, calculated from the regression equation)

Thus we can calculate the standard error of the mean prediction, $\hat{SE}(\hat{Y})$, as follows:

$$\hat{SE}(\hat{Y}) = s_e \sqrt{\frac{1}{N} + \frac{(X - \bar{X})^2}{(N-1)s_x^2}}$$

$$= 2.26 \sqrt{\frac{1}{928} + \frac{(72 - 68.30)^2}{927 \times 3.29}}$$

$$= 0.17$$

Then the 95% confidence interval of the predicted mean height of children with parental height 72 inches is:

$$CI_{0.95} = 70.44 \pm 1.963 \times 0.17$$
$$= 70.44 \pm 0.33$$
$$= [70.11, 70.77]$$

If we do this calculation for a series of X-values in the range of X, we can draw the confidence range around the regression line. In practice, good statistical software is able to make these calculations and draw the confidence range.

Prediction and prediction intervals

In the section 'Confidence Range for a Regression Line', we saw how to calculate a confidence range for a regression line. This gives us an indication of the uncertainty around the predictions we make about the *mean* of Y, given X. In our example, for all children of parents with the same height X, the confidence range shows us where these children's mean height is likely to be. However, regression is also sometimes used for predicting *individual* data points. Here, the question is: 'given that the parents have height X, what is the expected height Y of an *individual* child'? As we will see, there is much more uncertainty in the prediction of an individual's outcome, compared to the prediction of a group mean. A situation where we could apply individual prediction is imputation of missing values. For example, let's suppose there is an individual in our data set whose height has not been measured for some reason. If however the parents' height has been recorded, we might substitute a predicted value from the regression of child's height on parents' height for the missing observation.[15]

As we have seen, the predicted value of Y given X can be calculated from the regression equation:

$$\hat{Y} = \hat{\beta}_0 + \hat{\beta}_1 X$$

As statisticians, we are concerned with the uncertainty around a prediction. To quantify the uncertainty, we can construct a prediction interval. For example, if we construct a 95% prediction interval for predicting the height of an individual child, we expect that 95% of true heights fall within the bounds of this interval.[16] The calculations are shown in Box 2.6. The 95% prediction intervals for all parental heights are illustrated in Figure 2.9. Notice that the prediction intervals are much wider than the 95% confidence intervals for the regression line. This is because a confidence interval for the regression line is calculated on the assumption that we only care about getting it right *on average*. Given an X value, the confidence interval tells us a range in which we can expect the *mean of Y* to lie. In contrast, the prediction interval gives us a range in which, given an X value, we can expect an *individual value of Y* to lie. There is more uncertainty when trying to predict an individual case, compared to predicting the average of a sample. Like the confidence interval for the mean prediction,

---

[15] It's not advisable to simply go about substituting predictions from a model for missing values and then to analyse the data set as if it had been complete from the start. Such an approach underestimates the uncertainty in the prediction and thus leads the researcher to be overconfident in their conclusions. Multiple imputation is a sophisticated method that aims to take this additional uncertainty into account (see also Chapter 6).

[16] Alternatively, of course, we could construct a prediction interval with some other confidence level, for example, 99% or 90%.

the individual prediction interval is wider for X-values further away from the mean, but this fanning-out effect is small relative to the width of the interval in our example, which is why in Figure 2.9 it is barely visible.

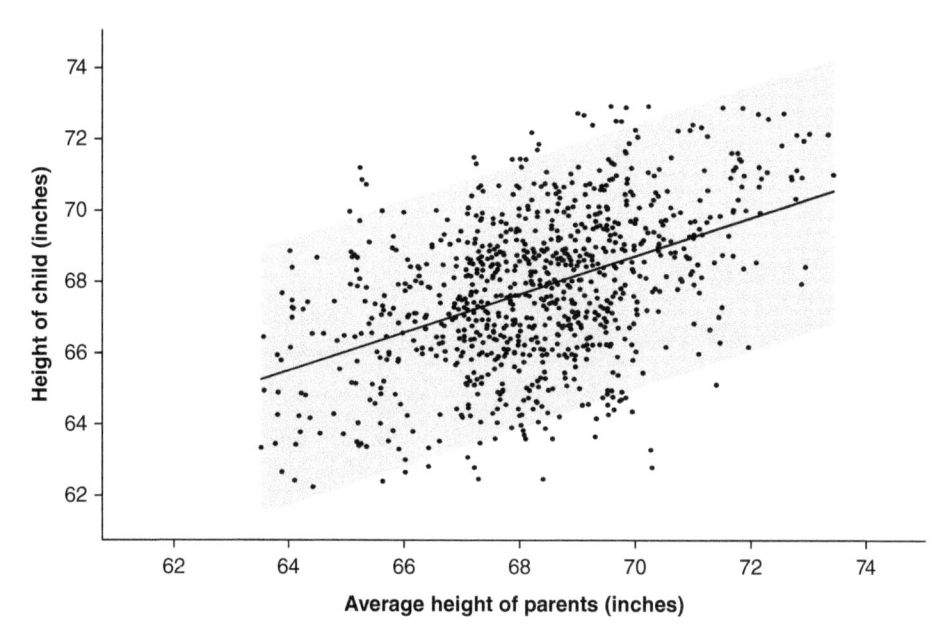

Figure 2.9   Regression line with 95% prediction intervals

Box 2.6

How to Calculate a Prediction Interval

How is the prediction interval (for predicting an individual Y-value from a predictor X) calculated? The calculation is similar to that for the confidence interval of the regression line, but taking into account the larger uncertainty that results when we try to predict the value of an individual.

It can be shown that the standard deviation of the predicted value, $\hat{Y}$, for a given X can be estimated by the following:

$$\hat{SD}_{ind}(\hat{Y}) = s_e \sqrt{1 + \frac{1}{N} + \frac{(X - \bar{X})^2}{(N-1)s_x^2}}$$

Note that the estimation of $\hat{SD}_{ind}(\hat{Y})$ is the same as the estimation for $\hat{SD}(\hat{Y})$ shown in Box 2.5, except that '+1' is added to the term under the square root. This accounts for the additional uncertainty we incur when we try to predict the height of an individual,

(Continued)

rather than the average height for a group. The prediction interval (PI) is then calculated as follows:

$$PI_{0.95} = \hat{Y} \pm t_{n-2, 0.975} \times \hat{SD}_{ind}(\hat{Y})$$

For the same example value as in Box 2.5, predicting the height of an individual child with parental height 72 inches, $\hat{SD}_{ind}(\hat{Y})$ is:

$$\hat{SD}_{ind}(\hat{Y}) = 2.26 \sqrt{1 + \frac{1}{928} + \frac{(72-68.30)^2}{927 \times 3.29}}$$
$$= 2.27$$

Then the 95% prediction interval can be calculated as follows:

$$PI_{0.95} = 70.44 \pm 1.963 \times 2.27$$
$$= [65.99, 74.89]$$

This is considerably wider than the 95% confidence interval in Box 2.5.

To further illustrate the different interpretations of the confidence interval (Box 2.5) and the prediction interval (this box), consider the following. From the confidence interval, we can conclude with 95% confidence that the group of children whose parents are 72 inches tall are shorter than their parents *on average* (since the confidence interval [70.11, 70.77] does not contain the value 72). However, we cannot predict with equal confidence that any *individual* child of such parents will be shorter than their parents, since the 95% prediction interval [65.99, 74.89] does contain the value 72, as well as higher values.

Regression in practice: things that can go wrong

When you apply linear regression, it is wise to be aware of some traps that, if you fall into them, can make your regression model worthless or misleading. Such mistakes are particularly likely to occur in three types of situations:

1. When the researcher doesn't think clearly about her or his research question but simply decides "let's predict Y by X and see what happens"
2. When the researcher fails to look at plots of the data before, or alongside, the fitting of the model
3. When the researcher does not fully consider the limitations of regression models

It is easy to fall into these traps these days, because statistical software can do all the calculations for you, and it takes little effort to produce standard output (e.g. a table like Table 2.2) and achieve the *appearance* of a sophisticated statistical analysis without actually doing one. If you are tempted to follow that route, let this section be a warning.

Influential observations

The estimated regression model can sometimes be influenced strongly by a single observation that is very different from all the others (Anscombe, 1973). The same can happen if a small subset of the observations differs very much from the others. The potential influence of a single observation is illustrated in Figure 2.10. In these hypothetical data, the influential observation (black dot) either suppresses a strong relationship among the grey dots (case a) or artificially gives the appearance of a positive relationship when in fact there is a negative correlation, or no correlation at all (case b).

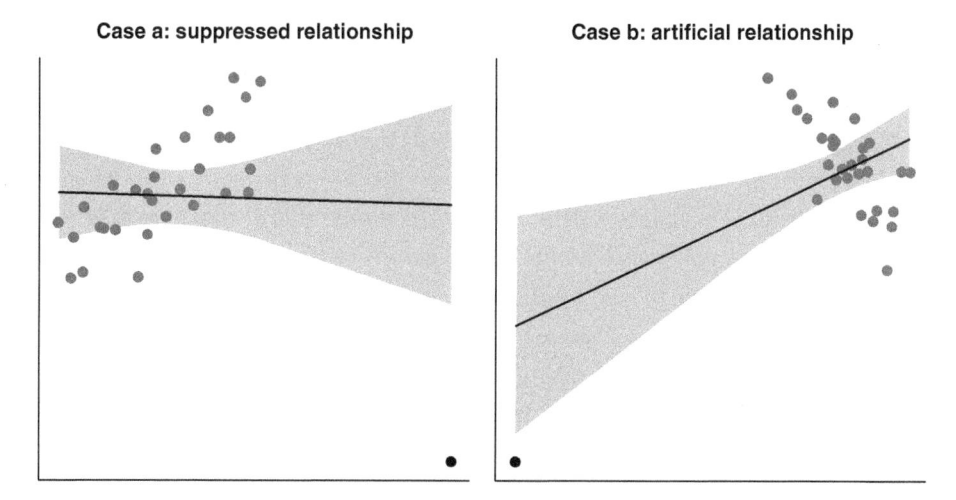

Figure 2.10 Misleading regression lines resulting from influential observations

Note. Simulated data. The influential observation (black dot) leads to a misleading regression line that does a poor job at representing the data. The shaded areas give 95% confidence regions for the regression lines.

What should we do if our data look something like in Figure 2.10? The first thing to do would be to find out more about the influential observation. Sometimes untypical observations are the result of measurement or coding errors. For example, you may have coded missing values as '999' and entered observations with this code into the regression model as if it was a real measurement (representing someone as being 999 inches tall, say). In such a case, the apparently influential observation is erroneous, and the mistake is easily rectified.

However, it is possible to have untypical observations even if your measurements are accurate and your coding impeccable. For example, among a sample of 500 households from the United Kingdom, 499 might have an annual income between £15,000 and £100,000, but the 100th household may include a pop star earning millions of pounds per year. This outlier value could then have a strong influence on any model featuring household income, either as a predictor or as an outcome. It may be appropriate to remove the pop star from the data set before modelling. That would restrict the applicability of the model to households with income ranges between £15,000 and £100,000, and such a restriction might be perfectly appropriate.

Selecting the right group

Sometimes a linear model may be perfectly appropriate for a subgroup of the data but not for the whole data set. Consider Figure 2.11, which shows the relationships between GDP (gross domestic product) per capita and life expectancy for two groups of countries from the same data set: in the left panel, only European countries are included; in the right panel, African countries are added to the European data. Each time, a linear model is fit on the data displayed. A linear model works well for Europe alone, suggesting that there is a slight linear increase in life expectancy as GDP per capita rises from around US$5900 (the GDP per capita in Albania in 2007) to around $49,000 (Norway). The model estimates that for every additional $10,000 in GDP per capita, life expectancy rises by about 2 years. We may want to try a curvilinear model to see whether that improves the fit (see Chapter 3), but the linear model doesn't do a bad job.

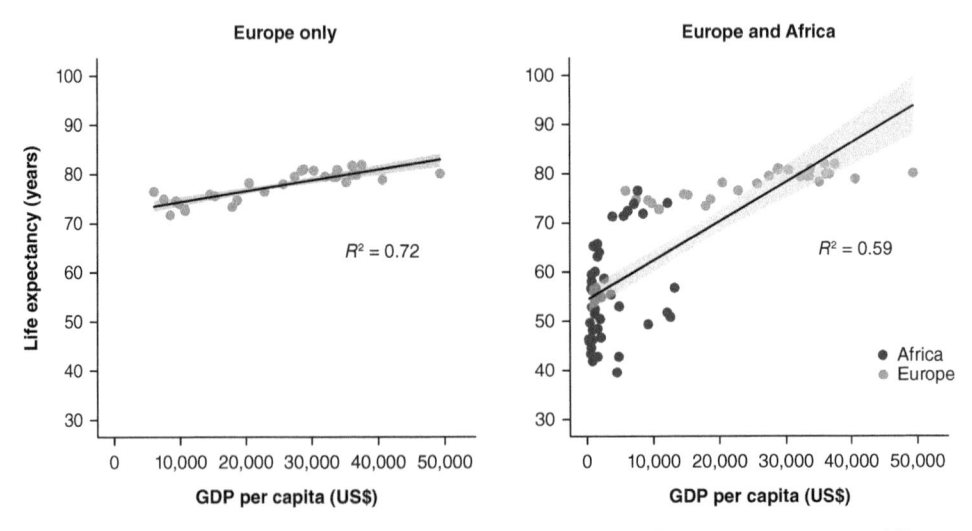

Figure 2.11 The relationship between GDP per capita and life expectancy, in two different selections from the same data set

Note. Data provided by the Gapminder Foundation (Bryan, 2017). GDP = gross domestic product.

When we include African countries in the data set, things change profoundly: the regression equation now estimates life expectancy to rise by about 8 years for every additional $10,000. But the model fits poorly – R^2 is lower than for the European data alone, and there is a clear non-linear pattern in the data which the straight regression line does not capture. In general, how we should address such a situation depends on the context. However, in the example two options we might consider are (1) to analyse the two groups separately and (2) to use a non-linear model that can accommodate the relationship between GDP and life expectancy for both groups (an example of the latter strategy is included in Chapter 3).

One important issue to note here is that graphical exploration is often necessary to detect the inapplicability of linear regression for the data containing two groups. In particular, looking at the R^2 value alone would not necessarily have alerted you that something is wrong with the analysis in the right panel of Figure 2.11. Here, $R^2 = 0.59$, which looks like a strong linear relationship (it corresponds to *Pearson's r* = 0.77). Thus, without looking at the graph, the unwary analyst may well have concluded that a linear regression achieves an adequate fit and a good prediction of life expectancy via GDP in this group of countries.

The dangers of extrapolation

Sometimes analysts attempt to use a regression model to predict what happens outside the range of the data that were used to estimate the model. This is called extrapolating beyond the data. In general, it is a difficult thing to do well, and, if done without thought, can lead to severe misprediction and erroneous conclusions.

Consider Figure 2.12. This illustrates a regression of life expectancy on GDP, using only data from the 12 Asian countries with the highest GDP. Their GDP per capita values range from about $11,600 (Iran) to $47,300 (Kuwait). Now, we might expect that the predictions from this model might be reasonably accurate for countries with GDPs between $11,600 and $47,300, even for countries other than the 12 that were included in the original sample. Such an expectation would be plausible if the new countries were similar to those included in the original sample, but possibly not otherwise (beware the 'different-groups' fallacy from the previous section).

But can we extrapolate the predictions from our regression to countries with GDPs outside the range of the original data – that is, to countries with GDPs smaller than $11,600 or larger than $47,300? Imagine that the researchers had access only to data from the 12 richest Asian countries but would like to use their model to predict the life expectancies of countries with GDP values below $10,000 per capita. They might

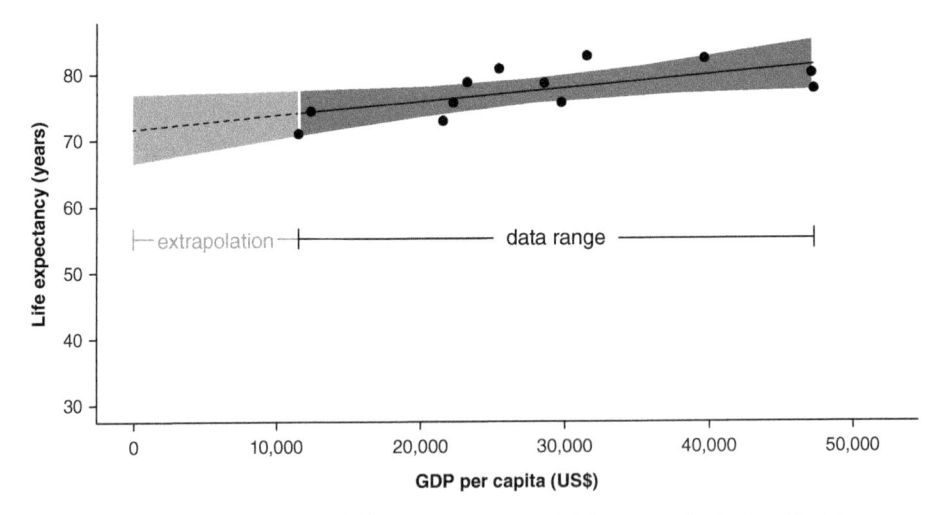

Figure 2.12 Linear regression of life expectancy on GDP per capita in the 12 Asian countries with highest GDP, with extrapolation beyond the data range

Note. Data provided by the Gapminder Foundation (Bryan, 2017). GDP = gross domestic product.

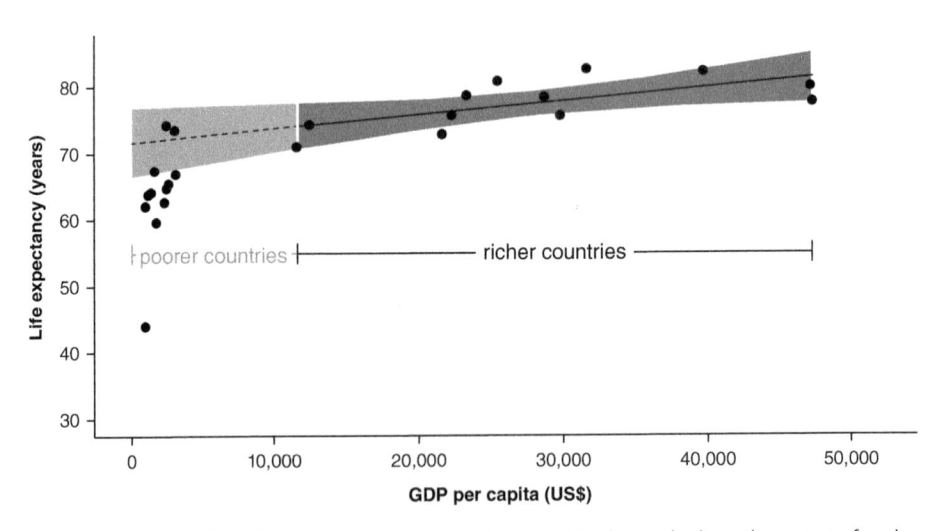

Figure 2.13 Checking the extrapolation from Figure 2.12 by including the points for the 12 Asian countries with the lowest GDP per capita

Note. The regression model is based on the 12 Asian countries with the highest GDP (see Figure 2.12). The extrapolation to lower GDP values tends to overestimate the life expectancy in the 12 Asian countries with the lowest GDP. Data provided by the Gapminder Foundation (Bryan, 2017). GDP = gross domestic product.

then extend the regression line (and its confidence range) as shown in Figure 2.12. The extrapolation suggests that countries with GDPs under $10,000 per capita will generally have only slightly lower life expectancies than the 12 richest Asian countries. However, in reality, this extrapolation is widely off the mark. This is shown by Figure 2.13, where I have added the 12 Asian countries with the lowest GDP values. The majority of these have life expectancies far below the extrapolated prediction. The regression line based on data from the richest 12 countries clearly does not fit the data when the 12 poorest countries are also included.

In this example, it was easy for me to check that the extrapolation leads to misleading predictions for the poorest countries, because I had access to the relevant data. Of course, in practice a researcher would consider extrapolation only in a situation where they do *not* have access to additional data. (If they had, they would simply include those data in their model estimation in the first place.) Thus, by definition, extrapolation requires a leap of faith into the unknown: we need to make the assumption that our model will work well for cases on which we don't have data, and whose characteristics are different to the cases on which we do have data. Unfortunately, in reality that assumption is often not justified.

Another example of the dangers of extrapolation is provided by financial crises. In a period of economic stability, prices of stocks may rise steadily. Financial models of stock prices based on data gathered in such 'good times' for investors may confidently predict that the future will look like the past. Complicated-looking equations and nice-looking graphs may be used to illustrate the increasing value of certain stocks and may form the basis of predictions of future gains to be had from purchasing the stocks. But as we know, financial crises may interfere, and there is no guarantee that a trend of the past may continue in the future. The belief in the trustworthiness of a model outside of the range of data from which it was built may come at a high cost.

Chapter Summary

- This chapter has introduced simple linear regression: a model for a straight-line relationship between a single numeric predictor and a continuous outcome.
- This chapter has also introduced inferential procedures for simple linear regression, namely statistical hypothesis tests and confidence intervals for regression coefficients. These inferential procedures are only valid, however, when our data meet certain statistical assumptions.
- The next chapter introduces these assumptions and also considers what to do when they are not met. Chapters 4 and 5 then extend the simple linear regression model by introducing models that involve more than one predictor.

Further Reading

Rowntree, D. (1981). *Statistics without tears. A primer for non-mathematicians.* Penguin.

Rowntree's book gives an intuitive explanation of the idea of regression, which makes do with a minimum of mathematics.

Krzanowski, W. J. (1998). *An introduction to statistical modelling.* Wiley.

If you wish to study the mathematical aspects of linear regression in more depth (but without actually doing a full course in mathematical statistics), then this book will repay careful study.

3

ASSUMPTIONS AND TRANSFORMATIONS

Chapter Overview

The assumptions of linear regression	52
Investigating assumptions: regression diagnostics	54
Regression diagnostics: application with examples	56
What if assumptions do not hold? An example	71
Types of transformations, and when to use them	79
Further Reading	85

All statistical models make assumptions about the processes that have generated the data and about the characteristics of the population distribution that the data were sampled from. If the assumptions are wrong, then estimates from the statistical model may be meaningless or misleading. In practice, it is not always possible to conclusively establish whether the data meet the assumptions that we have made for a particular model. However, we can consider whether our assumptions are plausible or not. Sometimes we can use statistical theory, and our knowledge of how the data were collected, to deduce how likely it is that assumptions are met. To some extent, we can also use the data themselves to put assumptions to the test.

This chapter starts with a brief overview of the assumptions that underlie linear regression. In the rest of the chapter, I further explain and illustrate some of the assumptions and show how to investigate our data to evaluate how plausible the assumptions are. We also consider what we can do in situations where model assumptions are not met. In particular, the second half of this chapter discusses **variable transformations**, a mathematical technique that can sometimes enable us to change our model so that it can meet its assumptions and can help to specify a plausible model even when there is a non-linear relationship between the predictor and the outcome.

The assumptions of linear regression

In this section, I briefly introduce seven key assumptions that underlie simple linear regression, as described in Chapter 2. Subsequent sections will consider each of them in more detail. The assumptions are:

1. *Linearity: The relationship between the predictor and the outcome is linear.* If this assumption is not met, the linear model misrepresents the true shape of the relationship between the predictor and the outcome.
2. *Normality of errors: The errors follow a normal distribution.* If the errors are not normally distributed, hypothesis tests and confidence intervals about model coefficients and predictions may yield misleading results.[1]
3. *Homoscedasticity of errors: The variance of the errors around the regression line is the same at every point of the regression line.* '**Homoscedasticity**' is a compound word made of classical Greek roots meaning 'same variance'. The opposite of homoscedasticity is **heteroscedasticity** ('different variance'). If the errors are heteroscedastic,

---

[1] In this book, I assume that you have come across the normal distribution before. I provide reminders of the properties of the normal distribution in the section 'Regression Diagnostics: Application With Examples' – see in particular Boxes 3.1 and 3.3.

hypothesis tests and confidence intervals around model coefficients and model predictions may yield misleading results.
4. *Independence of errors: The errors are independent of one another.* If there is dependency between some or all errors, hypothesis tests and confidence intervals around model coefficients and model predictions may yield misleading results.
5. *Randomness of errors: The errors are the result of a random process.* If the errors are not in fact random, then inferences from the sample to a population or process might be illusory. A random process may be built into the design of our study, such as when we employ random sampling to select survey respondents. But we may also assume randomness in social or natural processes. For example, Galton's data on heights, used in Chapter 2, were not a random sample of child–parent pairs. Nonetheless, our model assumed that the variations of children's heights around the predicted values were the result of a random process. Given our knowledge of genetics today (which Galton himself did not have), we might argue that the selection of parent genes that are passed on to their children is such a random process.
6. *The predictor is measured without error: The linear regression model has no error term for the predictor variable, and thus it implicitly assumes that the predictor variable has no measurement error.* This assumption cannot be tested within the framework of linear regression itself. Structural equation models (see *The SAGE Quantitative Research Kit*, Volume 9) are one way to analyse data while taking into account measurement errors in both predictor and outcome variables.
7. *Absence of extremely influential observations: There are no extreme outliers in the data that distort the observed relationship between the predictor and the outcome.* If this assumption is not met, coefficient estimates, as well as hypothesis tests and confidence intervals, may be misleading.

An illustration of the important assumptions of linearity, normality and homoscedasticity is given in Figure 3.1, which shows Galton's data and the fitted regression line, as discussed in Chapter 2. Three normal distribution curves are drawn around the predicted child's height for parental heights of 65, 68 and 71 inches, respectively. There is nothing special about these three parental heights; they are merely examples. Think of the three normal curves as growing out of the page towards you. A full three-dimensional illustration would resemble an elongate hill rising up from the page, its cross-section shaped like the normal distribution and its top ridge sitting exactly over the regression line.

Figure 3.1 illustrates the assumption that, for a sample of families with the same parental height, the heights of the children follow a normal distribution, whose mean is the predicted value. So children's heights close to the predicted values are more likely than children's heights further away from the predicted value. Note also that the normal distributions all have the same variance. The children's heights are spread around the predicted values evenly, the variation being the same around every predicted value. This illustrates the assumption of homoscedasticity.

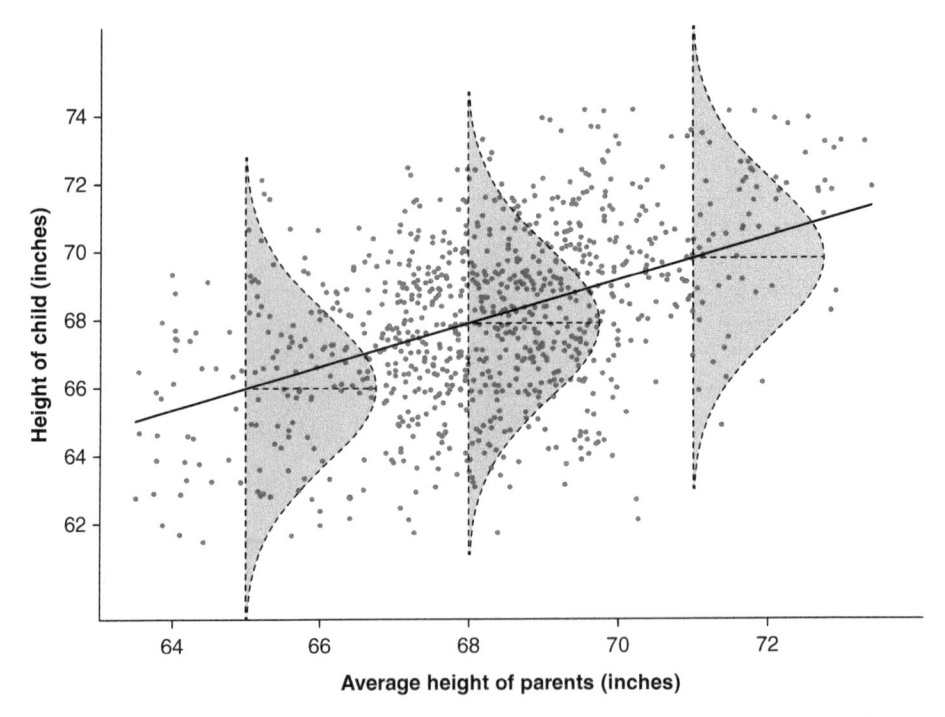

Figure 3.1 Illustration of the assumptions of normality and homoscedasticity in Galton's regression

Note. Think of the three normal distributions as growing out of the page towards you.

Investigating assumptions: regression diagnostics

Errors and residuals

How can we determine whether our assumptions are plausible or not? Some of the assumptions listed above concern the errors. However, recall from Chapter 2 that we do not observe the errors directly. Because we never observe the 'true' regression line, we also never know for sure exactly how large the error is for any given observation.

But we do observe the residuals, which are our estimates of the errors. It would thus be nice if we could use the residuals to draw conclusions about the errors and thereby put the regression assumptions to the test. It turns out, however, that this is not straightforward, because it can be shown mathematically that the residuals

- are correlated with one another (and therefore not independent)[2] and
- don't have the same variance at all levels of the predictor (i.e. the residuals are heteroscedastic).[3]

Thus, the residuals do not conform to some of the regression assumptions and therefore cannot be used directly to investigate the plausibility of these assumptions. However, we can use the residuals indirectly, by transforming them into standardised residuals. How that works is the topic of the next section.

Standardised residuals

Standardised residuals[4] are calculated as follows:

$$stdres_i = \frac{e_i}{s_e \sqrt{1 - h_{ii}}}$$

where

- $stdres_i$ is the standardised residual of the ith observation,
- e_i is the (unstandardised) residual of the ith observation,
- s_e is the residual standard error and
- h_{ii} is the **leverage** of the ith observation. The leverage is a number between $1/n$ and 1 that indicates how *un*typical the predictor value of the ith observation is. The further a predictor value is from the sample mean, the larger is its leverage. The image used here is that of a lever. The difference between the predictor value and the sample mean represents the length of the lever: the longer the lever, the more force you can exert. Analogously, the further away a predictor value is from the mean, the stronger is its influence on the slope of the regression line.[5]

---

[2] That the residuals depend on one another is maybe not too difficult to understand. Imagine a scatter plot with a regression line. Now imagine that we discovered that the outcome value of one observation had been recorded wrongly. Let's imagine that we therefore correct this value, redraw the scatter plot and estimate a new regression line. This corrected line will have a different slope than the one that was based on the incorrect observation. This means that all the residuals will change, including, of course, the residual of the observation whose value we have corrected. This shows that a change in one residual affects all other residuals: they depend on one another.
[3] The further away the value of the predictor variable is from the mean, the smaller is the variance of the residual. This is because observations with predictor values further away from the mean have a larger influence on the estimated regression equation than those close to the mean.
[4] Standardised residuals are sometimes called 'studentised residuals' or 'internally studentised residuals'.
[5] See also Chapter 4 for a definition of the leverage in the context of multiple regression. The leverage h_{ii} has the letter i in the subscript twice, because it is an element of a matrix, the so-called 'hat matrix', denoted H. The first i denotes the matrix row, the second the column in which the leverage can be found. In this book, I will not show how the leverage is calculated, and it is not necessary to understand what precisely the hat matrix is in order to understand this book. For those interested in mathematical details, Krzanowski (1998, p. 101ff) may be a good start.

The standardised residuals, by definition, have a mean equal to 0 and a standard deviation equal to 1. If the model assumptions hold, the standardised residuals are independent of one another, are approximately homoscedastic, and approximately follow a standard normal distribution. We can therefore use the standardised residuals to evaluate whether model assumptions are plausible: if the standardised residuals are heteroscedastic or depart quite clearly from the normal distribution, this may be an indication that model assumptions are violated.

The process of checking assumptions via the inspection of standardised residuals and other aspects of the data is called *regression diagnostics*. This is the topic to which we now turn.

Regression diagnostics: application with examples

This section considers how to use standardised residuals to investigate how plausible some of the assumptions underlying linear regression are. We look at the assumptions of normality, homoscedasticity, linearity, independence, and absence of influential observations, each in their turn.

Normality

In this book, I assume that you have encountered the normal distribution before. *The SAGE Quantitative Research Kit*, Volume 3, gives an introduction. If you wish to remind yourself of the properties of the normal distribution, and of the concept of a *standard normal distribution*, please consult Box 3.1.

Box 3.1

The Normal Distribution and the Standard Normal Distribution

The normal distribution is of primary importance in statistical science. It is a probability distribution that describes a continuous variable. When graphed, it has a characteristic shape that some people call a 'bell curve'. Figure 3.2 shows an illustration.

Some important characteristics of the normal distribution are:

- *Two parameters:* The normal distribution is completely characterised by its two parameters, the mean (usually denoted by μ) and the standard deviation (σ). That is to say, if I know the mean and the standard deviation of a normal distribution, I know exactly what it looks like. Other types of distributions are characterised by just one parameter, or more than two parameters. For example, the Poisson distribution has just a single parameter, which is equal to both its mean and its variance – see *The SAGE Quantitative Research Kit*, Volume 8.

ASSUMPTIONS AND TRANSFORMATIONS | 57

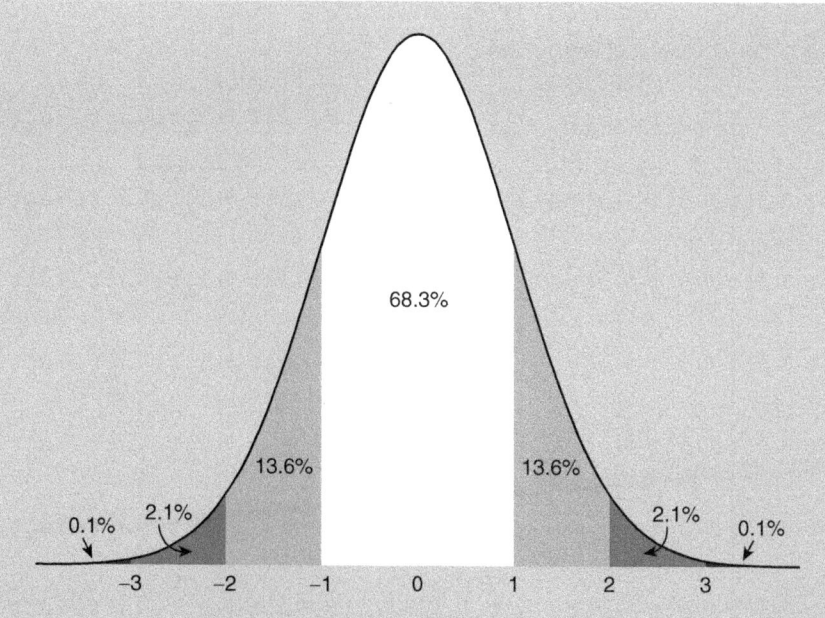

Figure 3.2 An illustration of the normal distribution

Note. The illustration shows a standard normal distribution, with mean equal to 0 and standard deviation equal to 1.

- *Symmetry:* A normal distribution is symmetric around the mean, and values close to the mean are more likely than values further away from the mean. This implies that its mean, median and mode are the same value. The mean is 0 in Figure 3.2.
- *Unboundedness:* The normal distribution is unbounded. That means that a normally distributed variable can in principle take any value, from −∞ to ∞, although values very far away from the mean are very unlikely.

An area under the curve describes the probability of values falling within a certain interval. These probabilities are expressed as percentages in Figure 3.2. For example, 68.3% of the values of a normally distributed variable fall in the interval ±1 standard deviations (*SD*) either side of the mean. To give another example, only about 0.1% of values are larger than the mean + 3 *SD*.

Figure 3.2 shows a standard normal distribution, which is the name for a normal distribution with $\mu = 0$ and $\sigma = 1$. We can transform any normal distribution, for a given variable X, into a standard normal distribution by z-standardising X such that $Z = \frac{X - \mu}{\sigma}$.

Many measurements in the physical world are approximately normally distributed. This is the case, for example, for babies' birth weight and the height of human adults (separately for each gender). The importance of the normal distribution for statistics derives chiefly from a mathematical result called the *central limit theorem*. Simplifying a little, the central limit theorem states that the sampling distribution of the mean of a variable X will be approximately normal, whatever the distribution of X, if the sample size is large enough. That is an important reason why the normal distribution is so useful in statistical inference. Box 3.3 gives more detail on the normal distribution.

If the assumption of normality of errors holds, the standardised residuals should follow a standard normal distribution. We will look at two types of plots commonly used to assess normality: histograms and normal quantile–quantile plots (q–q plots).

Figure 3.3 shows the standardised residuals from Galton's regression (Chapter 2). The fit between the standardised residuals and the normal distribution is quite good here. So we have no reason, from these data, to doubt the normality assumption for Galton's regression.

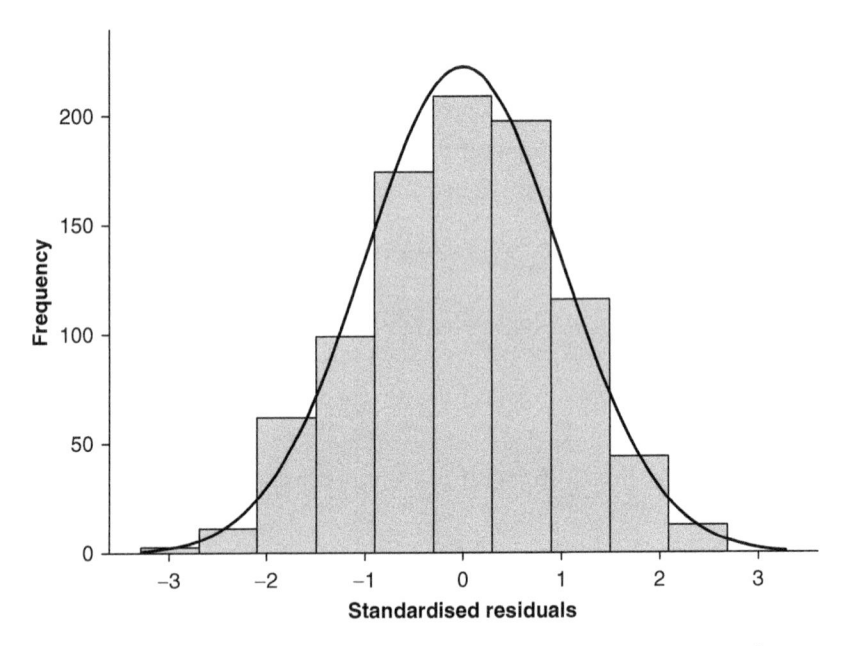

Figure 3.3 Histogram of standardised residuals from Galton's regression, with a superimposed normal curve

How would the histograms look in cases where the normality assumption was not met? Figure 3.4 shows a selection of histograms for a variety of distribution shapes. If the standardised residuals deviate widely from the normal distribution, this is an indication that the assumption of normality of errors may not hold.

Histograms are useful and have the advantage that they are intuitively interpretable. One problem with histograms, however, is that the fit between the bars and the curve can look better or worse, depending on how many bars you choose to draw and depending on your choice of breakpoints. A second problem is that it can sometimes be difficult to see deviations from normality at the tails of the distribution in a histogram. Therefore, it is often preferable to assess normality using the so-called normal quantile–quantile plot, or *normal q–q plot*. The normal q–q plot displays the observed

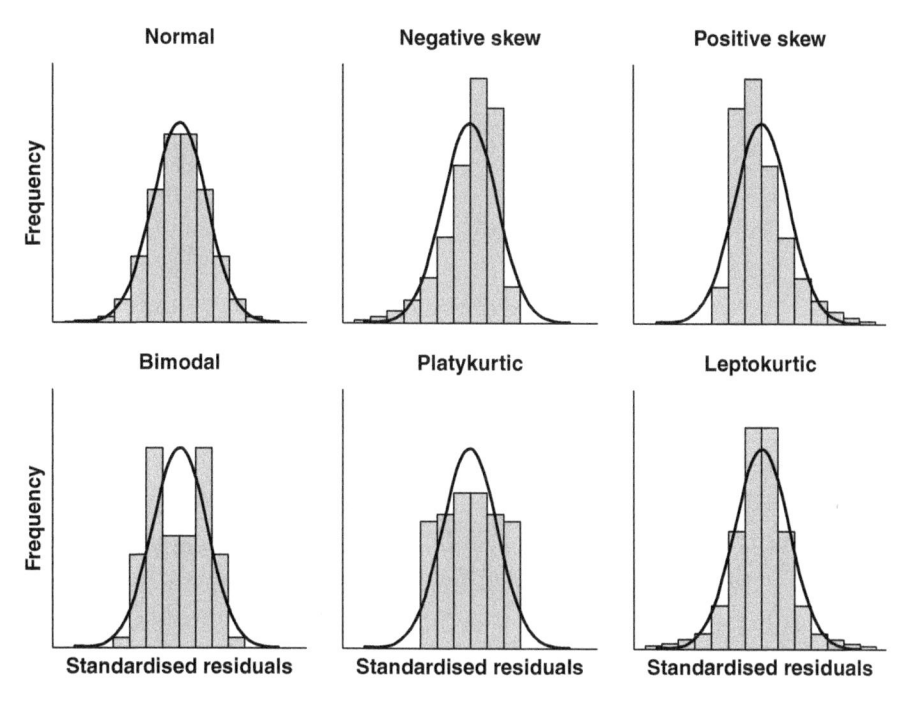

Figure 3.4 Histograms of standardised residuals illustrating six distribution shapes

Note. Simulated data. These histograms show the same data as the normal q–q plots in Figure 3.6.

Box 3.2

Regression Diagnostics and Uncertainty

I use cautious language when talking about the graphical evaluation of assumptions ('no reason to doubt the assumption' and 'the assumption may not hold'), rather than confidently asserting from a histogram or some other plot that 'the normality assumption is met' or '… not met', as the case may be. I do this because regression diagnostics in general involve the subjective judgement of the analyst to some extent. Rarely is absolute certainty to be had. For example, it is often difficult to assess the normality assumption in small samples (with $n < 100$, say, although there is no precise definition of 'small'). In small samples, even when the errors are in reality perfectly normally distributed, the distribution of the standardised residuals can look ambiguous, or even decidedly non-normal. Thus, in small samples, a non-normal distribution of standardised residuals isn't necessarily strong evidence against the normality assumption (although it is not evidence in favour of the assumption either).

standardised residuals against their theoretical quantiles. The theoretical quantiles are the values we would expect if the standardised residuals were perfectly normally distributed.

Figure 3.5 shows the normal q–q plot for the standardised residuals from Galton's regression. Each dot represents a standardised residual. The y-axis represents the value of the standardised residual. The x-axis represents the theoretical quantiles of the standard normal distribution. The diagonal line indicates the expected positions of the dots. If the distribution of the standardised residuals is perfectly normal, all the points fall exactly on this line. Deviations from the line indicate deviations from the normal distribution. Here, the normal q–q plot confirms what the histogram suggested: the distribution is quite close to normal. Note, however, that there is a slight deviation from normality in the right-hand tail of the standardised residuals (top right corner of the graph): we have fewer large positive residuals than expected under the normal distribution. Slight deviations from normality among a small number of observations in the tails of the distribution are common and should not overly concern us. To give you an idea of what severe departures from normality look like in a normal q–q plot, Figure 3.6 gives an illustration.

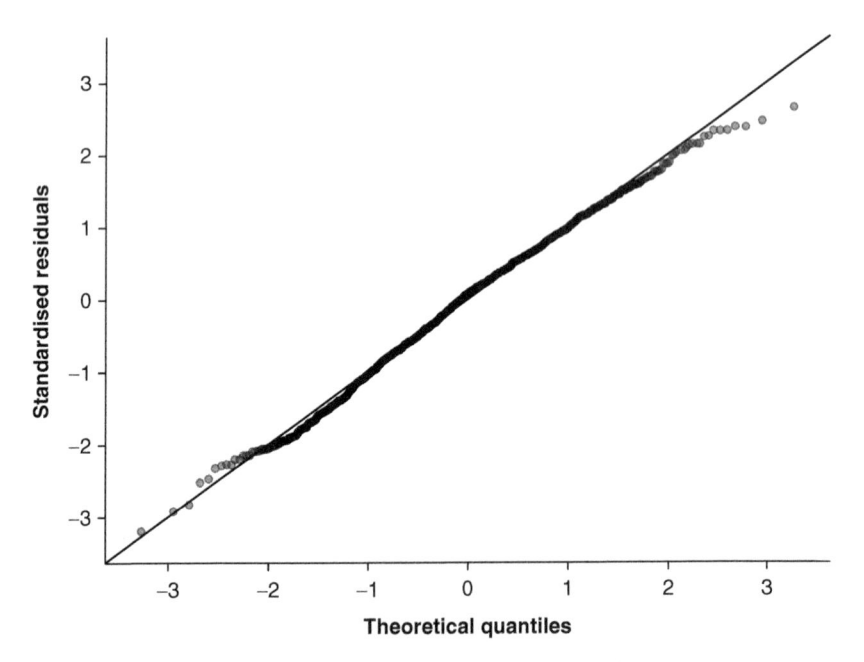

Figure 3.5 Normal q–q plot of standardised residuals from Galton's regression

Note. The theoretical quantiles are the values you would expect the standardised residuals to have if they followed a normal distribution. In a perfect normal distribution, all data points fall on the diagonal line.

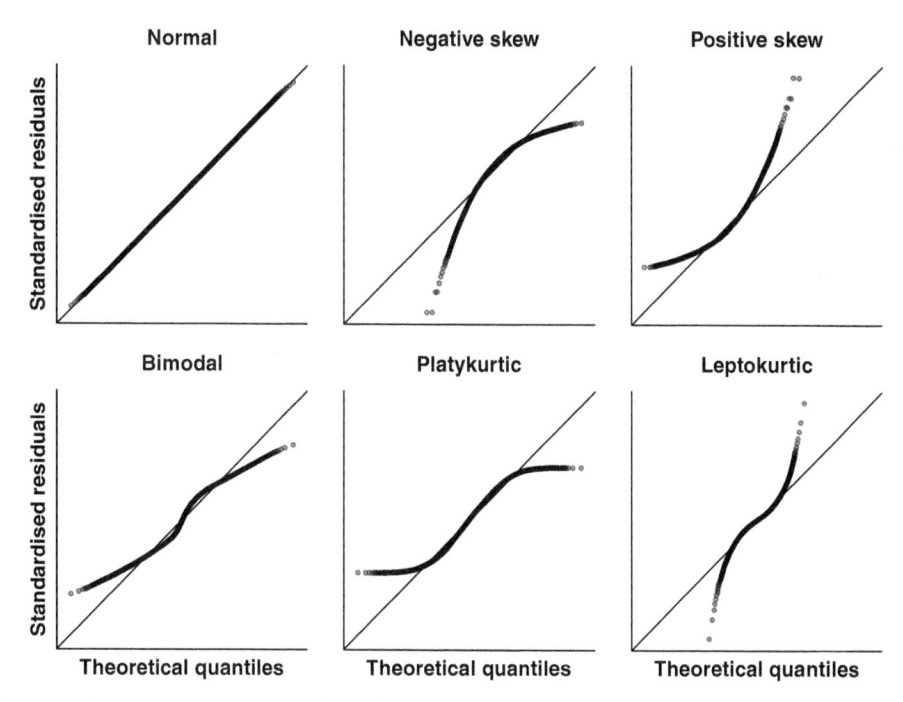

Figure 3.6 Normal q–q plots of standardised residuals for six distribution shapes

Note. Simulated data. These plots show the same data as the histograms in Figure 3.4.

Homoscedasticity and linearity: The spread-level plot

Now let's consider the assumptions of homoscedasticity and linearity. Both can be assessed by the *spread-level plot*. The spread-level plot is a scatter plot that displays the standardised residuals against the predicted outcome values. For each observation i, we are plotting the standardised residual ($stdres_i$) on the vertical axis and the predicted outcome ($\hat{Y}_i$) on the horizontal axis.[6] Consider Figure 3.7, which shows this plot for Galton's regression. The black line represents the regression line, swivelled to a horizontal position.

We can use the spread-level plot to assess the assumptions of homoscedasticity and linearity. Let's first consider homoscedasticity. Figure 3.7 shows that the standardised residuals have about the same variation at every level of the predicted value (i.e. in the graph, the vertical spread of the points is fairly even as we move from left to right). This suggests that the assumption of homoscedastic errors is plausible.

---

[6] You will often see the spread-level plot using standardised predicted values on the X-axis, instead of the 'raw' predicted values used in Figure 3.7. For the purpose of regression diagnostics, both methods are equally valid and produce essentially the same pattern of points.

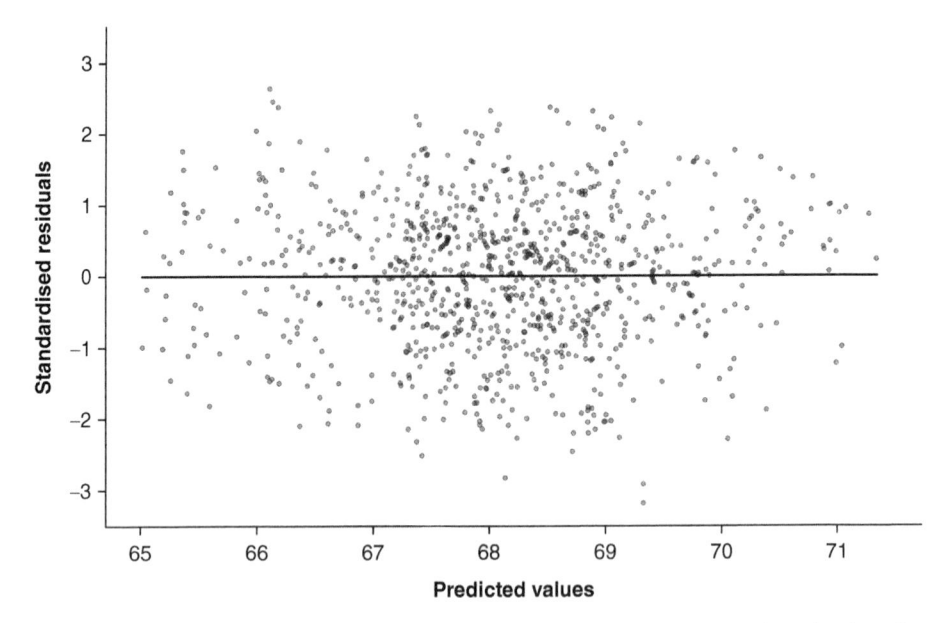

Figure 3.7 Spread-level plot: standardised residuals and regression predicted values from Galton's regression

Figure 3.7 also suggests that the relationship between the predictor and the outcome is linear. If there was a non-linear relationship, we would see some non-linear pattern in the spread-level plot. The absence of such a pattern confirms the linearity assumption.

A healthy spread-level plot – one that suggests that regression assumptions are met – should display no pattern in the data at all, as in Figure 3.7. For comparison, consider Figure 3.8, which features examples of plots indicating heteroscedasticity, non-linearity and skewed residuals alongside the scatter plots of the raw data (with regression lines) from which the spread-level plots were derived:

- In the example for heteroscedasticity, the standardised residuals have a small variance when the predicted value is small, but the variance gets larger for larger predicted values. This suggests that the error variance depends on the predicted value and thus that the errors are heteroscedastic.
- In the example for non-linearity, the standardised residuals follow a curvilinear pattern.
- In the example showing skewed residuals, the normality assumption is violated. This would also be seen in a normal q–q plot, for example.

(a) Spread-level plots

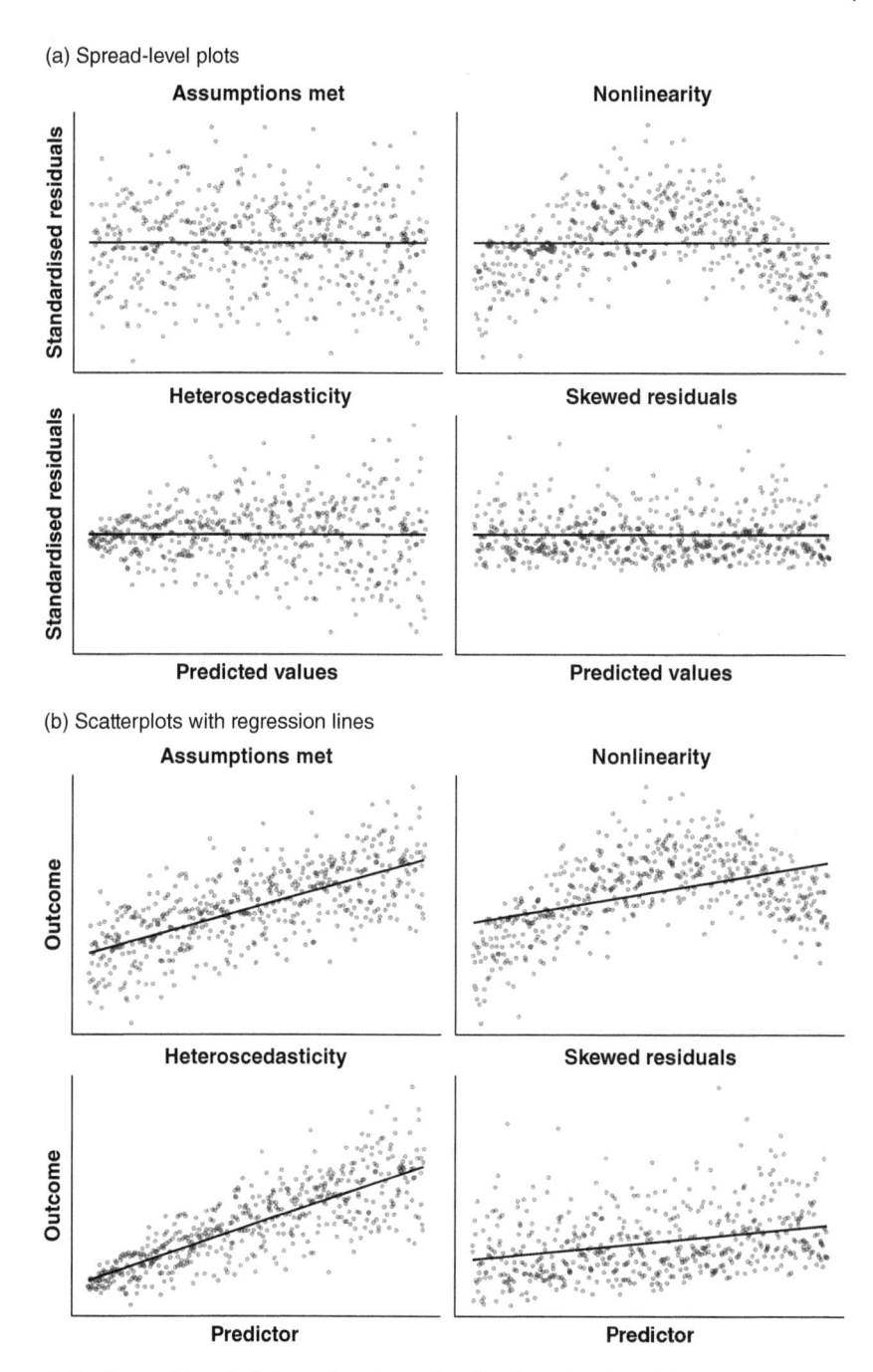

Figure 3.8 Spread-level plots and scatter plots for four simulated data sets

Note. The design of this graph was inspired by a similar one in the excellent textbook by Tabachnick and Fidell (2013).

Considering Figure 3.8, you may wonder why we bother making a spread-level plot at all, since the plots of the raw data seem to lead us to the same conclusion. It is true that for regression with a single predictor, a scatter plot of the data and a spread-level plot are usually equally informative. However, the spread-level plot will become essential for multiple regression models, which feature more than one predictor variable. We see why in Chapter 5.

Outliers and influential observations

We can also inspect standardised residuals to identify outliers and influential observations. An outlier is an observation that has an unusually large standardised residual. A large standardised residual for an observation implies that this observation has an unusual combination of outcome and predictor values. In Galton's regression, an outlier might be a short child of tall parents, or a tall child of short parents. An influential observation is one that has a large influence on the estimated coefficients of the regression line. An influential observation is usually an outlier, but not all outliers are equally influential.

Outliers

To consider what constitutes an outlier, let us remind ourselves how we expect the standardised residuals to be distributed. If all model assumptions are met, then the standardised residuals should follow approximately a standard normal distribution. Box 3.3 serves as a reminder of some properties of the standard normal distribution that are relevant here.

Box 3.3

Further Properties of the Normal Distribution

Box 3.1 stated some of the properties of the normal distribution, including percentages of values that fall within the intervals of ±1 SD either side of the mean, between 1 and 2 SD away from the mean and so forth. Another way to think about the normal distribution is to consider the intervals that enclose certain percentages of values, such as 95%, 99% and 99.9%. This is shown in Figure 3.9.

ASSUMPTIONS AND TRANSFORMATIONS | 65

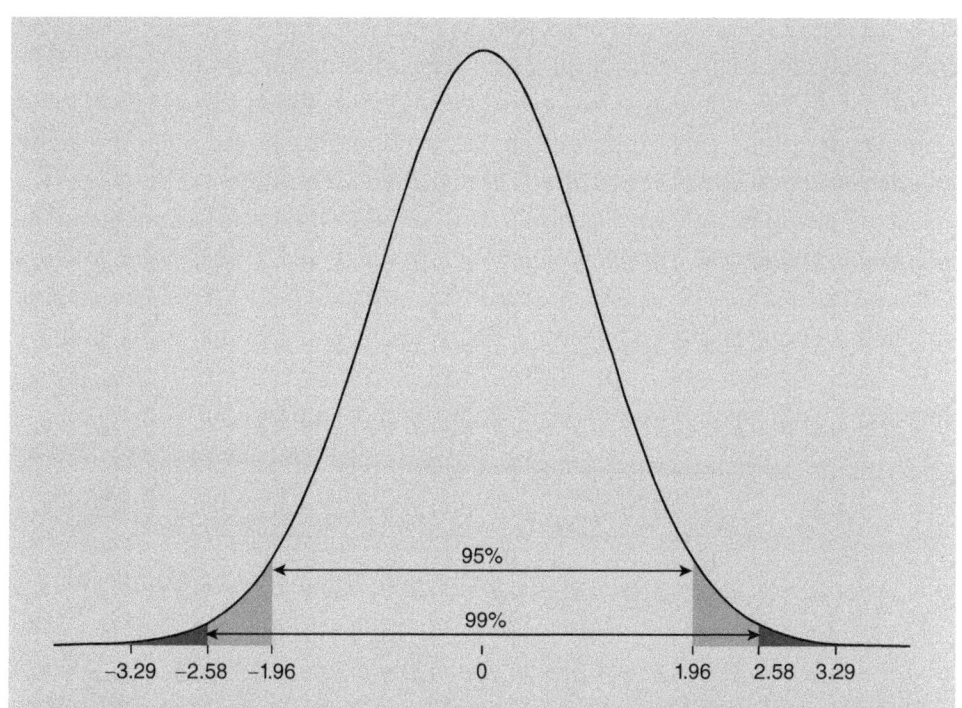

Figure 3.9 Illustration of a standard normal distribution, with conventional critical values

In a standard normal distribution, the mean is equal to 0 and the standard deviation is equal to 1. Figure 3.9 illustrates that, in a standard normal distribution,

- about 95% of values fall in the interval between −1.96 and 1.96,
- about 99% of values fall in the interval between −2.56 and 2.56 and
- about 99.9% of values fall in the interval between −3.29 and 3.29.

The critical values for statistical hypothesis tests based on the normal distribution are derived from these properties. Thus,

- the critical values for a z-test at the 5% level of significance are −1.96 and 1.96,
- for a z-test at the 1% level of significance they are −2.56 and 2.56, and
- for a z-test at the 0.1% level of significance they are −3.29 and 3.29.

The same critical values are used in the calculation of 95%, 99% and 99.9% confidence intervals around a statistic, respectively, when it can be assumed that the statistic has a normal sampling distribution.

From the information in Box 3.3, we can conclude that if the normality assumption holds, we would expect about 1% of standardised residuals to be larger than ±2.56 (in absolute terms), and about 0.1% of standardised residuals (1 in 1000) to be larger than ±3.29 (in absolute terms). If such large (negative or positive) residuals occur more often than expected, we might suspect them of being outliers.

We may inspect the largest negative and positive residuals to scan for outliers. Galton's regression had a sample size of 928. So we would expect at most one standardised residual (about 0.1% of 928) to be larger than 3.29 in absolute terms, and 9 or 10 standardised residuals (about 1% of 928) to be larger than 2.56 in absolute terms.

Table 3.1 shows the largest negative and positive standardised residuals from Galton's regression. The largest standardised residual is −3.19. Four standardised residuals are larger than 2.56 in absolute terms.

Table 3.1 The largest positive and negative standardised residuals from Galton's regression

Five Largest Negative Standardised Residuals	Five Largest Positive Standardised Residuals
−3.19	2.65
−2.92	2.46
−2.83	2.38
−2.52	2.38
−2.47	2.33

Table 3.1 gives us no reason to be suspicious of any observation. Although there are some large standardised residuals, they are not more numerous than we expect in a normal distribution. If anything, we have slightly fewer large standardised residuals than we would expect.

Influential observations

As we saw in Chapter 2, the estimated regression line can sometimes be influenced strongly by a small number of observations, or even by a single observation. In general, we should avoid having a small number of observations dominating our estimation of the regression line. If such influential observations are present, this should make us doubt whether our findings truly represent the population or process that we are trying to study.

What makes an observation influential? An observation will be the more influential

- the more untypical its value on the predictor variable (this is measured by the leverage, h_{ii}; see the section 'Standardised Residuals') and
- the larger its standardised residual.

A measure of the influence of an observation is *Cook's distance*, which takes account of both the leverage and the standardised residual of an observation. Cook's distance, D_i, is calculated as follows:

$$D_i = \frac{stdres_i^2}{(p+1)} \times \frac{h_{ii}}{(1-h_{ii})}$$

where

- D_i is the Cook's distance of the *i*th observation,
- $stdres_i^2$ is the squared standardised residual of the *i*th observation,
- *p* is the number of predictors in the regression model (for simple linear regression, *p* = 1) and
- h_{ii} is the leverage of the *i*th observation (see the section 'Standardised Residuals').

The larger the leverage, the larger Cook's distance will tend to be. Also, the larger the standardised residual, the larger Cook's distance will tend to be. A large Cook's distance, then, indicates an influential observation.[7]

Ideally, we would like the Cook's distances of all observations to be 'small'. But how small is small? This is not easy to say. The absolute values of Cook's distances are influenced by the sample size (since the leverages tend to have smaller values for larger sample sizes). In some statistics books, you may find various recommendations regarding how big is 'too big' for a Cook's distance. But these are just rules of thumb and do not have a theoretical justification. Also, these rules often don't work very well in practice. My advice is instead to inspect the observations with the largest Cook's distances and check whether they are unusual in some way.

For Galton's data, the seven largest Cook's distances are 0.015, 0.013, 0.012, 0.011, 0.011, 0.011 and 0.010. These seven observations are identified in Figure 3.10 as black dots.[8] They are 'unusual' in the sense that they are relatively far away from the regression line. In four cases, the children are unusually tall compared to their parents; in three cases, the children are unusually short compared to their parents. However, none of these seven seems so unusual as to seem likely to exert an undue influence on our regression results.

---

[7] Cook's distance also has another neat interpretation: the Cook's distance of the *i*th observation is a measure of how much the regression line would change if we removed the *i*th observation from the data set.

[8] The choice of displaying seven potentially influential observations, rather than some other number, is somewhat arbitrary. In practice, it is advisable to make several sensible checks. See also Figure 3.11, where there are four clear outliers.

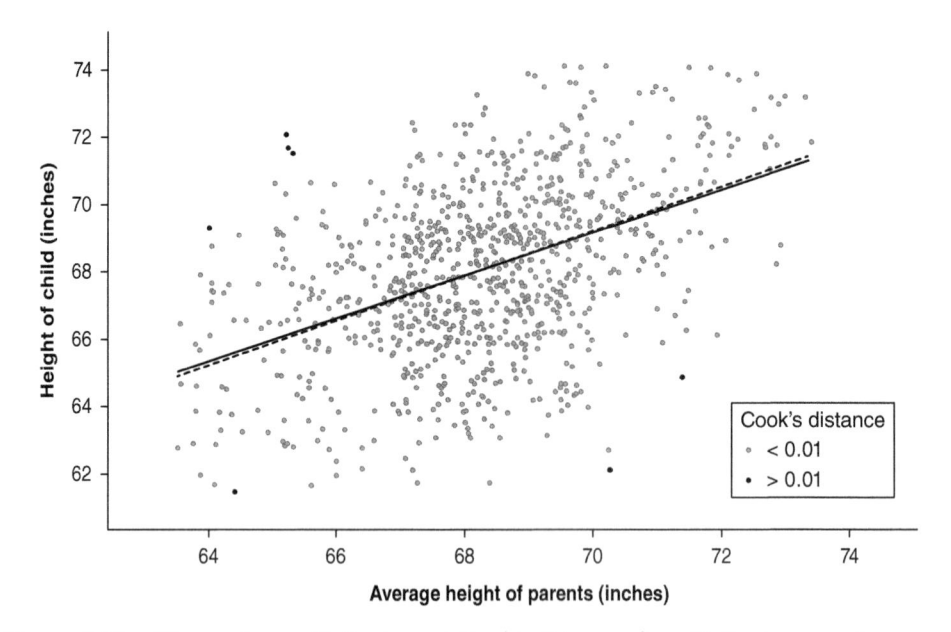

Figure 3.10 Observations with the largest Cook's distances from Galton's regression

Note. Solid line: regression line based on the full data set (n = 928). Dashed line: regression line based on all data except the seven observations with the largest Cook's distances (n = 921).

Another way to check whether some observations are highly influential is to estimate the regression model on the data with the suspect observations removed and to compare whether this leads to different results than the regression on the full data. I have done this for Galton's data. After removing the seven observations with the largest Cook's distances, the slope estimate for the remaining data (n = 921) is $\hat{\beta} = 0.665$. This is similar to the slope estimate from the full data set ($\hat{\beta} = 0.638$). Figure 3.10 illustrates this: the dashed line is the regression line estimated on Galton's data minus the seven observation with the largest Cook's distances. The solid line is the regression line based on the full data set. There is almost no difference between the two lines. So there is no reason to think that our results are strongly influenced by a few unusual observations. This suggests that the seven observations with the largest Cook's distances can safely be included in the analysis, without distorting the results.

For contrast, let's look at a situation where we clearly have highly influential observations. Consider Figure 3.11. This shows, once again, Galton's data, but this time I have meddled with them: I have replaced one parental height and three children's heights by values above 80 inches (203 cm), thus artificially creating four outliers.

In these data, the four largest Cook's distances are 1.179, 0.195, 0.171 and 0.155. The next largest is 0.010, a lot smaller than the fourth largest. It is thus clear that four data points are a lot more influential than the remaining 924.

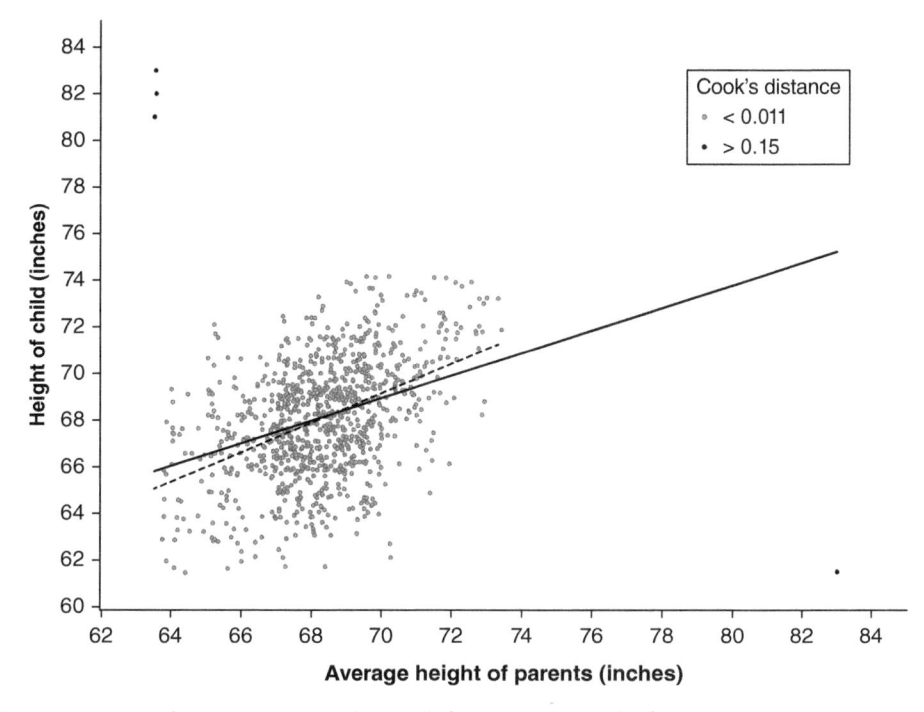

Figure 3.11 Galton's regression data with four hypothetical influential observations

Note. Solid line: regression line based on the full data set with four artificially created outliers (n = 928). Dashed line: regression line based on all data except the four observations with the largest Cook's distances (n = 924).

Figure 3.11 also shows how the outliers have influenced the estimated regression line. The solid line represents the regression of the whole data set, including the outliers. The dashed line is the regression line estimated on the remaining 924 values, excluding the outliers. The outliers have a clear effect on the slope estimate. With the outliers, the slope estimated is $\hat{\beta} = 0.484$. After removing the outliers, we have instead $\hat{\beta} = 0.630$, a clear difference.

What to do if you find an outlier or influential observation?

If you detect a highly influential observation in your analysis data set, you may want to investigate whether the outlying value is in fact correct. For example, a height measurement above 80 inches (203 cm), although certainly possible, may well be a mistake, possibly due to a typo in data entry. If you think that a measurement has been incorrectly recorded, of course this incorrect value should not be included in the regression.

On the other hand, the outliers could be perfectly valid observations. If the measurement is correct but unusual, then the decision whether to include the observation should be informed by the purpose of your research. There may be reasons to remove some or all of the influential observations: for example, if you think that they are so unusual that their inclusion would distort your findings regarding the relationship between the predictor and the outcome.

You may be wondering why I introduce Cook's distances at all, given that a graph like Figure 3.11 allows us to identify our outliers visually. It is true that for simple linear regression, a graph will usually show you whether your analysis is likely to be influenced by outliers, and there is not necessarily a need to consult Cook's distance. However, direct graphical inspection gets more difficult when we move on to multiple linear regression – that is, linear regression with more than one predictor. In that case, Cook's distances serve as a convenient indicator of the influence observations have on a model. Chapter 5 explains this in more depth.

Independence of errors

Independence of errors is the assumption that the value of one error won't influence the value of another. Errors can be dependent for a variety of reasons. A common type of dependence in social science data is clustering. For example, an educational research project may study children clustered in schools. Children going to the same school might be expected to be more similar to one another than they are to children going to a different school, and it is important to take such similarity into account when modelling clustered data. Clustering also occurs when we study households clustered in areas, patients clustered in hospitals, and so forth. When the research design involves collection of clustered data, linear regression as it is introduced in this book is usually not appropriate. More advanced techniques, such as the types of models called *mixed effects models* or *multilevel models*, may need to be applied (see also Chapter 6 in this book, and *The SAGE Quantitative Research Kit*, Volume 9).

Ignoring dependence may lead to serious mis-estimation of the standard errors of regression coefficients, and thus to incorrect confidence intervals, prediction intervals, and *p*-values. But how do we know if our observations are dependent or not? In the social sciences, we often rely on our knowledge of how the data were collected to think about the assumption of independence. Certain types of undesired dependency can be avoided by careful data collection procedures. In social surveys, for example, measures to ensure independence of observations include random sampling, selecting only one person per household contacted, training interviewers to promote standardisation of interviewing procedures (to reduce interviewer effects, another example of dependency), and so forth.

What if assumptions do not hold? An example

The regression analysis of Galton's data met all its underlying assumptions. But what if one or several assumptions are violated? This section presents an example where the linearity assumption does not hold and shows in detail how to address the problem by transforming a variable. The following section on 'Types of Transformations and When to Use Them' will then introduce variable transformations more formally.

A non-linear relationship

Consider again the relationship between GDP per capita and life expectancy, which we previously examined in Chapters 1 and 2. A subset of the data is shown in Figure 3.12.[9]

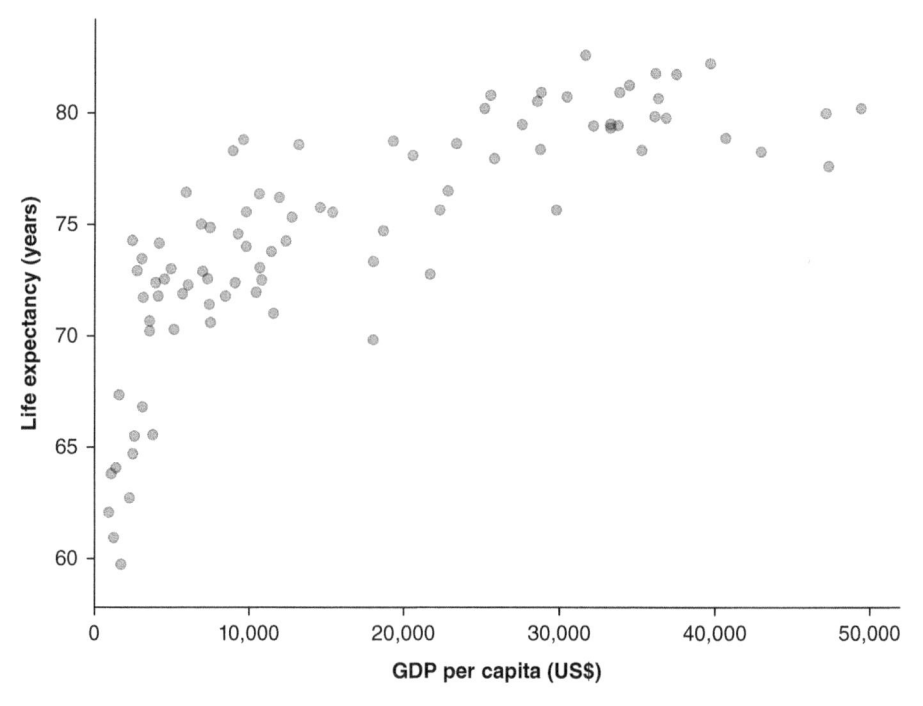

Figure 3.12 Life expectancy by GDP per capita in 88 countries

Note. GDP = gross domestic product.

---

[9] I have removed all African countries, as well as Afghanistan and Iraq. This is to simplify the relationship and remove outliers, which makes the example easier to explain. In a real research investigation, I would not necessarily have removed these countries from the data set.

LINEAR REGRESSION: AN INTRODUCTION TO STATISTICAL MODELS

It is easy to see that the relationship between GDP per capita and life expectancy is not linear. The points approximately follow a curve, not a straight line. So it is clear that a naïve linear regression won't fit these data well. I will nonetheless use linear regression here in order to illustrate two things:

1. How regression diagnostics look when assumptions are violated
2. How easy it is to come to false conclusions when fitting a model that violates assumptions

Let's suppose, then, that we hadn't looked at Figure 3.12 and had proposed a linear model of life expectancy predicted by GDP per capita as follows:

$$LifeExp_i = \alpha + \beta GDP_i + \varepsilon_i$$

The results of fitting this model to the data illustrated in Figure 3.12 are shown in Table 3.2.

Table 3.2 Estimates from a simple linear regression of life expectancy on GDP per capita

	Estimate	Standard Error	95% CI Lower	95% CI Upper
Intercept	69.424	0.574		
GDP (per US$10,000)	3.031	0.264	2.514	3.549

Note. $R^2 = 0.60$. GDP = gross domestic product; CI = confidence interval.

If you only looked at Table 3.2, you might consider this a perfectly sensible result. The coefficient of determination is $R^2 = 0.60$, which appears to suggest a strong linear relationship. The slope coefficient estimate and its confidence interval suggest that for every additional US$10,000 in GDP per capita, average life expectancy increases by between about 2.5 and 3.5 years. The linear model assumes that this increase in average life expectancy is the same, regardless whether we are talking about a GDP difference between $10,000 and $20,000, or between $40,000 and $50,000.

However, we know from Figure 3.12 that this conclusion from the linear model would be misleading. In fact, the relationship between GDP and life expectancy follows a curved line: at low levels of GDP, a $10,000 difference in GDP is associated with relatively large differences in life expectancy, whereas at high levels of GDP, the same difference in GDP is associated with much smaller differences in life expectancy, or possibly none at all. So the estimates in Table 3.2, although they are correctly calculated using least squares regression, are not a good description of the data.

Model diagnostics for the linear regression of life expectancy on GDP

Regression diagnostics for the naïve linear regression of life expectancy on GDP confirm that the assumption of linearity is not met. In Figure 3.13, the spread-level plot shows a clear non-linear pattern (an inverted 'U', albeit a lop-sided one), and the normal q–q plot suggests that the standardised residuals are negatively skewed (compare Figure 3.13 with Figure 3.6).

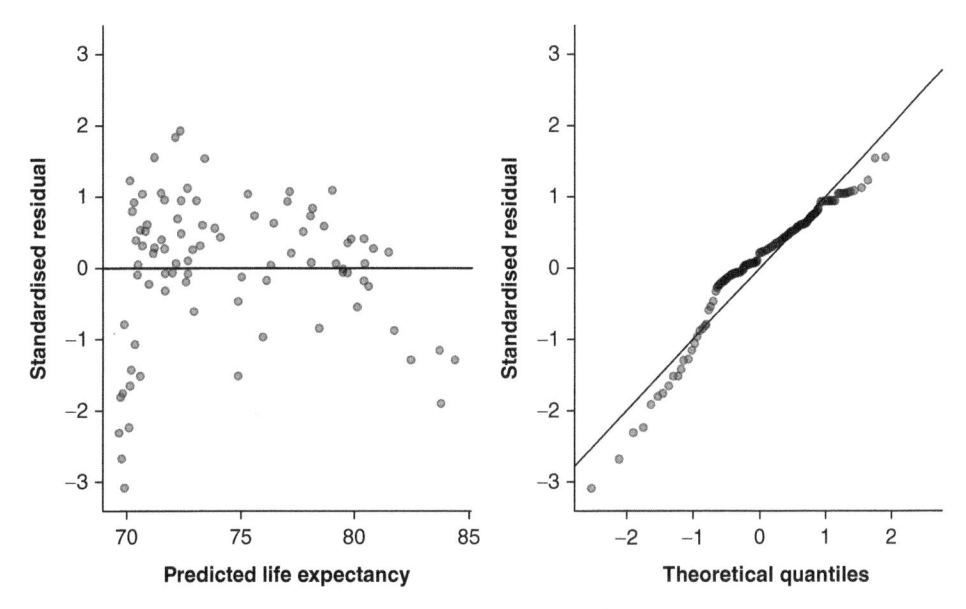

Figure 3.13 Diagnostic plots for the linear regression of life expectancy on GDP per capita

Note. GDP = gross domestic product.

So it is clear that this linear regression model is not appropriate for the data. What should we do?

Transforming a variable: logarithmic transformation of GDP

We will apply a technique called variable transformation. Rather than using the raw values of GDP per capita as a predictor of life expectancy, we use the **logarithm** of GDP per capita instead. So we propose the model

$$LifeExp_i = \alpha + \beta \log_2(GDP)_i + \varepsilon_i$$

You may not know, or may not remember, what logarithms are. If that is so, I recommend that you next read Box 3.4.

> **Box 3.4**

Logarithms

A logarithm is a mathematical function that has applications in many areas of science. Logarithms are also used in many statistical models, including in linear regression with transformed variables (as shown in this chapter), as well as in logistic and count regression models (see *The SAGE Quantitative Research Kit*, Volume 8). Most people, when they first encounter logarithms, learn about base-10 logarithms. A base-10 logarithm of a number *n* is the answer to the question '10 to the power of what equals *n*?'

We write $\log_{10}(n)$ to denote the logarithm of *n* to base 10. For example,

$\log_{10}(100) = 2$, because $10^2 = 100$

$\log_{10}(1000) = 3$, because $10^3 = 1000$

$\log_{10}(0.1) = -1$, because $10^{-1} = 0.1$

One scientific application of logarithms is the Richter Scale for measuring the strength of earthquakes, which uses base-10 logarithms. This means that the Richter Scale is a *multiplicative scale*: an earthquake of strength 3 on the Richter Scale is 10 times as strong as an earthquake of strength 2, which in turn is 10 times as strong as an earthquake of strength 1.

In general, we write $\log_b(n)$ to denote the logarithm of *n* to base *b*. Any positive number can be a logarithmic base. Thus, $\log_2(n)$ is the base-2 logarithm. For example,

$\log_2(8) = 3$, because $2^3 = 8$, and

$\log_2(0.5) = -1$, because $2^{-1} = 0.5$

An important type of logarithm is the *natural logarithm*, whose base is Euler's number $e = 2.71828 \ldots$ The natural logarithm has useful mathematical properties and is therefore commonly used in many statistical techniques. Since the natural logarithm is the most important for mathematicians, it is assumed that if someone writes $\log(n)$ without specifying the base, the natural logarithm is what is meant.[10]

Note the following general results, which hold for any base *b*:

$\log_b(b) = 1$

$\log_b\left(\dfrac{1}{b}\right) = -1$

$\log_b(1) = 0$

---

[10]Euler's number *e* is an *irrational number*, which means that it cannot be expressed as a fraction, that it has an infinite number of digits, and that the digits never settle on a repeating pattern. The best known irrational number is $\pi = 3.14159 \ldots$, which is the ratio of a circle's circumference to its diameter.

The logarithm is only defined for positive numbers. That is, $\log_b(0)$ has no result, and neither does $\log_b(-1)$. Table 3.3 gives a few example results for logarithms of different bases.

Table 3.3 Logarithms for bases 2, 10 and Euler's number e

n	$\log_2(n)$	$\log_{10}(n)$	$\log(n) = \log_e(n)$
0	Not defined	Not defined	Not defined
0.1	−3.322	−1	−2.303
0.5	−1	−0.301	−0.693
1	0	0	0
2	1	0.301	0.693
e = 2.718...	1.443	0.434	1
4	2	0.602	1.386
8	3	0.903	2.079
10	3.322	1	2.303
100	6.644	2	4.605
1000	9.966	3	6.908

This is how we apply the transformation: first, we make a new variable in our data set, which is the transform of the original variable. In our example, we calculate $trans(GDP) = \log_2(GDP)$, where $trans(GDP)$ denotes 'transformed GDP per capita'. I use the base-2 logarithm (denoted by $\log_2$) for reasons that will become clear soon. Tables 3.4 and 3.5 show raw and transformed values of GDP, for some example values and a selection of countries in the data set, respectively.

Table 3.4 Calculating the base-2 logarithm for a selection of GDP per capita values

GDP per Capita (US$)	$\log_2(GDP)$
500	≈ 9
1000	≈ 10
2000	≈ 11
4000	≈ 12
8000	≈ 13
16,000	≈ 14
32,000	≈ 15

Note. $\log_2(GDP)$ is given to the nearest whole number. To three decimal points, the values are 8.966, 9.966, 10.966 and so forth. GDP = gross domestic product.

Table 3.5 Raw and log-transformed GDP per capita values for six countries

Country	GDP per Capita (US$)	log₂(GDP)
Bangladesh	1391	10.4
Nicaragua	2749	11.4
Albania	5937	12.5
Argentina	12,779	13.6
Oman	22,316	14.4
Singapore	47,143	15.5

Note. GDP per capita values are rounded to whole numbers; log₂(GDP) is given to one decimal point. GDP = gross domestic product.

Now we can plot the transformed version of GDP against life expectancy. This is shown in Figure 3.14. This relationship looks closer to linear than the relationship between life expectancy and untransformed GDP.

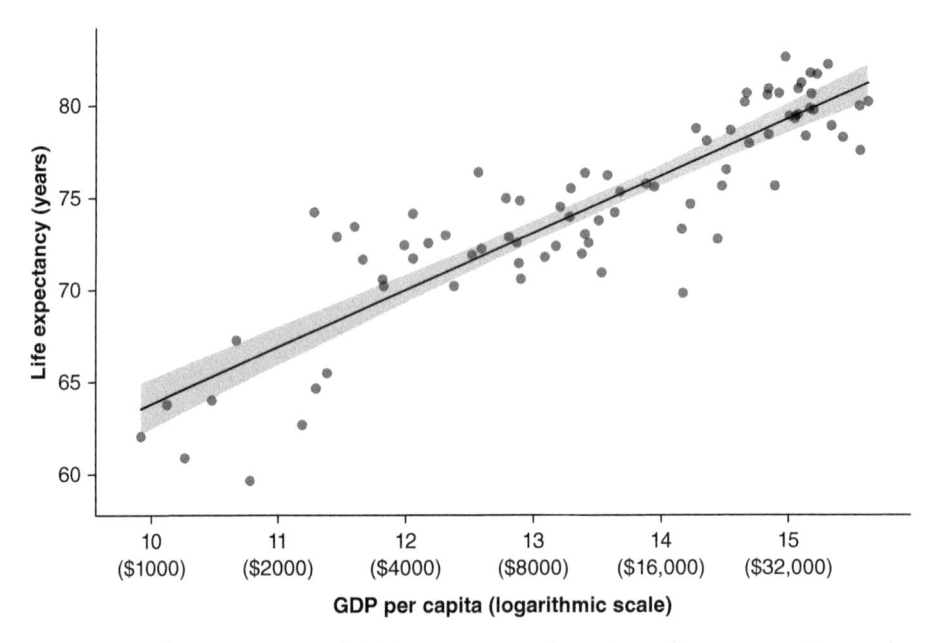

Figure 3.14 Life expectancy and GDP per capita – illustrating a linear regression on the logarithmic scale

Note. GDP = gross domestic product.

How does this transformation technique work? One way to understand the effect of the logarithmic transformation is to consider that it replaces an additive scale with a multiplicative scale. Without transformation, Figure 3.12 shows GDP per capita on an *additive scale*: a 1-unit distance on the *x*-axis means a difference in GDP of $10,000. In contrast, Figure 3.14 shows GDP on a *multiplicative scale*: a 1-unit distance on the *x*-axis means 'multiply by 2', so that the distance between $1000 and $2000 is the same as the distance between $2000 and $4000, the same as the distance between $4000 and $8000, and so forth.

Since Figure 3.14 suggests that the logarithmic transformation of GDP results in a linear relationship with life expectancy, we propose the following linear regression model:

$$LifeExp_i = \alpha + \beta \log_2(GDP)_i + \varepsilon_i$$

The difference between this model and the naïve linear regression (see the section 'A Non-Linear Relationship') is that this time our predictor variable is log-transformed. Otherwise this model works just the same as any linear regression, and the coefficients can be estimated in the same way. The estimated coefficients are shown in Table 3.6, and the resulting regression line is shown in Figure 3.14. Note that $R^2 = 0.77$, which is considerably higher than the $R^2 = 0.60$ that we found for the model using untransformed GDP per capita (compare Table 3.2). So the model using $\log_2(GDP)$ as a predictor accounts for a greater proportion of the variance of life expectancy than the naïve model using the untransformed GDP variable.

Table 3.6 Estimates from a simple linear regression of life expectancy on $\log_2(GDP)$

	Estimate	Standard Error	95% CI Lower	95% CI Upper
Intercept	32.988	2.462		
$\log_2(GDP)$	3.097	0.182	2.740	3.454

Note. $R^2 = 0.77$. CI = confidence interval; GDP = gross domestic product.

How do we interpret these estimates? The estimated intercept $\hat{\alpha} = 32.988$ is the predicted life expectancy for a country with $\log_2(GDP) = 0$ – that is, a country with a GDP per capita of $1 (because $\log_2(1) = 0$). In itself, this is not a very useful value, because there is no country with a GDP per capita of $1.

More interesting is $\hat{\beta} = 3.097$, the estimate of the effect of $\log_2(GDP)$. Technically, this means 'for a 1-point difference on $\log_2$-transformed GDP, life expectancy is predicted to differ by 3.097 years'. This interpretation is not very helpful, however, because most of us don't find it easy to think on a log scale. A more intuitive interpretation uses the multiplicative property of the logarithmic scale: the estimate $\hat{\beta} = 3.097$ means that if GDP per capita is *doubled*, the model predicts an increase in life expectancy of 3.097 years.

So if GDP per capita in your country is $1000, then to gain about 3 years of predicted life expectancy you would need to increase GDP per capita by $1000, according to this model. But if your country's GDP per capita is $10,000, then an extra $1000 won't be nearly enough to raise predicted life expectancy by 3 years. Rather, it would require an increase of $10,000 (resulting in a total GDP of $20,000, double your starting point) to raise the predicted life expectancy by 3 years.

In general, for a regression with a log-transformed predictor, using the logarithm with some base b, the regression coefficient estimate $\hat{\beta}$ can be interpreted as follows: if I multiply X by b, Y is predicted to change by $\hat{\beta}$. This multiplicative relation is most intuitively interpretable when we choose $\log_2$ or $\log_{10}$, say, compared to the natural logarithm with base 2.7172 . . . So when log-transforming a predictor, it is often wise to choose an easily interpretable base for the logarithm, such as base 2 or base 10.

One way to visualise the results of the regression with the log-transformed predictor is to plot the regression line on the original, untransformed scale. This is shown in Figure 3.15, which again features the regression line based on the estimates in Table 3.6. This line appears as a curve because the X-axis uses the untransformed GDP. Figure 3.15 thus illustrates the non-linear relationship between GDP and life expectancy that is assumed by the model with log-transformed GDP. Among countries with relatively low GDP, small differences in GDP are associated with large predicted differences in life expectancy. But the bigger the GDP gets, the smaller the gain in life expectancy for the same difference in GDP. This result may imply that for a poor country, doing the sort of things that raise GDP per capita will have a considerable effect on the life expectancy of its citizens. For a country that is already quite rich, however, additional economic output has relatively little effect on life expectancy; for rich countries, maybe other things matter more.

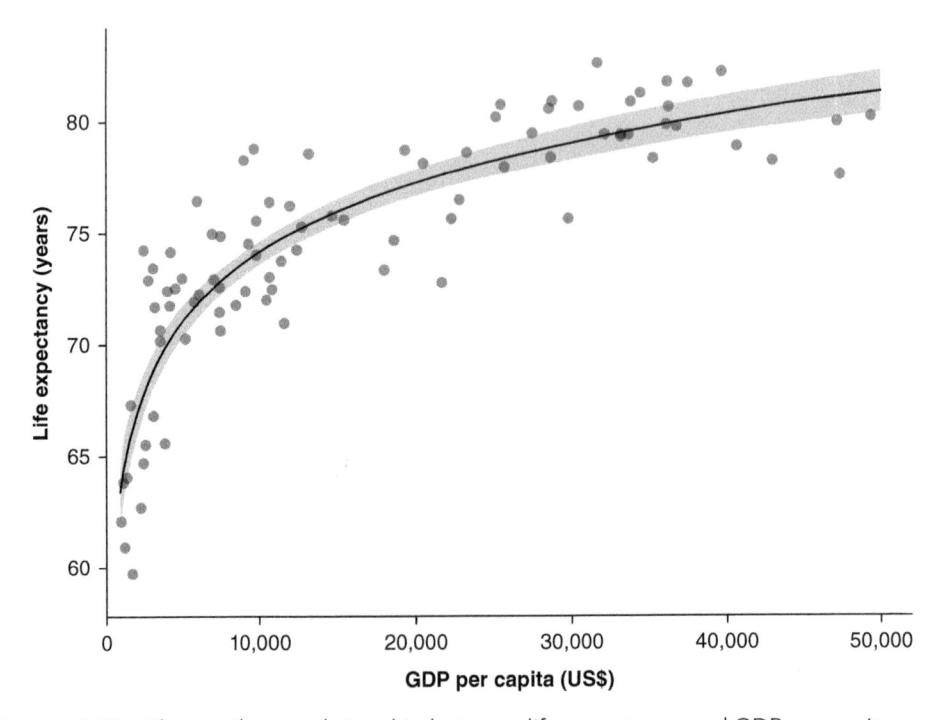

Figure 3.15 The curvilinear relationship between life expectancy and GDP per capita

Note. The black line represents the regression line from a linear regression of life expectancy on $\log_2(GDP)$ – see Table 3.6. GDP = gross domestic product.

Regression diagnostics for the linear regression with predictor transformation

We should apply regression diagnostics to check whether the data are consistent with the assumptions of linear regression with log-transformed GDP. Figure 3.16 shows the spread-level plot and the normal q–q plot of the standardised residuals.

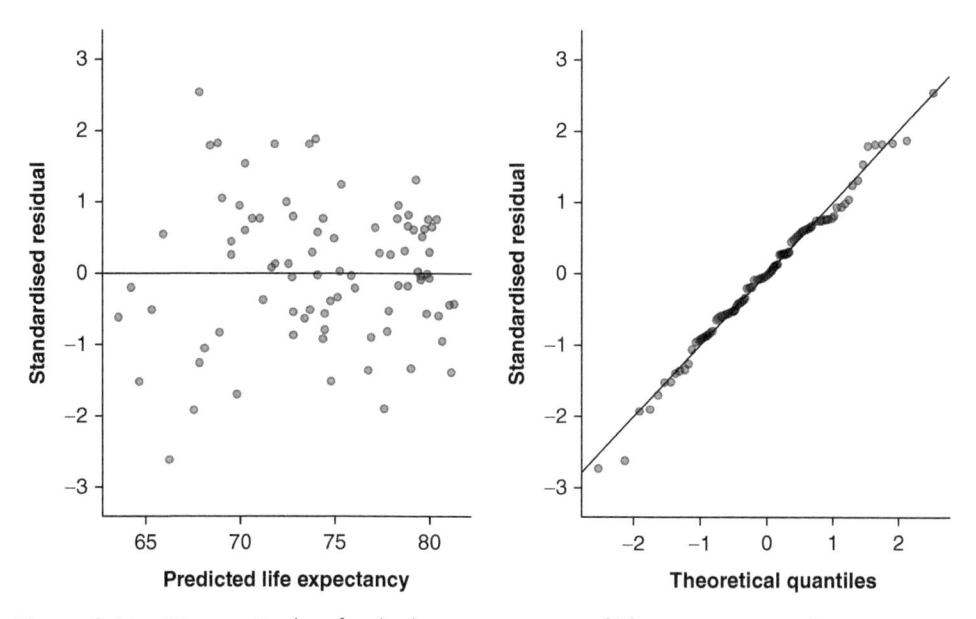

Figure 3.16 Diagnostic plots for the linear regression of life expectancy on $\log_2(GDP)$

Note. GDP = gross domestic product.

The spread-level plot suggests that log-transforming GDP has been successful at linearising the relationship, since there is now much less of a curvilinear pattern than in the standardised residuals of the untransformed model (compare Figure 3.13). The normal q–q plot suggests that the standardised residuals approximately follow a normal distribution – certainly much more closely than their counterparts without the transformation of GDP (again, compare Figure 3.13). All standardised residuals are between –3 and +3, which is what we would expect in a sample of size $n = 88$. There does not seem to be an outlier. In summary, then, our regression diagnostics suggest that we can have confidence in the results from this regression model.

Types of transformations, and when to use them

Let us now consider variable transformations more formally. This section introduces the most common types of transformation and discusses how to choose an appropriate one.

When our data fail to meet one or several assumptions of linear regression, it is sometimes possible to resolve the problem by applying a transformation to either the predictor or the outcome, or both. A transformation changes a variable by applying a mathematical function. For example, the logarithmic transformation uses $trans(x) = \log(x)$, where $trans(x)$ stands for 'the transformed version of x'. In the square transformation, we have $trans(x) = x^2$. And the inverse transformation is $trans(x) = 1/x$. In principle, there is an infinite number of potential transformations from which we might choose.[11]

Choosing a transformation is an art as much as a science. There is no generally applicable rule that we could apply automatically and without thought (e.g. by implementing it in software and recommending to software users to 'let the computer decide'). However, there are a few general guidelines as well as advanced techniques for making data-driven choices. This section will give a short introduction to the most important transformations and point you to more advanced literature that can help you to delve more deeply into the topic.

Common transformations

An important general point is that if we transform either a predictor or an outcome in a linear model, we are implicitly assuming a non-linear relationship. In the previous section, we saw how transforming the predictor (GDP) helped us to model its non-linear relationship with an outcome (life expectancy). The principle holds for all transformations. In fact, one way to understand different types of transformations is to understand the shape of the relationship between the predictor and the outcome they allow us to model.

Logarithmic transformations

The logarithmic transformation is defined as $trans(x) = \log_b(x)$, for some base b. It is often applied to variables that measure *amounts*, such as

- amounts of money (incomes, debts, prices, GDP, etc.) and
- amounts of goods (tons of steel produced, tons of waste recycled, litres of water used, etc.).

---

[11] A simple transformation, which you may already have encountered in *The SAGE Quantitative Research Kit*, Volume 3, is the standardisation of the variable, where $trans(x) = \dfrac{x - \bar{x}}{s_x}$. This is often called the z-standardisation and creates a new variable (usually denoted as z) that has a mean of 0 and a standard deviation of 1. z-Standardisation does not help with addressing problems with model assumptions, because it does not affect the shape of the distribution of the variable, or the shape of the relationship between the transformed variable and other variables. However, z-standardisation is sometimes employed to help with interpretation of model results (see Chapter 5).

Amount variables are often positively skewed, and the log-transformation will tend to make the distribution more closely symmetric, and therefore closer to normal. In fact, many amount variables follow the so-called log-normal distribution, which can be defined as the distribution of a variable whose log-transform is normally distributed.

Logarithmic transformation of the predictor: $\hat{Y} = \alpha + \beta \log(X)$

In the previous section, we looked at a logarithmic transformation of GDP as a predictor of life expectancy. The logarithmic transformation of a predictor implies a particular shape of the relationship between the predictor and the outcome: the larger the predictor values, the smaller the effect of a given difference in predictor values on the predicted outcome. For an illustration, see the illustrations of the 'log transform of X' in Figure 3.17: the curve of best prediction is steep for small values of X but flattens with larger values of X. This holds true when the association between Y and $\log(X)$ is positive, as well as when it is negative.

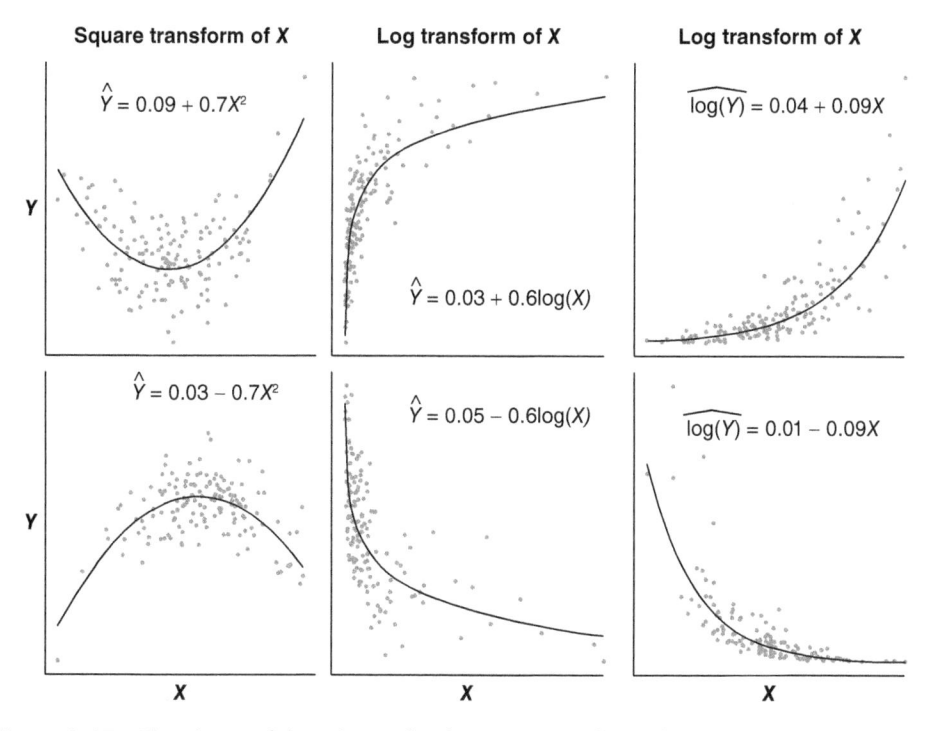

Figure 3.17 The shape of the relationship between Y and X in three common transformations, with positive slope coefficient (top row) and negative slope coefficient (bottom row)

Note. Regression equations are shown in each plot. Note that the slope coefficients are all positive in the top row of plots but negative in the bottom row. The intercepts are arbitrary.

The slope coefficient β of a log-transformed predictor can be interpreted as the predicted difference in Y associated with multiplying the predictor X by the base of the logarithm that was used in the transformation. For example, in the previous section, we used $trans(GDP) = \log_2(GDP)$, the base-2 logarithm. Accordingly, β indicated the predicted difference in Y associated with doubling X. If we had instead used the base-10 logarithm, $trans(GDP) = \log_{10}(GDP)$, then the resulting β would have to be interpreted as the predicted difference in Y associated with multiplying X by 10.

When log-transforming a predictor variable, the choice of the base b is important only for the interpretation of the model coefficients. It does not affect the model predictions or the model fit. That is, regardless which base we choose, the predicted outcome values, the standardised residuals and R^2 will all be the same.

Logarithmic transformation of the outcome: $\log(Y) = \alpha + \beta X$

Log-transforming the outcome implies either a J-shaped relationship between the predictor and the outcome or an inverted J-shape (depending on whether the slope coefficient of the predictor is positive or negative; see the illustrations of the 'log transform of Y' in Figure 3.17).

The slope coefficient β of a linear regression model with a log-transformed outcome has the following interpretation: for a 1-unit change in the predictor, the outcome is predicted to be multiplied by b^β, where b is the base of the logarithm employed. For example, imagine that we have log-transformed an outcome Y as $trans(Y) = \log_2(Y)$ and aim to predict this by a predictor X. Imagine further that we have estimated this model on a data set and that the estimated regression equation is as follows:

$$\widehat{\log_2(Y)} = 1 + 0.5X$$

So $\hat{\beta} = 0.5$, which suggests that a 1-unit difference in X is associated with Y being multiplied by $2^{0.5} = \sqrt{2} \approx 1.41$.

The choice of logarithmic base does not affect the predicted values of untransformed Y, the residuals, or R^2. For example, if we had instead used the logarithm with base 10 (i.e., $trans(Y) = \log_{10}(Y)$), then the model estimated on the same data would have yielded

$$\widehat{\log_{10}(Y)} = 1 + 0.15X$$

So $\hat{\beta} = 0.15$, which suggests that a 1-unit difference in X is associated with Y being multiplied by $10^{0.15} \approx 1.41$. This is the same result we obtained above when using $trans(Y) = \log_2(Y)$.

Quadratic transformation of the predictor: $\hat{Y} = \alpha + \beta X^2$

Quadratic transformations of a predictor variable can be useful for modelling U-shaped and inverted U-shaped relationships (see the illustrations of the 'square transform of X' in Figure 3.17). The slope coefficient β is to be interpreted as the predicted difference in Y associated with a 1-unit change in X^2.

Some examples of U-shaped relationships are:

- *Diastolic blood pressure and heart disease:* the risk of heart disease is lowest for people whose diastolic blood pressure is in the normal range, but the risk of heart disease is higher when diastolic blood pressure is either lower or higher than normal (Herrington et al., 2017). This is a U-shaped relationship.
- *Age and delinquency:* for the period since crime statistics disaggregated by age are available (since the 19th century), a repeated finding is that delinquency is rare among young children, rises in adolescence, peaks at young adulthood, and thereafter declines as age increases (Ulmer & Steffensmeier, 2015). Age and delinquency thus have an inverse U-shaped relationship.

In order for a model with a quadratic transformation to work as intended, it is often useful to **mean-centre** X before computing the square, such that $trans(X) = (X - \bar{X})^2$. The mean of a mean-centred variable, $X - \bar{X}$, is zero.

Techniques for choosing an appropriate transformation

Besides the logarithmic and square transformations, some other common transformations are:

- Inverse transformation: $trans(x) = 1/x$
- Square root transformation: $trans(x) = \sqrt{x}$
- Cubic transformation: $trans(x) = x^3$, or $trans(x) = (x - \bar{x})^3$

It is sometimes necessary to add a constant to the variable to be transformed before applying the transformation. For example, the logarithm is only defined for positive numbers, so it may be necessary to set up the transformation as $trans(X) = \log(c + X)$, where the constant c is chosen so that $(c + X)$ is always positive. A similar consideration applies to the square root transformation, which cannot take negative values. On the other hand, the inverse transformation can deal with positive as well as negative values, but not with zero (since $1/x$ is not defined for $x = 0$).

How might you go about choosing an appropriate transformation? A few guidelines are given below:

- *Consult theory and published evidence:* For example, the U-shaped relationship between diastolic blood pressure and the risk of heart disease is now well established, so a square transformation of diastolic blood pressure should probably be considered when investigating this relationship on new data.
- *Consider the type of variables you wish to model:* For example, as we said above, amount variables can often (although not always) be modelled using a logarithmic transformation.
- *Explore your data:* For example, make a scatter plot of the two variables and investigate the shape of the relationship. If it is curvilinear, try a plausible transformation and check whether this renders the relationship linear. The disadvantage of this approach is that you are using your data twice: first to decide on the shape of your model and then again to estimate the model. This can lead to *overfitting*. To overfit a model means to optimise the model to the particular data set at hand, which carries the risk that the results won't generalise to the population or process under study. (*The SAGE Quantitative Research Kit*, Volume 8, gives more details on overfitting.)

Some rules of thumb may be helpful for deciding which transformations to try when using exploratory data analysis to identify a suitable transformation for a linear model.

The general principle is that it often helps to transform variables so that the result is a normal distribution, or at least a symmetric distribution. Note that normality of the outcome variable is not strictly an assumption of linear regression. The normality assumption applies to the errors of prediction, not the predictor or the outcome. However, in practice, often a normally distributed outcome will lead to normally distributed errors. Also, it is often the case that a highly skewed predictor has a non-linear relationship with a normally distributed outcome.

So how can we render variables closer to normally distributed? The following rules of thumb may be helpful:

If the variable is positively skewed, try

- the logarithmic transformation, $trans(X) = \log(c + X)$, or
- the square root transformation, $trans(x) = \sqrt{c+x}$, or
- the inverse transformation, $trans(x) = 1/(c+x)$,

where c denotes a constant chosen so as to ensure that all sample values of x can be transformed.

If the variable is negatively skewed, try

- the reflected logarithmic transformation, $trans(x) = \log(c + max(x) - x)$, or
- the reflected square root transformation, $trans(x) = \sqrt{c + max(x) - x}$, or
- the reflected inverse transformation, $trans(x) = \dfrac{1}{c + max(x) - x}$,

where $max(x)$ denotes the maximum value of x observed in the data set. The 'reflection' $max(x) - x$ has the effect of reversing the x-values: the smallest x-value becomes the largest value of $trans(x)$ and so forth. The reflection turns a negatively skewed variable into a positively skewed one, so that a transformation that removes a positive skew can be applied.

Chapter Summary

- Nowadays, statistical software makes it relatively easy to fit a regression model to a set of data with just a few clicks. This has many advantages, but it also carries a risk: if the analyst thinks that they can leave all the difficult work to a computer, and take the software output table of the first model they estimate as the 'correct' result, they may well adopt an inadequate or even nonsensical model and draw erroneous conclusions.
- In particular, failure to consider and investigate assumptions is a common mistake in statistical analysis. When a model fails to meet its underlying assumptions, the conclusions drawn from the results may be misleading, and statistical hypothesis tests and confidence intervals may be inaccurate.
- This chapter has considered the assumptions underlying simple linear regression, has introduced regression diagnostics for checking the plausibility of some of these assumptions, and has shown how transforming a variable can aid in developing an appropriate statistical model. Although this chapter has discussed these issues in the context of linear regression, the principles apply more generally. Whenever you fit a statistical model of any kind, you should consider the plausibility of the assumptions underlying the model and use diagnostic procedures to aid you in this.

Further Reading

Royston, P., & Sauerbrei, W. (2008) *Multivariate model-building: A pragmatic approach to regression analysis based on fractional polynomials for modelling continuous variables*. Wiley.

A principled data-driven way to choose transformations for predictor variables is the technique of fractional polynomials, described in this book by Royston and Sauerbrei. The idea is to select a moderately large set of transformations to try to use statistical hypothesis tests to choose the one that appears to fit the data best. Fractional polynomials are a rather advanced technique, but they are useful when little prior knowledge about suitable transformations exists. You will find more information on fractional polynomials in Chapter 6.

4
MULTIPLE LINEAR REGRESSION: A MODEL FOR MULTIVARIATE RELATIONSHIPS

Chapter Overview

Confounders and suppressors 88
Multivariate relationships: a simple example with two predictors............. 93
Simple examples of multiple regression models 97
Dummy variables for representing categorical predictors....................... 117
Further Reading 123

This chapter introduces multiple linear regression: linear regression with more than one predictor variable. Multiple linear regression is a model that we might consider when we have one continuous outcome variable and more than one predictor. The predictors are assumed to be numeric variables, but as we will see, we can accommodate categorical predictors via the use of so-called dummy variables.

Most social phenomena have more than one cause. In order to describe, predict and explain what happens in the social world, it is usually not sufficient to look at the relationship between two variables only. Multivariate analysis involving more than two variables is thus immensely important in many areas of research. Social scientists might use multivariate models for purposes such as the following:

- *Consider multiple influences in combination:* We may be interested in the relative importance of several variables for explaining an outcome, possibly to gauge the evidence for or against specific theories about the social world. For example, a simple such question might have the form: what has a stronger influence on Y – variable X or variable Z?
- *Develop precise predictions:* Our interest may be in the prediction of some outcome, and we may hypothesise that using multiple predictors, rather than just one, will render our prediction more precise (by reducing prediction errors).
- *Adjustment for confounders:* We may be interested in the relationship between just one predictor and an outcome, but may be concerned that there are confounding variables at play, which interfere with the relationship of interest, and which we need to take into account if we want to obtain a precise estimate of the relationship of interest.

Confounders and suppressors

Let's consider in more detail what multivariate relationships may look like in social science data. In particular, we should get familiar with two important concepts: (1) **confounding** variables, or **confounders**, and (2) **suppressor** variables.

Spurious relationships and confounding variables

One reason to go beyond a single predictor in a regression model, and instead consider multiple predictors, is the possibility of confounding. Confounding is said to occur if the true relationship between two variables only becomes apparent once we take a third variable into account. This third variable is called a *confounding* variable, or *confounder*. Most commonly, when researchers talk about confounding, they mean that an apparent association between two variables, X and Y, turns out to be due, in part or entirely, to the influence of a confounder, Z. This can occur when Z

is associated with both X and Y. We call a third variable, Z, a confounder if we have reason to believe that it is causally related to both X and Y, and that it explains, completely or partially, the observed association between X and Y. On the other hand, if a variable Z is on the causal path from X to Y (X causes Z, and Z causes Y), then Z is not a confounder, but rather a *mediator*.

Let's think through an example of confounding. There is an association between birth order and the chance of Down syndrome in the child: a mother's second child is more likely to be born with Down syndrome than a mother's first child; the third child is more likely to have Down syndrome than the second child, and so forth. Does this mean that having older siblings increases the probability of having Down syndrome? In fact, despite the statistical association, there is no causal relationship between birth order and Down syndrome. The confounding variable at play here is mother's age, which is associated with both Down syndrome and birth order. The probability of a child being born with Down syndrome increases with the age of the mother. And, by definition, mothers are older when they give birth to their second child than they were when they had their first child.

It can be seen from this example that confounding is a causal concept. To identify the confounder, we need to know, or make the assumption, that it is mother's age that is a causal factor involved in Down syndrome, rather than birth order. Statistical data analysis alone cannot show whether a variable acts as a confounder or not.

Let's look at an example of confounding from the point of view of a researcher who wishes to investigate the relationship between two variables, X and Y, using a regression model. A scatter plot of X and Y might look something like Figure 4.1.

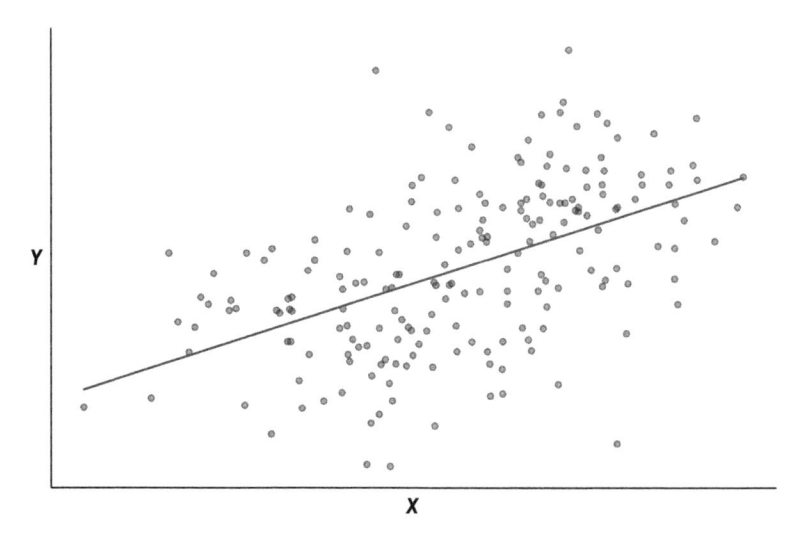

Figure 4.1 A hypothetical scatter plot of two apparently correlated variables

Figure 4.1 appears to indicate a moderately strong relationship. In fact, the observed correlation between X and Y in this picture is $r = 0.52$. If we had reason to believe that X is a cause of Y, we might conclude that Y is moderately strongly influenced by X. However, now consider Figure 4.2. This illustrates the possibility that the association between X and Y might be explained by the influence of a confounding variable. The data displayed are exactly the same as in Figure 4.1. The difference is that in Figure 4.2 the points are coloured according to their value on the confounder. The confounding variable here is a categorical variable with two values: Group 1 and Group 2. In general, a confounder can be a variable of any type: numerical (e.g. mother's age or number of older siblings) or categorical (e.g. gender or ethnicity).

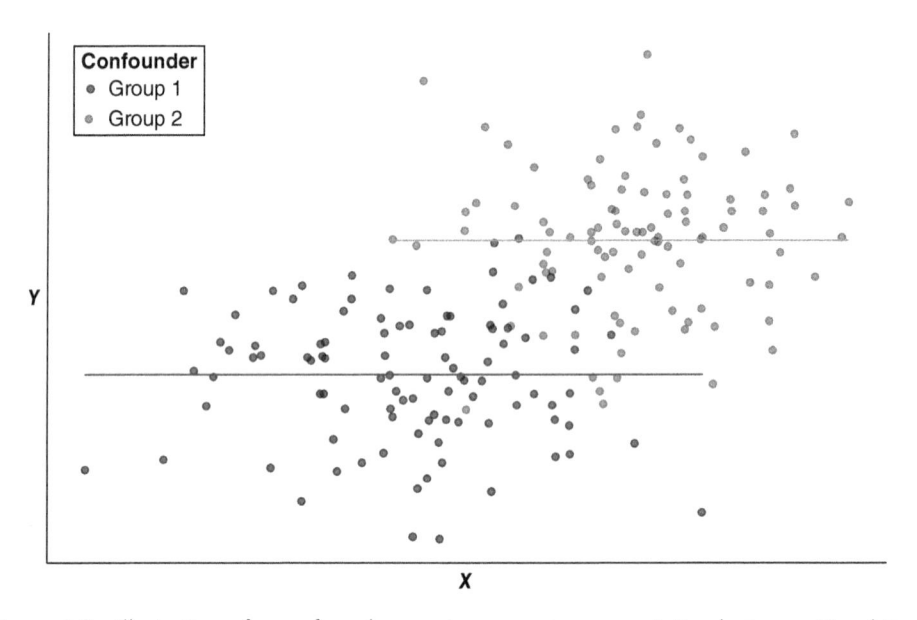

Figure 4.2 Illustration of a confounder causing a spurious association between X and Y

The confounder is associated with both X and Y: members of Group 1 tend to have low values on both X and Y. Members of Group 2 tend to have high values on both X and Y. Within each group, there is no relationship between X and Y (the observed correlation is about $r = 0$ in each group).

In some cases, as in Figure 4.2, the apparent association between X and Y completely disappears once a confounder is controlled for. Researchers then speak of a *spurious relationship* between X and Y. In other cases, a confounder may only explain some, but not all, of the relationship between X and Y, such that, after controlling for the confounder, the correlation between X and Y is smaller than without controlling for the confounder, but not zero.

Masked relationships and suppressor variables

A suppressor variable might be considered as the opposite of a confounder. When a suppressor is at play, then two variables, X and Y, seem uncorrelated (or weakly correlated), but a (stronger) relationship between them becomes visible once a third variable is accounted for. In such a case, the third variable is called a *suppressor variable*, because it is said to suppress the true relationship between X and Y. Suppression is illustrated in Figures 4.3 and 4.4.

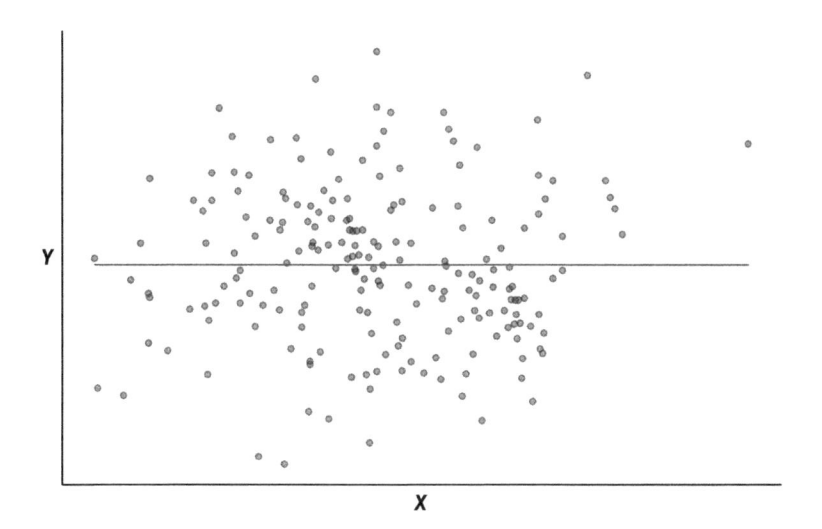

Figure 4.3 A hypothetical scatter plot of two apparently unrelated variables

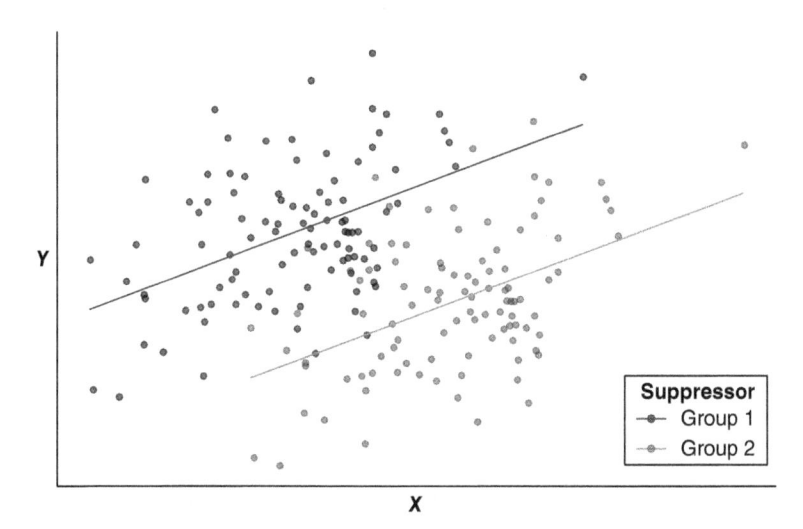

Figure 4.4 Illustration of a suppressor variable masking the true relationship between X and Y

Figure 4.3 displays the bivariate relationship between X and Y, without considering a third variable. It seems as if there is no association ($r \approx 0$). However, Figure 4.4 suggests that a third variable may be at work that suppresses the true relationship between X and Y. Within each group of the suppressor variable, there is in fact a moderately strong association between X and Y ($r \approx 0.47$ within each of Group 1 and Group 2).

The phenomenon of a suppressed relationship between two variables, X and Y, might occur when a third variable, the suppressor, is associated with the predictor X, and is also associated with Y, but in the opposite direction. For example, the suppressor might have a positive association with X, and a negative association with Y. When a suppressor variable suppresses the true association between two variables, we call this a *masked relationship*, and the suppressor is sometimes called a *masking variable*.

As an example of a masked relationship consider the Sure Start programme, a UK government initiative designed to assist families with preschool children by providing childcare and early education (example inspired by Williams, 2015). The intention of the programme is to improve educational achievement. So it is an interesting research question whether a family's participation in the programme is in fact associated with the subsequent educational achievements of their child, or children. When analysing relevant data, you might find, maybe to your surprise, that Sure Start children have worse educational achievements than children whose families did not attend Sure Start centres. Should we conclude that Sure Start is bad for children's education, and that the programme results in the opposite of its intended effect? We should not. There is a suppressor variable at work here, namely poverty: poorer families are more likely to participate in Sure Start, and children from poorer families on average have worse educational achievements than children from richer families. In other words, the suppressor (poverty) is positively associated with Sure Start attendance (X), but negatively associated with educational achievement (Y). Once we control for family poverty in the analysis, a positive association between Sure Start attendance and educational achievement becomes visible. Thus, to adequately estimate the effect of Sure Start attendance on educational achievement in observational data (i.e. outside a randomised controlled trial), we need to statistically control for poverty. If we do not, we might obtain a misleading estimate of the effect of the Sure Start programme.

Just like confounding, suppression is a causal concept. We call a variable a suppressor only when we have reason to believe that the masked relationship is indeed a causal one. Thus, seeing a potential 'suppression pattern' such as in Figure 4.4 is in itself not sufficient to conclude that a 'true association' between X and Y exists that is masked by the suppressor. To draw such a conclusion, we need to make further assumptions about the causal relationships between the three variables involved.

Multivariate relationships: a simple example with two predictors

Confounding and suppression are important concepts and can be a motivation for multivariate analysis. On the other hand, often in social science we might not have a clear causal theory that would allow us to decide, for example, which of two predictors of an outcome is a cause, and which a confounder. Sometimes we might more simply be interested in investigating how two (or more) variables act together in their relationships with an outcome. This section introduces a simple research example that helps us think about different types of multivariate relationships we might find in practice.

Consider what determines how happy people are in their lives, how well they feel mentally. Is it money? Status? Success? Physical health? Romantic love? Relationships with friends and family? Being part of a community? Studies into mental wellbeing have investigated many contributing factors, and of course these factors don't need to be mutually exclusive. Let's begin by focusing on just two potential predictors of mental wellbeing:

- *Social participation:* taking part in voluntary, political or charitable organisations, sports clubs, neighbourhood associations and so forth. We might theorise that this fosters mental wellbeing by providing a sense of community and purpose for one's life.
- *Health:* the state of one's physical health. One indicator of health is the presence of a limiting illness or disability, which prevents people from leading an active life in some respects.

Suppose we wanted to investigate both these issues together, and wished to ask whether mental wellbeing was associated with either social participation or the presence of a long-standing limiting illness, or both. For the moment, let's put aside the question of causality. We are not claiming that either social participation or the presence of a long-standing limiting illness has a causal effect on mental wellbeing. We are simply describing the statistical associations between these variables.

Suppose that we have the following two hypotheses:

- *Hypothesis 1:* People who participate more in social life tend to have better mental wellbeing than people who participate less, and this is true for people with a limiting illness as well as for those without.
- *Hypothesis 2:* People who have a limiting illness tend to have worse mental wellbeing than people without a limiting illness, and this is true for people at all levels of social participation.

Note that the two hypotheses involve multivariate relationships: In Hypothesis 1, we are not simply hypothesising that 'more social participation predicts higher mental wellbeing', but that it does so even if we take the presence or absence of a limiting illness into account. Thus, the hypothesis implies that the relationship between social participation and mental wellbeing exists among people who have a limiting illness, as well as among people who do not. Similarly, Hypothesis 2 asserts that a limiting illness will predict worse social wellbeing for people who don't participate socially, for those who participate a lot, as well as for everyone in between.

Let's look at this problem from a formal standpoint. Three variables are involved:

- Mental Wellbeing (*MWB*), which we assume is a numeric outcome.
- Social Participation (*SocPart*), a numeric predictor.
- Limiting Illness (*Limill*). This is a dichotomous predictor, and is coded 0 for those who don't have a limiting illness, and 1 for those who do. We can use a numeric variable with the codes 0 and 1 to represent a categorical variable in a regression model. Such a binary '0/1' predictor is called a **dummy variable**. (We will look at dummy variables in detail in the section 'Dummy Variables for Representing Categorical Predictors'.)

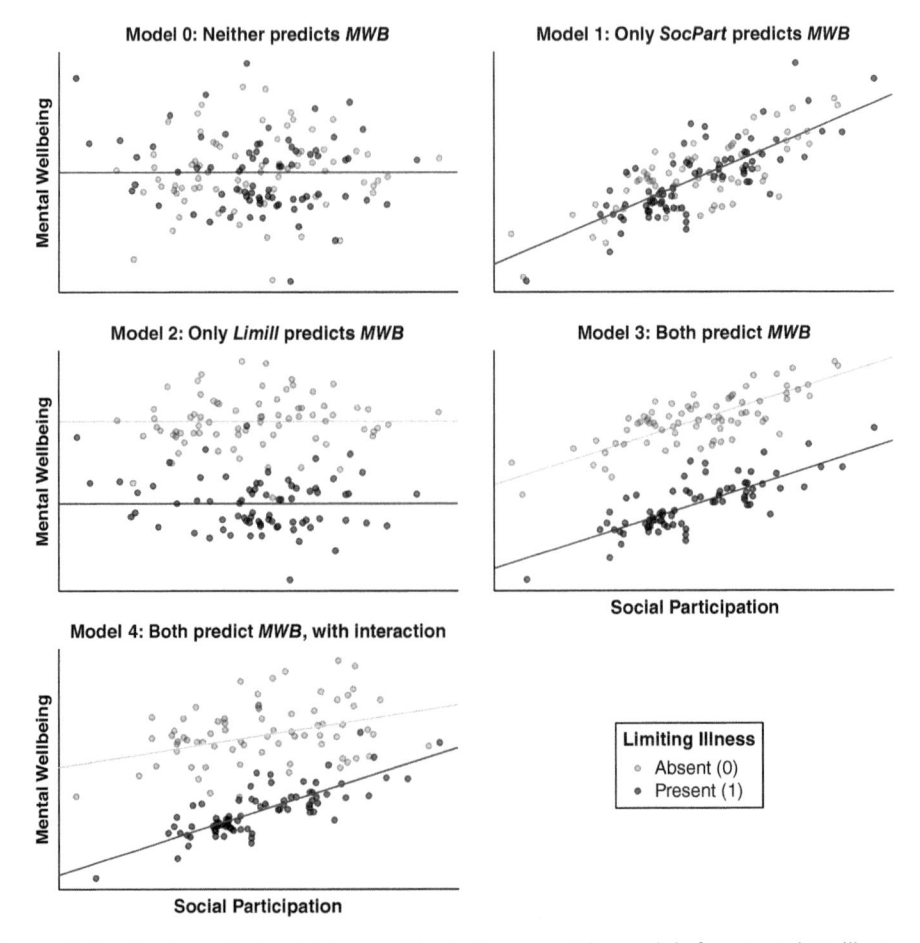

Figure 4.5 Five hypothetical data sets illustrating possible models for Mental Wellbeing predicted by Social Participation and Limiting Illness

Note. MWB = Mental Wellbeing; SocPart = Social Participation; Limill = Limiting Illness.

What might a suitable model be? Before we look at data, let's consider the possibilities. There are five types of hypothetical models involving these two predictors. These hypothetical models are illustrated in Figure 4.5. The data were simulated to conform to each model. Figure 4.5 thus illustrates a thought experiment: for each of the five models, we consider what the data might look like *if* that model was correct.

Let's have a look at the five models in turn.

- *Model 0* proposes that Mental Wellbeing is not related to either Social Participation or Limiting Illness.
- According to *Model 1*, Social Participation predicts Mental Wellbeing, but Limiting Illness does not, once Social Participation has been taken into account.
- *Model 2* represents the hypothesis that Limiting Illness predicts Mental Wellbeing, but Social Participation does not, once Limiting Illness has been taken into account. We have two regression lines, one for each group (*Limill* = 0 or *Limill* = 1), but both lines are horizontal, so there is no relationship between Social Participation and Mental Wellbeing in either group.
- *Model 3* posits that both Social Participation and Limiting Illness predict Mental Wellbeing. There are separate regression lines for those with a limiting illness and those without. The two lines have different intercepts, but share the same slope. This model thus assumes that the relationship between Social Participation and Mental Wellbeing is the same for people with a limiting illness as it is for those without a limiting illness.
- Finally, in *Model 4* both Social Participation and Limiting Illness predict Mental Wellbeing, as in Model 3. The difference is that in Model 4 those with a limiting illness have a different slope for Social Participation than those without a limiting illness. In other words, Model 4 proposes that the relationship between Social Participation and Mental Wellbeing is different among people with a limiting illness, compared to people without a limiting illness. This phenomenon, when the relationship between two variables depends on a third variable, is called an *interaction* (see also Box 4.2, later in this chapter). Model 4 assumes that Social Participation and Limiting Illness *interact* in their relationships with Mental Wellbeing.

These five models represents the basic possibilities for a regression with two predictors. Of course, the theoretical possibility exists that the relationships are of different strengths than those illustrated in Figure 4.5, or even have opposite signs: such that, for example, less social participation may predict more mental wellbeing (which we might call the misanthropic theory of happiness). The five model types above thus only illustrate the five possible combinations of predictors, not all the possibilities of the strengths or directions of the relationships. In the section 'Simple Examples of Multiple Regression Models', we consider how to estimate these five models using real data. Before we do that, it helps to formally define multiple linear regression.

Multiple regression: general definition

Multiple linear regression is a model of the form:

$$Y_i = \beta_0 + \beta_1 X_{1i} + \beta_2 X_{2i} + \cdots + \beta_p X_{pi} + \epsilon_i$$

This model looks very similar to simple linear regression. The main difference is that instead of one predictor variable X, we now have multiple predictor variables, which we call X_1, X_2, and so forth. The number of predictors is denoted by p, and so the last predictor variable is called X_p. Each predictor has its own slope coefficient, and the slope coefficients are numbered in the same way as the predictor variables (β_1, β_2,..., β_p). We also have an intercept, which I call here β_0 (it is also sometimes called α, as in Chapters 2 and 3).

As in simple linear regression, in multiple regression we assume that the errors ϵ_i are independent from one another, that they follow a normal distribution and that they are homoscedastic (see Chapter 3). These assumptions are sometimes written as follows:

$$\epsilon_i \sim NID(0, \sigma^2)$$

which should be read as 'the errors are normally and independently distributed (NID), with mean zero and variance σ^2'. The tilde symbol (~) means 'is distributed as'. The homoscedasticity assumption is expressed here by the term σ^2, which does not have a subscript i, indicating that the variance is the same for all errors, no matter what the predicted value is. The error variance, σ^2, is the square of the error standard deviation, σ, which in turn is estimated by the residual standard error, s (see Chapter 2, section 'Residual Standard Error').

We also assume that the relationship between each predictor X_1, X_2,..., X_p and the outcome Y is linear. The predictors may be numeric variables, dummy variables (coded 0 or 1, such as Limiting Illness) or interactions between predictors. In principle, there is no limit to the number of predictors in a multiple linear regression model.[1]

Predicted values of the outcome are given by the following equation:

$$\hat{Y}_i = \beta_0 + \beta_1 X_{1i} + \beta_2 X_{2i} + \cdots + \beta_p X_{pi}$$

The coefficient β_0 is called the *intercept* (or, alternatively, the *constant*). It represents the predicted value of the outcome Y for a case whose values on *all* predictors are zero. The coefficients β_1, β_2, ... are called the *slopes*. The concept of the slope is familiar from simple linear regression. However, in multiple regression, the interpretation

---

[1] However, the more predictors you have, the greater a sample size you will need to estimate the model reliably. Also, a larger model (with more predictors) is not necessarily a better one, a point to which we will return below.

of the slope is different in an important way. In a model with more than one predictor, the slope represents the effect of a predictor *when all other predictors are taken into account*. You will find researchers acknowledging this interpretation using any of the following formulations. They might say that a slope coefficient for X_1 in a multiple regression with additional predictor X_2 represents:

- the effect of X_1 *controlling for* X_2 (this is a typical formulation in social science),
- the effect of X_1 *adjusting for* X_2 (medical and epidemiological research),
- the effect of X_1 *holding X_2 constant* (statistical textbooks),
- the effect of X_1 *in the presence of* X_2 (also statistical textbooks), or
- the effect of X_1 *after X_2 has been taken into account* (everyone).

All these formulations are synonyms in this context.

The coefficients of a multiple linear regression model can be estimated from a set of suitable data by ordinary least squares (OLS) regression (see Chapter 2). This procedure finds the coefficients that result in the smallest sum of squared residuals for a given data set. Residuals are given by

$$e_i = Y_i - \hat{Y}_i$$

for $\hat{Y}_i$ based on estimates of the coefficients.

As in simple linear regression, how well the model predicts the outcome in a set of data is indicated by the residual standard error and the R^2 statistic.

1. The residual standard error (s) is an estimate of the standard deviation of the errors, σ. It is calculated as $s = \dfrac{\Sigma e_i^2}{n-p-1}$, where n is the sample size and p is the number of predictors. We can think of the residual standard error as a gauge of the precision of our predictions. The smaller the residual standard error, the better the prediction. The residual standard error is not a standardised measure, so it depends on the scale and the variance of the outcome variable, and can't necessarily be compared between models estimated on different data sets.
2. The R^2 statistic can be interpreted as the proportion of the variance of Y explained by the predictors in the data set at hand. We saw how it is calculated in Chapter 2. The R^2 statistic is a standardised measure (it does not depend on the scale of the outcome), and thus can be compared between models estimated on different data sets.

Simple examples of multiple regression models

We will now look at an application of multiple regression to real data. The example takes inspiration from a study by Elliott et al. (2014), who used data from the UK National Child Development Study (NCDS) to investigate predictors of mental wellbeing. NCDS is a birth cohort of UK residents born in 1958. The data used in this example are from a survey conducted in 2008, when the cohort members were about 50 years old.[2] The examples that follow use the same data set as Elliott et al., but I have simplified the analysis in some respects, and I don't replicate the methods of the published study exactly.

Example 1: One numeric predictor, one dichotomous predictor

Let's begin by investigating the relationship between mental wellbeing, social participation and the presence of a limiting illness, as above in the section 'Multivariate relationships: a simple example with two predictors'. This exemplifies a model with two predictors, one of which is numeric, while the other is dichotomous. Figure 4.6 shows the distributions of the three variables.

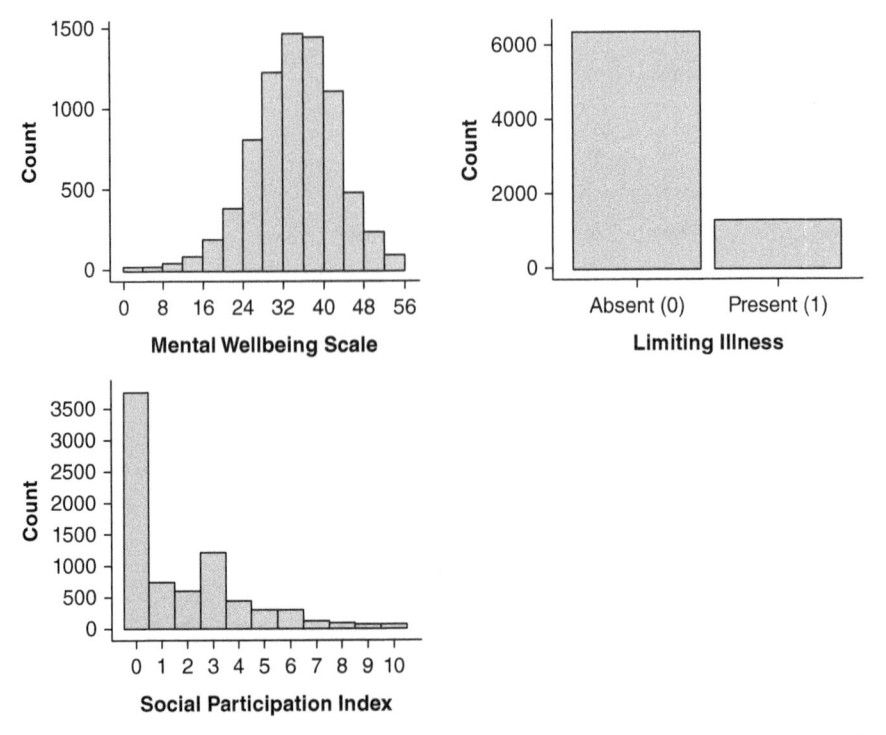

Figure 4.6 The distributions of Mental Wellbeing, Social Participation and Limiting Illness

Note. N = 7603. Data were taken from the National Child Development Study, 2008 sweep.

---

[2] I am grateful to the Centre for Longitudinal Studies (CLS), UCL Institute of Education, for permitting the use of these data and to the UK Data Service for making them available. However, neither CLS nor the UK Data Service bear any responsibility for the analysis or interpretation of these data.

Mental Wellbeing and Social Participation are both numeric variables, derived by summing the answers to multiple survey questions. Higher scores indicate better mental wellbeing and more social participation. Limiting Illness is a dichotomous variable. For the purpose of multiple regression, we need to turn its values into numbers. We will give respondents who report a limiting illness the value 1, and all others the value 0. Box 4.1 tells you a bit more about how these variables were measured in the NCDS survey.

> **Box 4.1**
>
> **Variables From the National Child Development Study Used in Example 1**
>
> *Mental Wellbeing Scale (MWB):* The Edinburgh–Warwick Mental Wellbeing Scale is a 14-item questionnaire that asks respondents to rate 14 statements (e.g. 'I've been feeling good about myself'), using five response options (from 'Never' to 'Always'). I have coded the responses to each question 0 to 4. A total score is calculated as the sum of the 14 items, so that a person's mental wellbeing score may vary between 0 and 56. A higher score indicates higher mental wellbeing. This variable is not truly continuous, since it can take only whole numbers as its values. However, we can regard it as a discrete measurement of an underlying continuous characteristic. (The official scoring for this scale is to code the item responses from 1 to 5, so that the total score can range from 14 to 70. I find it more intuitive to make the minimum score 0.) Figure 4.6 shows that *MWB* is approximately normally distributed in this sample, although there is a slight negative skew.
>
> *Social Participation (SocPart):* Social participation was measured by showing respondents a card with 16 types of organisations (e.g. political party, religious group, neighbourhood association). Respondents were asked to indicate, for each of the 16 types, whether they were a member of an organisation, and how often they went to meetings ('at least once a week', 'about once a month', 'less often', 'never', coded 3 to 0). Responses to the 16 questions were summed to give a score that theoretically varies between 0 and 48. There were very few respondents with scores over 10, however, and I recoded those to be equal to 10, to avoid problems with outliers in the analyses that follow. Figure 4.6 shows that the mode of Social Participation is 0, indicating that many respondents are either not members of any organisation, or if they are, that they don't attend meetings.
>
> *Limiting Illness (Limill):* The presence of a limiting illness was assessed by a single question, asking the respondent to indicate whether poor health limits their daily activities compared to most people their age, with response options 'yes' (coded 1) or 'no' (coded 0). Figure 4.6 shows that about 17% of respondents reported having a limiting illness.

Figure 4.7 illustrates how the three variables are related in this data set. Since both Social Participation and Mental Wellbeing can only take integer values, most combinations of scores occur many times in the data. For example, there are 190 people who had a wellbeing score of 31 and a social participation score of 0. I have jittered the points out of position, so that you can get a sense of how many there are for each combination of variable values. With that many data points, it can be difficult to discern the shape and the strength of a relationship – or indeed whether there are any relationships at all. This is particularly true in social science, where we often find that the relationships between variables are not very strong.

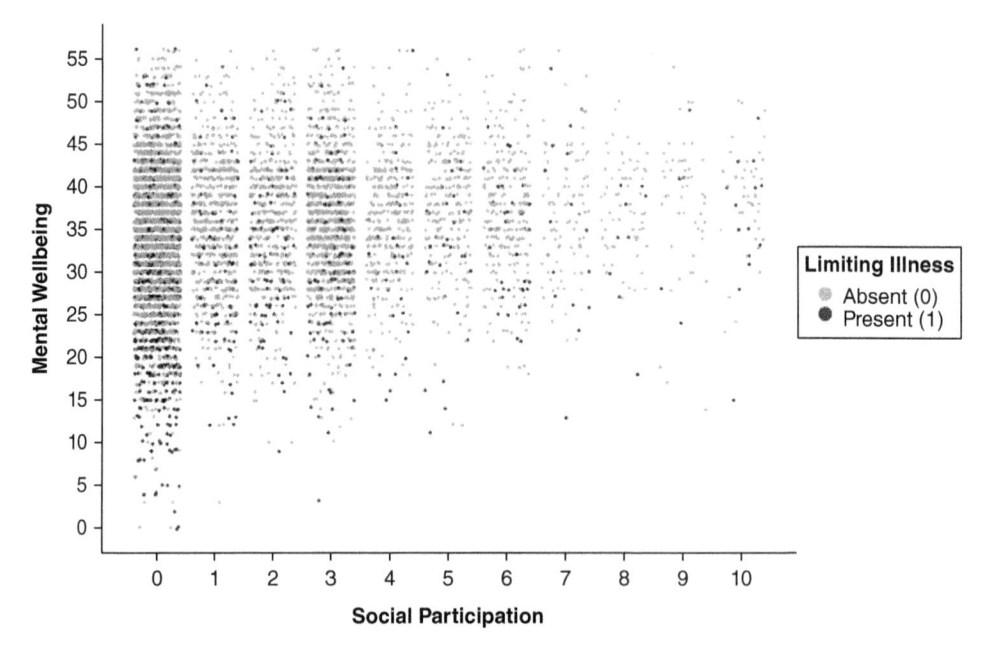

Figure 4.7 Scatter plot of Mental Wellbeing by Social Participation, grouped by Limiting Illness

Note. N = 7603. Data were taken from the National Child Development Study, 2008 sweep.

We will now estimate each of the five models outlined in the earlier section on 'Multivariate Relationships: A Simple Example With Two Predictors'. This is to illustrate how multiple regression works. In a real research investigation, you might not necessarily estimate all these models. Instead, guided by your research questions, you might consider one, two, or maybe three plausible models that represent particular hypotheses.

Table 4.1 shows the coefficient estimates from each of five models based on the NCDS data. Figure 4.8 illustrates the data and the regression lines implied by each of these sets of estimates. Different regression lines are drawn in each panel, corresponding to the model estimates shown in Table 4.1. The different panels thus show different interpretations of the data depending on the model proposed. Let's look at each of these models in turn.

Table 4.1 Coefficient estimates for five models predicting Mental Wellbeing

	Model				
	0	1	2	3	4
Intercept	34.994	34.189	35.801	35.054	35.133
Social Participation (SocPart)		0.478		0.427	0.382
Limiting Illness (Limill)			−4.819	−4.657	−5.075
Interaction: SocPart × Limill					0.293
Residual standard error (s)	8.111	8.043	7.909	7.854	7.851
R^2	0.000	0.017	0.049	0.063	0.064

Note. N = 7603. Data were taken from the National Child Development Study, 2008 sweep.

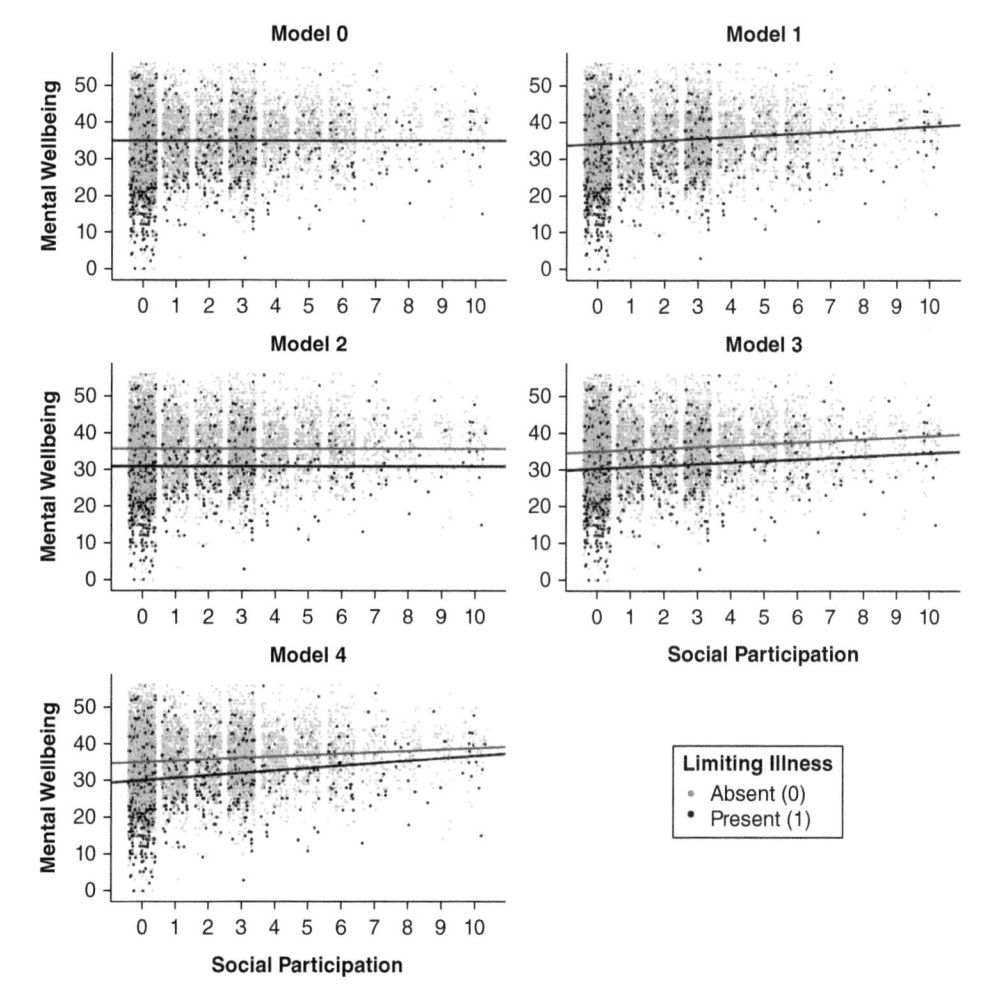

Figure 4.8 Mental Wellbeing, Social Participation and Limiting Illness: an illustration of five possible models for the National Child Development Study data

Note. N = 7603. Data were taken from the National Child Development Study, 2008 sweep. Each panel shows the same data. The regression lines in each panel illustrate the model estimates shown in Table 4.1.

Model 0: Neither Social Participation nor Limiting Illness predict wellbeing

Model 0 has no predictors. The model can be written as follows:

$$MWB_i = \beta_0 + \epsilon_i$$

$$\epsilon_i \sim NID(0, \sigma^2)$$

where *MWB* stands for Mental Wellbeing. There are only two parameters to estimate: (1) the intercept (β_0) and (2) the error variance (σ_2). Note that the normality assumption about the errors here implies that the variable *MWB* is normally distributed with mean β_0 and variance σ_2.

The least-squares estimate for this model is easy to calculate: the best estimate of the intercept is the sample mean of Mental Wellbeing ($\overline{MWB}$). Table 4.1 informs us that the estimated model equation is

$$\widehat{MWB_l} = 34.994$$

with residual standard error $s = 8.111$.

Model 0 estimates that *MWB* has a mean of 34.994 and a standard deviation of 8.111. According to Model 0, the mean *MWB* score is the same for the whole sample of participants, regardless of their social participation, whether they have a limiting illness or any other characteristic.

A model without predictors, such as this one, is often called a *null model*. It is rare that we are interested in the null model for its own sake. However, as we will see later on, we can use the null model as a comparison point when investigating the quality of some other model that we *are* interested in.

Model 1: Only Social Participation predicts wellbeing

Model 1 has one predictor, and can be written as follows:

$$MWB_i = \beta_0 + \beta_1 SocPart_i + \epsilon_i$$

$$\epsilon_i \sim NID(0, \sigma^2)$$

Table 4.1 shows that the estimated equation for Model 1 is

$$\widehat{MWB_l} = 34.189 + 0.478 \times SocPart_i$$

The estimates from Model 1 imply that the average wellbeing of those who don't participate socially at all (with a social participation score of 0) is 34.189, but that the average wellbeing is predicted to be greater by 0.478 points for every additional point on the social participation scale. Model 1 is, of course, a simple linear regression (see Chapter 2). This model assumes that having a limiting illness is not related to wellbeing, once social participation has been taken into account.

Model 2: Only Limiting Illness predicts wellbeing

Model 2 also has one predictor, and can be written as follows[3]:

$$MWB_i = \beta_0 + \beta_1 Limill_i + \epsilon_i$$

Model 2 assumes that the average wellbeing score is different for those without a limiting illness, compared to those with a limiting illness, and that Social Participation is unrelated to Mental Wellbeing once Limiting Illness has been taken into account. Table 4.1 gives us the model estimates:

$$\widehat{MWB_i} = 35.801 - 4.819 \times Limill_i$$

Model 2 predicts that the average wellbeing of those who *don't* have a limiting illness (such that their *Limill* score equals zero) is 35.801, and that the average for those who *do* have a limiting illness is 4.819 points lower – that is, 35.801 – 4.819 = 30.982. The coefficient β_1 here represents the difference between the means of the two groups. Model 2 corresponds to the alternative hypothesis of a *t*-test for independent samples (see Chapter 1).

Model 3: Both Social Participation and Limiting Illness predict wellbeing

Model 3 has two predictors, and can be written as follows:

$$MWB_i = \beta_0 + \beta_1 SocPart_i + \beta_2 Limill_i + \epsilon_i$$

Model 3 posits that the average mental wellbeing score is different for those with and without a limiting illness, and that mental wellbeing also depends on the level of social participation. The coefficient estimates from the NCDS data are:

$$\widehat{MWB_i} = 35.054 + 0.427 \times SocPart_i - 4.657 \times Limill_i$$

These estimates imply the following predictions: the predicted wellbeing score among those without a limiting illness and with a social participation score of zero is $\hat{\beta}_0 = 35.054$. A person with a limiting illness is predicted to have a wellbeing score that is 4.657 points lower (since $\hat{\beta}_2 = 4.657$) than a person without, if both have the same social participation score. Finally, a 1-point difference on the social participation scale is

---

[3] From this point onwards and for the remainder of this chapter, I will leave out the term $\epsilon_i \sim NID(0, \sigma^2)$ when defining a model, since it is the same for all linear regression models.

associated with a difference of $\hat{\beta}_1 = 0.427$ points on the wellbeing score, controlling for limiting illness. According to these estimates, people who engage in more social participation tend to report better mental wellbeing, controlling for limiting illness.

Have a look at Table 4.1 again and note the following:

- The coefficient for Social Participation in Model 3 is not the same as the coefficient for Social Participation in Model 1.
- The coefficient for Limiting Illness in Model 3 is not the same as the coefficient for Limiting Illness in Model 2.

In both cases, the estimated effect of the predictor is weaker when controlling for the other predictor, compared to a model without the control variable. This is because the two predictors are themselves associated with one another. Those with a limiting illness are less likely to engage in social participation than those without. Thus some of the association between Social Participation and Mental Wellbeing overlaps with the association between Limiting Illness and Mental Wellbeing.

Model 4: Interaction between Social Participation and Limiting Illness

Model 4 also has two predictors and allows for an interaction between the two. We can write it as follows:

$$MWB_i = \beta_0 + \beta_1 SocPart_i + \beta_2 Limill_i + \beta_3 (SocPart_i \times Limill_i) + \epsilon_i$$

Model 4 posits that both Social Participation and Limiting Illness predict wellbeing, and that the slope of Social Participation depends on whether a Limiting Illness is present or not. Note that the interaction term, $SocPart_i \times Limill_i$, is formed by multiplying the two variables involved. A formal definition of interactions in multiple linear regression is given in Box 4.2.

Box 4.2

Interactions in Regression Models

An interaction between two predictor variables occurs when the strength and/or the direction of the relationship between one of the predictors and the outcome depends on the other predictor. Let's call the outcome Y and the predictors X and Z. If the strength and/or direction of the relationship between X and Y is different for different values of Z, we say that X and Z interact in their effect on Y. Other terms that are sometimes used to describe interactions are *effect modification* ('Z modifies the effect of X on Y') and *moderation* ('Z moderates the relationship between X and Y').

An example of an interaction is given by Hamilton and Saito (2015) in their study of belief in human-made climate change in the US state of New Hampshire. One relevant predictor is party affiliation: generally, supporters of the Democratic Party are more likely to believe in human-made climate change than supporters of the Republican Party. Education also plays a role: the better educated a person, the more likely they are to accept the scientific consensus on human-made climate change. In addition, Hamilton and Saito found that education and party affiliation interact. Among Republican supporters, the relationship between education and belief in human-made climate change is weak; highly educated Republicans are only a little more likely to believe in human-made climate change than less well-educated Republicans. Among Democrats, this relationship is stronger, such that there is a relatively large difference between highly educated and less well-educated Democrats (for an illustration, see Figure 3 in Hamilton & Saito, 2015). In other words, education tends to make it more likely that a person accepts the scientific consensus on human-made climate change, but party affiliation moderates this relationship: the effect of education is weaker among Republicans than among Democrats. The reasons for this interaction are likely to be complex, as Hamilton and Saito (2015) explain.

We can model an interaction by adding the product (multiplication) of X and Z to our model as a predictor. Thus, a regression model involving an interaction between X and Z might be written as follows:

$$Y_i = \beta_0 + \beta_1 X_i + \beta_2 Z_i + \beta_3 (X_i Z_i) + \varepsilon_i$$

where $X_i Z_i$ is called an interaction term. In practice, you might create an interaction term in your data set by making a new variable that is equal to the product of X and Z. However, good statistical software programs, such as Stata or R, allow you to specify an interaction term as part of the command that estimates the regression model, without explicitly calculating the interaction term yourself.

In the presence of an interaction, you cannot interpret the relationship between X and Y in isolation. You must take account of the influence of Z on that relationship. (The same applies, vice versa, for the relationship between Z and Y, which must be interpreted in the light of the influence of X.) In our example model, the slope of X depends on Z, and the slope of Z depends on X. The slope of X is equal to $\beta_1 + \beta_3 Z_i$, and the slope of Z is equal to $\beta_2 + \beta_3 X_i$. Note, in particular, that β_1 is the slope of X when Z is zero, since $\beta_1 + \beta_3 \times 0 = \beta_1$. Analogously, β_2 is the slope of Z when X is zero.

The interaction described here is a two-way interaction, involving two predictors. Higher order interactions involving three or more predictors are also possible but are relatively rare outside of designed experiments, and I won't discuss them further here. A thorough introduction to interactions in multiple linear regression is given in Jaccard and Turrisi (2003).

When a model contains an interaction, the interpretation of coefficients is a little trickier than otherwise. Generally, in the presence of an interaction, slope coefficients for predictors involved in the interaction (here, $\hat{\beta}_1$ for *SocPart* and $\hat{\beta}_2$ for *Limill*) must be interpreted with reference to the other predictor involved. In our example, the slope coefficients should be interpreted as follows:

- $\hat{\beta}_1 = 0.382$: The slope coefficient for Social Participation represents the predicted difference in wellbeing for an additional point on social participation, *for those with no limiting illness*.
- $\hat{\beta}_2 = -5.075$: The slope coefficient for Limiting Illness represents the predicted difference between those with and without a limiting illness, *for those with a social participation score of zero*.
- $\hat{\beta}_3 = 0.293$: The coefficient of the interaction represents the *difference* in the slopes of Social Participation between those with a limiting illness and those without. Conversely, it can also be interpreted as the difference in the effect of Limiting Illness associated with a 1-point difference in Social Participation.

The next section explains the interpretation of this interaction in detail.

Interpretation of an interaction between a numeric and a dichotomous predictor

Let us look at the interaction in Model 4 more closely. The estimated model equation is

$$\widehat{MWB}_i = 35.133 + 0.382 \times SocPart_i - 5.075 \times Limill_i + 0.293(SocPart_i \times Limill_i)$$

This equation defines two regression lines: one line for those without a limiting illness (where *Limill* = 0), and another for those with a limiting illness (where *Limill* = 1):

- For *Limill* = 0, all terms involving *Limill* are zero and can be ignored, so the estimated regression line is

$$\widehat{MWB}_i = 35.133 + 0.382 \times SocPart_i$$

Thus, for those without limiting illness, the estimated slope of Social Participation is 0.382.

- For *Limill* = 1, the estimated regression line is

$$\begin{aligned}\widehat{MWB}_i &= 35.133 + 0.382 \times SocPart_i - 5.075 \times 1 + 0.293(SocPart_i \times 1) \\ &= (35.133 - 5.075) + (0.382 + 0.293)SocPart_i \\ &= 30.058 + 0.675 \times SocPart_i\end{aligned}$$

Thus, for those with a limiting illness, the estimated slope of Social Participation is 0.675, almost twice as steep as for those without a limiting illness. You can see this in Figure 4.8, in the panel for Model 4: the regression line for those with a limiting illness has a steeper slope than the line for those without limiting illness. Thus, from the estimates of Model 4 it looks as though the relationship between Social Participation and Mental Wellbeing is stronger among people with a limiting illness than among people without a limiting illness. (Whether this model is justified by the data is a different question, which we will discuss in Chapter 5.)

Let's assume for a moment that we have reason to believe that the interaction stipulated in Model 4 represents a real effect in the population, rather than just a fluke occurrence in a sample. Then we should ask ourselves what this interaction might mean. How can we understand it theoretically? Some possibilities might be the following:

- *Social Participation as a protective factor:* Social participation may, to some extent, protect an individual from the detrimental effects of a limiting illness on their mental wellbeing. People with a limiting illness may have fewer opportunities for engaging in communal activities than those without a limiting illness, so that for them social participation has special importance as a means of maintaining social relationships and feeling part of a group, which in turn may help them feel good mentally. This might be why the effect of social participation is stronger for people with a limiting illness than for people without such an illness.
- *Methodological artefact:* The measurement of limiting illness in this data set is rather simplistic. The survey question asks respondents to say whether they consider themselves to be limited by an illness or not, but does not allow them to specify *how much* they are limited. It might be that those with the severest illnesses are prevented from social participation, while those with less severe illnesses are relatively more likely to engage in social participation. On the other hand, more severe illnesses may tend to go hand in hand with poorer mental wellbeing. Therefore, what appears to be an association between level of social participation and mental wellbeing, among those with any limiting illness, may in fact partly reflect the association between *severity* of the illness and mental wellbeing. In other words, social participation may be acting as a proxy for severity of illness. To put the same thing in a different way: the interaction may be caused by unmeasured differences in the severity of limiting illnesses, which are partially reflected in respondents' social participation scores.
- Other interpretations may well be possible. Also, the two interpretations suggested above are not mutually exclusive.

In general, it is up to the researcher to think about whether an interaction makes theoretical sense, and what this sense might be. The statistical models themselves won't allow us to decide which, if any, of these interpretations are correct.

Example 2: Multiple regression with two numeric predictors

In the models involving Social Participation and Limiting Illness in Example 1 above, it was relatively easy to visualise the data and the regression predictions. But what if we have two numeric predictors? Figure 4.9 shows the distributions of two other variables that Elliott et al. (2014) hypothesised to be predictors of Mental Wellbeing. These variables are Neighbourhood Cohesion (*NC*) and Social Support (*SUPP*). As you can see, both are numeric variables. Box 4.3 describes how they were measured.

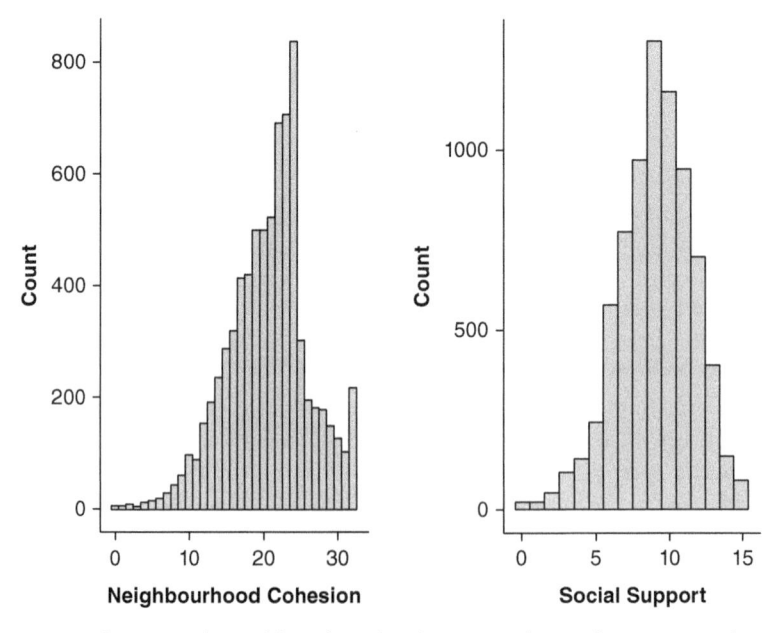

Figure 4.9 Distributions of Neighbourhood Cohesion and Social Support scales

Box 4.3

Measurement of Neighbourhood Cohesion and Social Support in the NCDS

Neighbourhood Cohesion (NC): Neighbourhood Cohesion was assessed by eight survey questions that asked respondents to rate how much they agreed or disagreed with statements such as 'I feel like I belong to this neighbourhood' or 'I would be willing to work together with others on something to improve my neighbourhood'. I scored responses on a scale from 0 ('strongly disagree') to 4 ('strongly agree'). The total score is calculated by summing the scores from the eight responses, so that the NC variable has a range from 0 to 32. A higher value indicates that a respondent feels their neighbourhood is more cohesive.

Social Support (SUPP): Social Support was measured by five items, which asked respondents to state how often they could count on people to help if they were sick in bed, had people around to listen to their problems and feelings, and how often in the last 2 weeks they had phone or letter contact with friends, had friends to visit or visited friends. Responses to each of these five items were scored from 0 to 3, and a total score was calculated by summing the five items, so that the Social Support variable has a range from 0 to 15. A higher value indicates more social support being available.

Two numeric predictors without interaction

For the moment, let's focus only on these two predictors and their relationship to Mental Wellbeing. A model we may propose is

$$MWB_i = \beta_0 + \beta_1 NC_i + \beta_2 SUPP_i + \varepsilon_i$$

I fitted this model to the NCDS data. Table 4.2 shows the estimated coefficients.

Table 4.2 Coefficient estimates from a regression of Mental Wellbeing on Neighbourhood Cohesion and Social Support

	Estimate
Intercept	24.124
Neighbourhood Cohesion (NC)	0.256
Social Support (SUPP)	0.611
Residual standard error	7.768
R^2	0.083

Note. N = 7603. Data were taken from the National Child Development Study, 2008 sweep.

Table 4.2 shows that the estimated model equation is

$$\widehat{MWB}_i = 24.124 + 0.256 \times NC_i + 0.611 \times SUPP_i$$

The slope coefficients are to be interpreted thus:

- A 1-point difference in Neighbourhood Cohesion is associated with an increase in Wellbeing by 0.256 points, when taking Social Support into account.
- A 1-point difference in Social Support is associated with a 0.611-point increase in Mental Wellbeing, when taking Neighbourhood Cohesion into account.

It is difficult to visualise relationships between three or more numeric variables on a two-dimensional sheet of paper. Nonetheless, I have attempted to do so, and Figure 4.10 is the result. I have selected only 25 respondents from the NCDS data set; their MWB, NC and SUPP scores are represented by points in three-dimensional space. The predicted outcome values from the regression equation now lie not on a line, but on a plane (a flat surface, like a table top). The plane outlined as a dashed grid in Figure 4.10 represents the predicted values of Mental Wellbeing from the regression model shown above. Note that the plane rises from left to right, reflecting the positive slope coefficient of Neighbourhood Cohesion. It also rises from front to back, reflecting the positive slope coefficient of Social Support.

It may be just about possible to get your head around a three-dimensional plot represented on a two-dimensional sheet of paper. (Although I struggle.) For models with

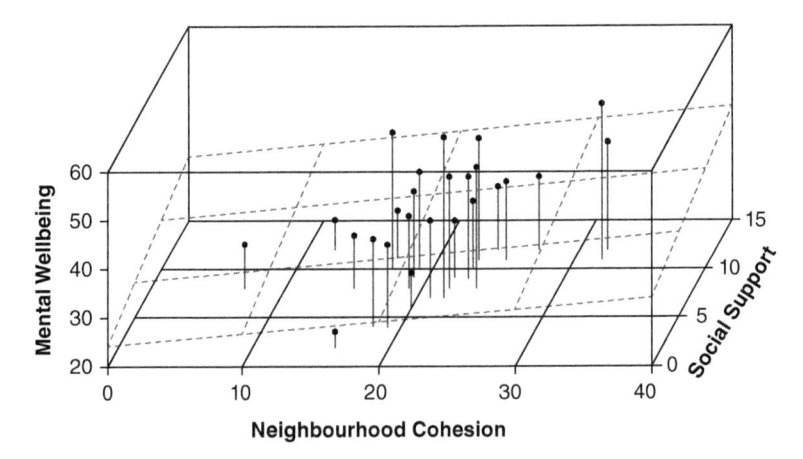

Figure 4.10 Three-dimensional representation of the relationship between Mental Wellbeing, Neighbourhood Cohesion and Social Support

Note. The regression plane is based on model estimates shown in Table 4.2. The dots represent 25 respondents to the National Child Development Study and their values on Mental Wellbeing, Neighbourhood Cohesion and Social Support. The Mental Wellbeing score is additionally represented by a vertical line anchoring each point to the 'floor' of the plot. The dashed grid represents the plane of predicted Mental Wellbeing scores, conditional on Neighbourhood Cohesion and Social Support.

more than two predictors, on-paper visualisation of the whole model becomes impossible. For example, with 10 predictors, we would be working in 11-dimensional space. Fortunately, mathematics and statistics can handle multiple dimensions, and so there is no limit, in principle, to the number of predictors we might include in a regression model, despite our human limitation in imagining multiple dimensions visually.

A two-dimensional way to visualise the estimates from a model with two numeric predictors is shown in Figure 4.11. Three regression lines illustrate the estimated relationship between Neighbourhood Cohesion and Mental Wellbeing at three different values of Social Support. The values 0, 9 and 15 are the minimum, median and maximum values, respectively, of Social Support in the NCDS data set. Of course, different example values could have been chosen. Also, with equal validity, I could have chosen to place Social Support in the *X*-axis of the plot, and draw example regression lines for different values of Neighbourhood Cohesion. In general, if you make such a plot, it is wise to design it so that it illustrates the result that is most important from a social scientific point of view.

Note that the three lines in Figure 4.11 are parallel: this reflects the assumption, made by the model reported in Table 4.2, that there is no interaction between Neighbourhood Cohesion and Social Support. In the next section, we will see how things change when we allow for an interaction between numeric predictors.

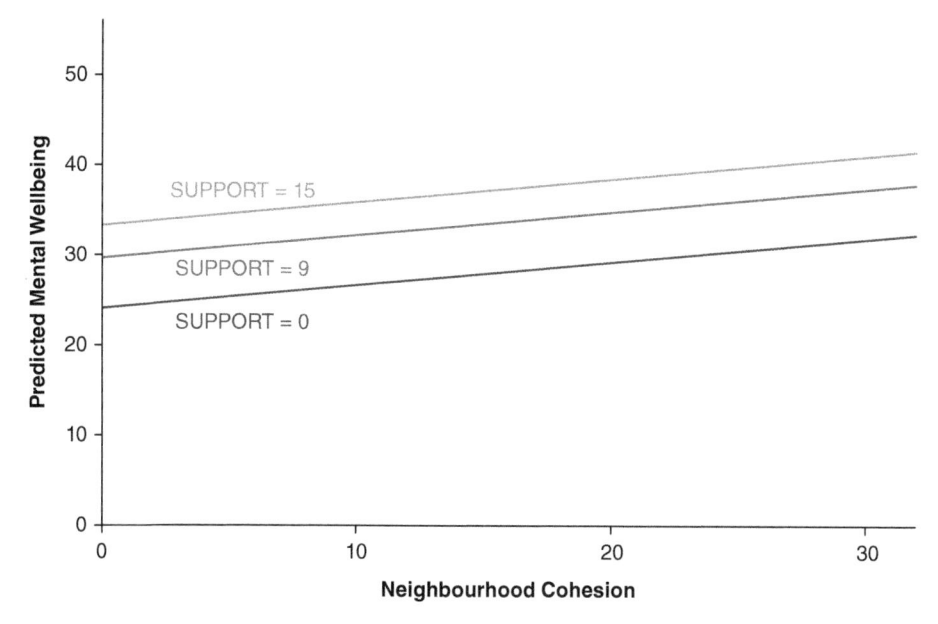

Figure 4.11 Three regression lines for the prediction of Mental Wellbeing by Neighbourhood Cohesion, for different values of Social Support

Note. Regression lines are based on model estimates shown in Table 4.2.

Interactions between two numeric predictor variables

It is possible to include interactions between numeric predictors in the regression equation. (For a formal definition of an interaction, see Box 4.2.) A model with an interaction between Neighbourhood Cohesion and Social Support has the equation

$$MWB_i = \beta_0 + \beta_1 NC_i + \beta_2 SUPP_i + \beta_3 (NC_i \times SUPP_i) + \varepsilon_i$$

As we saw in Box 4.2, the interaction term is formed as the multiplication of the two variables involved in the interaction. Table 4.3 shows the estimates of the coefficients from fitting this model on the NCDS data set. This shows that the estimated regression equation is

$$MWB_i = 21.644 + 0.381 \times NC_i + 0.890 \times SUPP_i - 0.014 \times NC_i \times SUPP_i + \varepsilon_i$$

The interaction is to be interpreted as the effect that one variable has on the slope of another. In this case, the estimated coefficient of the interaction is −0.014. This means that a 1-point difference in Neighbourhood Cohesion is associated with a decrease in the slope of Social Support by 0.014 units. With equal justification, we could say this the other way around: a 1-point difference in Social Support is associated with a 0.014 point decrease in the slope of Neighbourhood Cohesion.

Table 4.3 Coefficient estimates for the prediction of Mental Wellbeing by Neighbourhood Cohesion, Social Support and their interaction

	Coefficient
Intercept	21.644
Neighbourhood Cohesion (NC)	0.381
Social Support (SUPP)	0.890
Interaction: NC × SUPP	−0.014
Residual standard error	7.766
R^2	0.084

Note. N = 7603. Data were taken from the National Child Development Study, 2008 sweep.

To illustrate the interaction, we can use the estimated regression equation to deduce the slope gradients of one predictor for different levels of the other predictor. For example, for people with *SUPP* = 0, the estimated regression equation is

$$MWB_i = 21.644 + 0.381 \times NC_i + 0.890 \times 0 - 0.014 \times NC_i \times 0 + \varepsilon_i$$

$$= 21.644 + 0.381 \times NC_i + \varepsilon_i$$

That is, for *SUPP* = 0, the intercept is 21.644 and the slope of *NC* is 0.381.

Now consider, for example, people with *SUPP* = 9 (this happens to be the median *SUPP* score). For them, the estimated regression equation is

$$MWB_i = 21.644 + 0.381 \times NC_i + 9 \times 0.890 - 0.014 \times NC_i \times 9 + \varepsilon_i$$

$$= 21.644 + 8.010 + (0.381 - 0.014 \times 9) \times NC_i + \varepsilon_i$$

$$= 29.654 + 0.255 \times NC_i + \varepsilon_i$$

So for people with *SUPP* = 9, the intercept is 29.654 and the slope of *NC* is 0.255.

With similar calculations, we can find the estimated intercept and slope of *NC* for any value of *SUPP*. For example, for *SUPP* = 15, the intercept is 34.994 and the slope of *NC* is 0.171.

Figure 4.12 visualises the interaction by showing three regression lines for when *SUPP* equals 0, 9 and 15, respectively. Compare Figure 4.11, which illustrates a model without interaction, and features parallel regression lines, with Figure 4.12, where the presence of an interaction implies that the regression lines are not parallel.

From these estimates, then, it looks as if neighbourhood cohesion has a stronger effect on mental wellbeing for people with no or low social support, while for people with high social support, neighbourhood Cohesion is less important. We could also look at the results in another way and say that for people living in neighbourhoods with little cohesion, social support matters a great deal to their mental wellbeing, whereas for people living in more cohesive neighbourhoods, social support matters

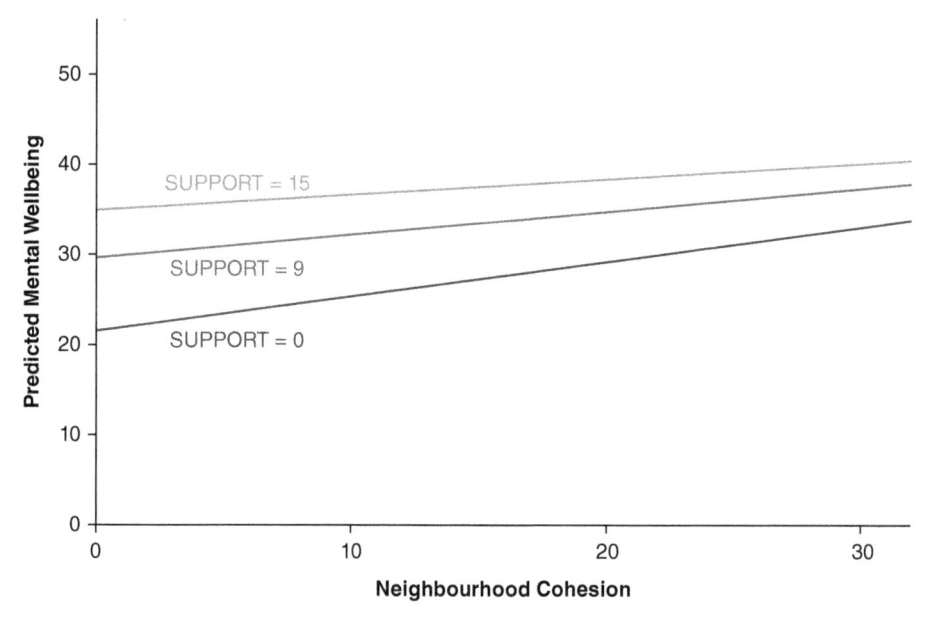

Figure 4.12 Three regression lines for the prediction of Mental Wellbeing by Neighbourhood Cohesion, Social Support and their interaction

Note. Regression lines are based on model estimates shown in Table 4.3.

less. If we believe that this interaction is important, we might look for a theoretical explanation. For example, we might speculate that a cohesive neighbourhood to some extent protects people who don't have a lot of social support from loneliness, and thus from poor mental wellbeing.

Research example: Neighbourhood cohesion and mental wellbeing

To illustrate the application of multiple regression to a social science research question, let's again consider the study by Elliott et al. (2014), which inspired the examples earlier in this chapter. Elliott et al. (2014) were interested in investigating the role that neighbourhood cohesion – a sense of belonging in one's neighbourhood – might play in mental wellbeing. This is an interesting sociological question, since it considers the possibility that a source of individual wellbeing may not necessarily only lie within the disposition and circumstances of the individual or their close family, but also in the quality of the community that they live in. The aim of the study was not to arrive at a comprehensive model for mental wellbeing, which would have to take into account a vast amount of potential causes, which researchers might struggle to all measure within a single study. Instead, Elliott et al. (2014) aimed at estimating the association between neighbourhood cohesion and mental wellbeing specifically.

A simple linear regression of Mental Wellbeing on Neighbourhood Cohesion would look like this:

Model 4.1:

$$MWB_i = \beta_0 + \beta_1 NC_i + \varepsilon_i$$

We might call this model, Model 4.1, an 'unadjusted model', because we are not adjusting the relationship between Mental Wellbeing and Neighbourhood Cohesion for any other variables. However, we might question whether this model is useful. What if the relationship between Neighbourhood Cohesion and Mental Wellbeing was really due to confounding by other variables? For example, people in more cohesive neighbourhoods may have more social support and more opportunities for social participation, and it may be these factors, rather than neighbourhood cohesion in itself, that explain any observed association between neighbourhood cohesion and mental wellbeing.

Because of such considerations, Elliott et al. (2014) adjusted their analysis for a range of potential confounding variables. For example, an adjusted model using the variables introduced in earlier sections of this chapter might be[4]

Model 4.2:

$$MWB_i = \beta_0 + \beta_1 NC_i + \beta_2 SUPP_i + \beta_3 SocPart_i + \beta_4 Limill_i + \beta_5 SocPart_i \times Limill_i + \varepsilon_i$$

Estimates from both the unadjusted and adjusted models, using the NCDS data, are displayed in Table 4.4. The simple linear regression of Mental Wellbeing on Neighbourhood Cohesion (Model 4.1, 'unadjusted model') yields an estimate for the regression coefficient of 0.334. In the adjusted model (Model 4.2), the slope coefficient estimate of Neighbourhood Cohesion controlling for the other variables in the model is 0.243. So if we believe the adjusted model (Model 4.2), our estimate of the effect of a cohesive neighbourhood on wellbeing will be considerably smaller than if we believe in the unadjusted model (Model 4.1).

In the publication of their study results, Elliott et al. (2014) estimated regression models of Mental Wellbeing similar to Model 4.1 and Model 4.2. In their journal article, they reported both the unadjusted and the adjusted coefficient of Neighbourhood Cohesion. They argued that the adjusted coefficient was likely to be a better estimate of the true relationship between Neighbourhood Cohesion and Mental Wellbeing, since the additional variables in the adjusted model likely represent confounders of that relationship.

---

[4]Elliott et al. (2014) adjusted for many more potential confounding variables. I have selected just a few to keep the example simple and easy to explain.

Table 4.4 Coefficient estimates, standard errors and confidence intervals for two regression models predicting Mental Wellbeing

	Model 4.1: Unadjusted Model			Model 4.2: Adjusted Model		
	Estimate	SE	95% CI	Estimate	SE	95% CI
Intercept	28.072	0.361		25.325	0.419	
Neighbourhood Cohesion (NC)	0.334	0.017	[0.301, 0.367]	0.243	0.017	[0.210, 0.276]
Social Support (SUPP)	—			0.552	0.036	[0.482, 0.622]
Social Participation (SocPart)	—			0.209	0.043	[0.124, 0.294]
Limiting Illness (Limill)	—			−4.853	0.280	[−5.402, −4.304]
Interaction: SocPart × Limill	—			0.265	0.109	[0.051, 0.479]
Residual standard error	7.910			7.559		
R^2	0.049			0.132		

Note. N = 7603. Data were taken from the National Child Development Study, 2008 sweep. SE = standard error; CI = confidence interval. Standard errors and confidence intervals are explained in Chapter 5.

Figure 4.13 illustrates the difference between the adjusted and the unadjusted models, by showing how the predicted Mental Wellbeing scores depend on Neighbourhood Cohesion, according to each model. The predictions from the unadjusted model are illustrated by a simple linear regression line. To illustrate the predictions for the adjusted model, I have fixed the numeric predictors (other than Neighbourhood Cohesion) at their sample medians. In other words, the two lines illustrating the adjusted model show the predicted wellbeing scores of people who have median social participation and social support scores. Two lines show how Mental Wellbeing depends on Neighbourhood Cohesion and the presence of a Limiting Illness, according to the adjusted model. These two lines are parallel, because there is no interaction between Limiting Illness and Neighbourhood Cohesion in this model.

The unadjusted model predicts a steeper slope than the adjusted model (numerically: 0.334 vs 0.243, as we saw from Table 4.4). Generally, the predictions from the unadjusted model fall somewhat between the predictions of the adjusted model for people with and without a limiting illness. The unadjusted model doesn't account for limiting illness, so its predictions ignore the distinction between people with and without a limiting illness. (Of course, the unadjusted model also ignores distinctions between people who differ in their social participation and social support scores.)

Regarding the main research question of Elliott et al.'s (2014) investigation, the conclusion from these analyses is that there is evidence of a positive association between Neighbourhood Cohesion and Mental Wellbeing, even after adjusting for

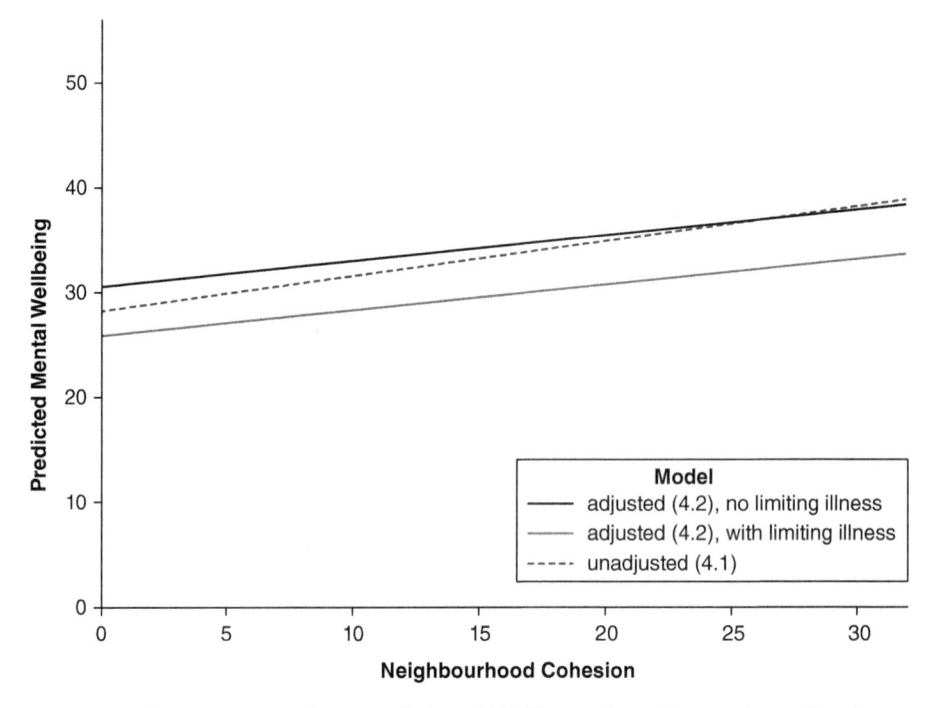

Figure 4.13 Comparing predictions of Mental Wellbeing from the unadjusted and adjusted models (Models 4.1 and 4.2)

Note. For Model 4.2, predictions are shown for people with median social participation (1) and social support scores (9), separately for those with and without a limiting illness.

a range of potential confounders. In order to estimate the approximate size of this association in the population, we should calculate a confidence interval; and in order to gauge the strength of the evidence for the association, we might conduct a hypothesis test of the slope coefficient of Neighbourhood Cohesion. We will do both in Chapter 5. For now, let's accept that there is evidence for this association. How do we interpret it?

Elliott et al. (2014) are careful to point out that their study only confirms evidence of an association, and does not in itself tell us what the causal mechanisms underlying this association are. It might be that good neighbourhood cohesion is conducive to mental wellbeing. Or it could be that people who feel well mentally tend to perceive their neighbourhoods as more cohesive than people who don't feel so well. It is also possible that there is no or little causal relation between neighbourhood cohesion and mental wellbeing, and that their observed association is really due to other confounders, which we have not controlled for in our analysis.

The observation of the association between Neighbourhood Cohesion and Mental Wellbeing becomes meaningful when we consider it in the light of other information. For example, Elliott et al. (2014) also analysed semi-structured interviews, using textual analysis of qualitative interview data. These data provide further indication, in the respondents' own words, of the importance that neighbourhoods can have for individuals' sense of wellbeing. Viewed together, the results from the statistical and qualitative analyses provide stronger evidence for the research hypothesis than either of them would have done on its own. For the researcher who applies linear regression, then, the lesson is that the result of a regression analysis is often best viewed as one piece of evidence within a larger research puzzle, rather than as a definitive answer that stands on its own.

Another piece of context information can further enrich our understanding of how we might interpret the regression analysis presented here. Elliott et al. (2014) in fact investigated the relationship between Neighbourhood Cohesion and Mental Wellbeing in three data sets. The NCDS data set, which I have used for the examples in this book, was just one of them. While the NCDS data contain information on 50-year-old UK residents, the respondents in Elliott et al.'s other two data sets were in their 60s and 70s, respectively. Elliott et al. found that the (adjusted) association between Neighbourhood Cohesion and Mental Wellbeing was stronger in the two older samples than in the younger NCDS sample.[5] This finding, if confirmed, might further illuminate our interpretation of the association: could it be that a sense of belonging to one's neighbourhood tends to become more important to people as they get older? From the regression analyses alone, we would not be justified in drawing this conclusion, but I hope that these considerations illustrate how the result of a regression analysis can become a piece of evidence within a wider theoretical argument. It is in linking the result of our regression analyses to our wider knowledge of the social world, and to the questions we have about it, that the coefficients become meaningful.

Dummy variables for representing categorical predictors

We may wish to use categorical predictors in a multiple regression model. For example, a survey question may have asked respondents to rate their own health as being either 'Poor', 'Fair', 'Good', or 'Very Good', thus creating an ordered categorical variable. Or we might wish to use a nominal predictor such as continent of birth, with categories Africa, Asia, Australia, Europe, North America and South America.

Categorical variables do not naturally fit into the framework of a linear regression analysis. However, there is a well-established method that allows us to include categorical predictors in multiple regression. We can use dummy variables.

---

[5]This is another example of an interaction: according to this finding, the strength of the relationship between neighbourhood cohesion and mental wellbeing varies with age.

What are dummy variables?

A dummy variable is a predictor that can assume either of two possible values: 0 or 1. We have already encountered a dummy variable in this chapter: the predictor Limiting Illness was coded 1 for the presence and 0 for the absence of a limiting illness. Representing the categories in numeric form allows us to include this variable in a regression model. The coefficient of limiting illness was then interpretable as the predicted difference between those with a limiting illness and those without, controlling for all other predictors in the model.

Limiting Illness was an easy variable to represent, since it only has two possible categories. But what about predictors with three or more categories? It turns out that we can represent a categorical variable with c categories by using $c - 1$ dummy variables. For example, we can represent a categorical variable with three categories by two dummies.

Let's consider a categorical variable with categories A, B and C. We define two dummy variables, Dummy a and Dummy b, as follows (see Table 4.5 for an illustration):

- People in category 'A' get the value 1 on Dummy a and 0 on Dummy b.
- People in category 'B' get 0 on Dummy a and 1 on Dummy b.
- Finally, people in category C get 0 on both dummies.

In this way, each category is uniquely represented by the two dummy variables, such that it is possible to infer, from a person's values on the two dummies, what their value on the original categorical variable is. In the example above, the category C is called the *reference category*. The reference category is not represented by its own dummy variable.

Table 4.5 A scheme for coding a categorical variable with three categories into two dummy variables

		Dummy Variables	
		Dummy a	Dummy b
Categorical variable	A	1	0
	B	0	1
	C	0	0

Research example: Highest Qualification coded into dummy variables

To illustrate how dummy variables work in the context of a regression model, let's look at a categorical variable in the NCDS data set. Consider 'Highest Qualification'. In British social science, this is customarily constructed to combine educational qualifications from both academic and vocational routes, which are graded on five National Vocational Qualification (NVQ) levels.[6] The distribution of this variable in the NCDS data is shown in Figure 4.14.

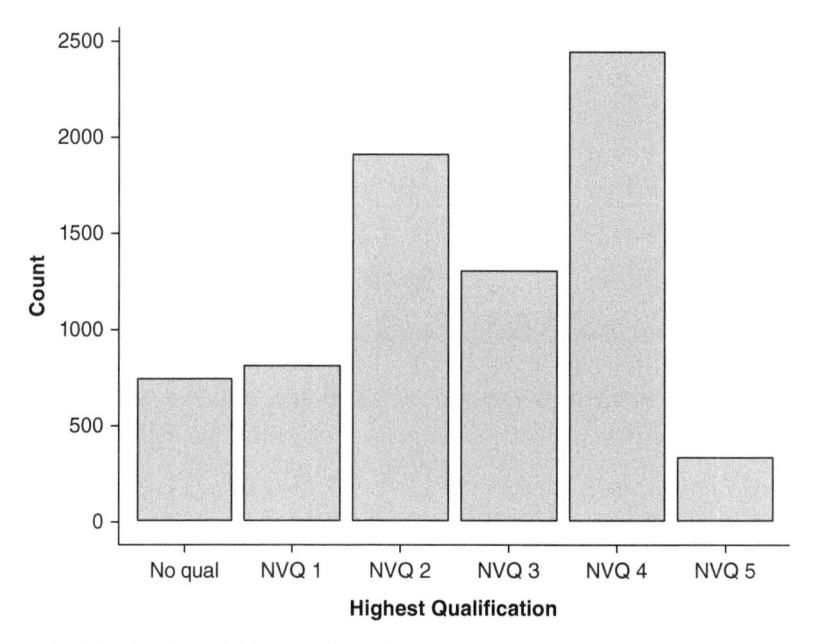

Figure 4.14 Distribution of 'Highest Qualification'

Note. N = 7603. Data were taken from the National Child Development Study, 2008 sweep. No qual = no qualification; NVQ = National Vocational Qualification.

This variable has six categories. Thus, in order to use it as a predictor, we will need to create five dummy variables (6 − 1). We select 'No qualification' to be the reference category. Thus, the respondents without qualifications will have the value 0 on all five dummies. Each of the other qualification levels is represented by one dummy: those with NVQ Level 1 (*NVQ1*) will have the value 1 on the first dummy and the value 0 on all others. Those with NVQ Level 2 (*NVQ2*) will have the value 1 on the second dummy and the value 0 on all others. And so forth. This results in the scheme shown in Table 4.6. Note that I have given each dummy a memorable name that identifies the category it represents.

---

[6] A higher NVQ level indicates a higher educational achievement. The precise definitions of NVQ levels are complicated, as they take into account changes in the UK education system over time, as well as multiple academic and vocational qualification types. Roughly, NVQ Level 1 is equivalent to completing primary school and some of secondary school, Level 2 is equivalent to completing secondary school, Level 3 corresponds to A-levels or high school. Level 4 represents bachelor degrees or equivalent, and Level 5 corresponds to postgraduate degrees or equivalent. The NVQ system of classifying qualifications was replaced by a new 8-level system in 2015. For details see: UK Government (n.d.).

Table 4.6 A scheme to represent Highest Qualification by five dummy variables

		Dummy Variables				
		NVQ1	NVQ2	NVQ3	NVQ4	NVQ5
Highest Qualification	No qualification	0	0	0	0	0
	NVQ Level 1	1	0	0	0	0
	NVQ Level 2	0	1	0	0	0
	NVQ Level 3	0	0	1	0	0
	NVQ Level 4	0	0	0	1	0
	NVQ Level 5	0	0	0	0	1

Note. NVQ = National Vocational Qualification.

A hypothetical data set containing the variable 'Highest Qualification' and five dummy variables is shown in Table 4.7. Depending on the statistical software you are using, it may or may not be necessary to actually create these variables through recoding your data. Some programmes, such as R and Stata, are able to use dummy variables automatically as part of the estimation of a multiple regression.

Table 4.7 Hypothetical data set with five dummy variables representing the categorical variable Highest Qualification

Participant ID	Highest Qualification	NVQ1	NVQ2	NVQ3	NVQ4	NVQ5	Other Variables
1	NVQ Level 3	0	0	1	0	0	...
2	NVQ Level 2	0	1	0	0	0	...
3	NVQ Level 5	0	0	0	0	1	...
4	NVQ Level 1	1	0	0	0	0	...
5	No qualification	0	0	0	0	0	...
6	NVQ Level 3	0	0	1	0	0	...
7	NVQ Level 4	0	0	0	1	0	...
8	No qualification	0	0	0	0	0	...
9	NVQ Level 1	1	0	0	0	0	...
⋮	⋮	⋮	⋮	⋮	⋮	⋮	⋮

Note. NVQ = National Vocational Qualification.

Using the dummy variables, we can estimate the relationship between Highest Qualification and Mental Wellbeing. We will do this while adjusting for the other variables from Elliott et al.'s (2014) analysis. Adding the five dummy variables to the adjusted model (Model 4.2) gives us Model 4.3.

Model 4.3:

$$MWB_i = \beta_0 + \beta_1 NC_i + \beta_2 SUPP_i + \beta_3 SocPart_i + \beta_4 Limill_i + \beta_5 SocPart_i \times Limill_i \\ + \beta_6 NVQ1_i + \beta_7 NVQ2_i + \beta_8 NVQ3_i + \beta_9 NVQ4_i + \beta_{10} NVQ5_i + \varepsilon_i$$

Let's think about how the dummy variables function within the regression equation. Each dummy has its own coefficient. This has the effect of giving each of the six qualification groups a different intercept.

First, consider the people with no qualifications. For them, all dummy variables are zero, so we can ignore all terms that involve the dummies. Thus, the model equation for the 'No qualification' group is

$$MWB_i = \beta_0 + \beta_1 NC_i + \beta_2 SUPP_i + \beta_3 SocPart_i + \beta_4 Limill_i + \beta_5 SocPart_i \times Limill_i + \varepsilon_i$$

and so the intercept for the 'No qualification' group is β_0.

Now consider people whose highest qualification is NVQ Level 1. For them, the dummy NVQ1 is equal to 1 and all other dummies are 0. So the model equation for this group is

$$MWB_i = (\beta_0 + \beta_6) + \beta_1 NC_i + \beta_2 SUPP_i + \beta_3 SocPart_i + \beta_4 Limill_i + \beta_5 SocPart_i \times Limill_i + \varepsilon_i$$

Thus the intercept for the 'NVQ Level 1' group is $\beta_0 + \beta_6$. The coefficient β_6 represents the difference in predicted Mental Wellbeing between the 'NVQ Level 1' group and the 'No qualification' group, when all other model predictors are held constant.

In an analogous way, we can work out the model equation for each of the remaining four qualification categories. The coefficients associated with the dummy variables (β_6, β_7, β_8, β_9, β_{10}) each estimate the difference in Mental Wellbeing between the group they represent and the 'No qualification' group, controlling for all other predictors in the model.

Estimating Model 4.3 using the NCDS data yields the results shown in Table 4.8. The coefficients of the dummy variables are to be interpreted as comparisons with the reference group. For example:

- The coefficient estimate for *NVQ5* is 3.288. This means a person with an NVQ Level 5 qualification is predicted to have a Mental Wellbeing score that is 3.288 points higher than that of a person who has no qualifications, when the two people have same values on all other predictors an NVQ Level 5.
- The estimate for *NVQ4* is 2.186. Thus people with NVQ Level 4 qualifications are predicted to have a Mental Wellbeing score 2.186 points higher than people with no qualifications, keeping all other predictors constant.
- And so forth for the other three dummy variables.

Thus, each dummy variable implies a comparison of the category it represents with the reference category. If we want to compare categories other than the reference category with each other, we can do so by calculating the difference between their dummy

Table 4.8 Estimates from a linear regression predicting Mental Wellbeing, with dummy variables representing Highest Qualification (Model 4.3)

	Estimate	SE	95% CI
Intercept	24.118	0.490	
Neighbourhood Cohesion (NC)	0.247	0.017	[0.214, 0.280]
Social Support (SUPP)	0.533	0.036	[0.464, 0.603]
Social Participation (SocPart)	0.107	0.045	[0.019, 0.194]
Limiting Illness (LimIll)	−4.628	0.280	[−5.178, −4.079]
Interaction: SocPart× LimIll	0.259	0.109	[0.047, 0.472]
Highest Qualification:			
NVQ1	0.124	0.380	[−0.621, 0.869]
NVQ2	1.243	0.325	[0.606, 1.881]
NVQ3	1.499	0.348	[0.817, 2.181]
NVQ4	2.186	0.323	[1.553, 2.819]
NVQ5	3.288	0.499	[2.310, 4.267]

Note. N = 7603. Data were taken from the National Child Development Study, 2008 sweep. Residual standard error = 7.52. R^2 = 0.14. SE = standard error; CI = confidence interval; NVQ = National Vocational Qualification.

coefficients. For example, the estimated difference between people with NVQ Level 5 and people with NVQ Level 4 is 3.288 − 2.186 = 1.102. Thus, the model estimates that people with NVQ Level 5 have an average wellbeing score that is 1.102 points higher than people with NVQ Level 4, controlling for all other variables in the model.

Choice of reference category for dummy variables

The choice of reference category for a set of dummy variables is arbitrary and does not substantially affect the model results. For example, the R^2 statistic, the residual standard error and the predicted values for any individual in the data set will be the same, no matter which reference category is chosen. However, in practice, it is useful to choose the reference category such that model estimates are convenient to interpret. By 'convenient to interpret' I mean that it is easy to see for the researcher and the reader what the coefficients imply for the research questions that motivate the analysis. For example, in our case choosing 'no qualification' as the reference group is convenient, as it allows us to easily read the coefficients of the five dummies as the differences in mental wellbeing associated with increasing levels of education.

When there is no conceptual reason to do otherwise, it is advisable to choose as the reference the category that occurs most frequently in our data, as this will tend to minimise the standard errors of the estimated dummy coefficients. Conversely, usually it is *not* advisable to make the reference category one with only a small number of cases, as this tends to result in large standard errors for the dummy coefficients.

Chapter Summary

- This chapter has introduced multiple linear regression as a model for the analysis of multivariate relationships, where the interest is in examining the relationships between a continuous outcome variable, and two or more predictors. This introduction is incomplete, since this chapter has not yet considered inference – hypothesis tests and confidence intervals – or the assumptions that we need to make in order for inferences to be valid. Chapter 5 will focus on these topics.
- Throughout this chapter, the relationships between the continuous outcomes and numeric predictors were assumed to be linear. This has made the examples easier to explain. It is, of course, possible to model non-linear relationships within multiple linear regression through the use of variable transformations, as described in Chapter 3.
- In textbooks on multiple regression, the topic of interactions is often introduced at a later stage than I have done here, and sometimes interactions are not discussed at all. It is true that interactions are relatively rarely reported in social science research publications based on multiple linear regression, but I am not sure that this suggests that interactions are in fact very rare in the social world. It may also be the case that interactions are under-researched because some researchers lack familiarity with techniques for estimating them.

Further Reading

Jaccard, J., & Turrisi, R. (2003). *Interaction effects in multiple regression* (2nd ed.). Sage. This book gives a thorough introduction to interactions in multiple linear regression. Further recommended readings on multiple regression are given at the end of Chapter 5.

5
MULTIPLE LINEAR REGRESSION: INFERENCE, ASSUMPTIONS AND STANDARDISATION

Chapter Overview

Inference about coefficients 126
The analysis of variance table and the *F*-test of model fit 131
Model building and model comparison 135
Assumptions and estimation problems 141
Standardisation 148
Further Reading 154

This chapter continues the introduction to multiple regression that the previous chapter began. So far, we have concerned ourselves with fitting multiple regression models to a data set and interpreting the estimated coefficients. Now we are ready to consider inference. We will look at confidence intervals and hypothesis tests about individual regression coefficients, as well as the systematic comparison of statistical models. This chapter also describes the application of residual diagnostics to evaluate the plausibility of the statistical assumptions underlying multiple regression. Finally, we will consider standardisation of slope coefficients as an aid to model interpretation. Throughout this chapter, we shall use the same research example and data set as in Chapter 4: the investigation of predictors of mental wellbeing in 50-year-old respondents to the NCDS cohort study.

Inference about coefficients

We begin with inference about individual regression coefficients: confidence intervals to estimate a plausible range for a coefficient and hypothesis tests to evaluate the evidence against a null hypothesis of interest. In most practical applications of multiple regression, we are more interested in slope coefficients than in intercepts, but the methods introduced in this section apply to intercepts also. To understand how inference about individual coefficients works, we first need to understand the concept of a standard error of a coefficient.

Standard errors of coefficient estimates

The standard error of a regression coefficient is a measure of how much the coefficient estimate would vary between different data sets. Estimates of standard errors can be calculated for all coefficients in a multiple regression from just a single data set. The mathematical details are beyond the scope of this book; in practice, any good statistical software will perform this calculation accurately. It is useful, however, to understand conceptually what the standard error of a coefficient estimate is.

Put formally, the standard error of a coefficient is the standard deviation of the sampling distribution of that coefficient. This is analogous, for example, to the standard error of a sample mean, which is a name for the standard deviation of the sampling distribution of the mean.

To think through what this means, imagine I could draw 10,000 random samples from the same population.[1] On each of these samples, I could then estimate the same multiple regression model. Then, if I looked at a particular coefficient estimate ($\hat{\beta}_k$,

---

[1] There is nothing special about the number 10,000 here. I could have also said 'a very large number'. To be mathematically precise, it should actually be an infinite number of samples, but this is more difficult to imagine.

say) across the 10,000 samples, I would find that the estimates of this coefficient differ from sample to sample. If the assumptions underlying my regression model are met, the coefficient estimates would approximately follow a normal distribution, whose mean would be close to the population parameter (β_k, the 'true' coefficient). The standard deviation of this distribution is a measure of the variability of the coefficient estimates across different random samples. It is this standard deviation that we call the standard error of a coefficient.

The smaller the standard error, the more precise is our coefficient estimate. In multiple linear regression, the size of the standard error for a slope coefficient depends on four things:

1. *Sample size:* the larger the sample, the smaller the standard errors tend to be.
2. *Model fit:* the better the model fit, the smaller the standard errors tend to be.
3. *Variance of the predictor variable:* the smaller the variance of a predictor, the smaller the standard error of its coefficient tends to be.
4. *Correlations between the predictor variables:* the smaller the correlations of a predictor with the other predictors in the model, the smaller the standard error of its coefficient tends to be.

Standard error estimates should usually be presented alongside coefficient estimates when presenting the results from a multiple regression model. Consider again the 'adjusted model' for the prediction of Mental Wellbeing by Neighbourhood Cohesion and potential confounders. This was Model 4.2 in Chapter 4, but since we are now in a new chapter, let's call it Model 5.1 from now on. I restate this model here for convenience:

Model 5.1:

$$MWB_i = \beta_0 + \beta_1 NC_i + \beta_2 SUPP_i + \beta_3 SocPart_i + \beta_4 Limill_i + \beta_5 SocPart_i \times Limill_i + \varepsilon_i$$

where the variables are defined as in Chapter 4. Estimating this model on the NCDS data set (as in Chapter 4) gives the results shown in Table 5.1.

Table 5.1 Coefficient estimates, standard errors and confidence intervals for a multiple regression predicting Mental Wellbeing (Model 5.1)

	Estimate	SE	95% CI
Intercept	25.325	0.419	
Neighbourhood Cohesion (NC)	0.243	0.017	[0.210, 0.276]
Social Support (SUPP)	0.552	0.036	[0.482, 0.622]
Social Participation (SocPart)	0.209	0.043	[0.124, 0.294]
Limiting Illness (Limill)	−4.853	0.280	[−5.402, −4.304]
Interaction: SocPart × Limill	0.265	0.109	[0.051, 0.479]
Residual standard error	7.559		
R^2	0.132		

Note. N = 7603. Data were taken from the National Child Development Study, 2008 sweep.
SE = standard error; CI = confidence interval.

Let's use SE to denote a standard error and SE_k to denote specifically the standard error of a slope coefficient (β_k), which relates a predictor (X_k) to an outcome (Y). We will use $\hat{SE}_k$ to denote the estimate of SE_k from a sample (using, once again, the 'hat' notation to indicate a sample estimate of a parameter). For example, the estimated standard error for the slope of Neighbourhood Cohesion (β_1) is $\hat{SE}_1 = 0.017$, as can be seen in Table 5.1.

Confidence interval for a coefficient

Using the standard error estimate, we can construct a confidence interval for the coefficient β_k. A 95% CI is calculated thus:

$$CI = \hat{\beta}_k \pm \hat{SE}_k \times t_{0.975, n-p-1}$$

where $t_{0.975, n-p-1}$, is the value that cuts off 2.5% of values in the right tail of the t-distribution with degrees of freedom (df) equal to $n - p - 1$, where n is the sample size and p is the number of predictors in the model. Our example Model 5.1 has $n = 7603$ and $p = 5$, and hence has $df = 7597$. The corresponding t-value to use in our confidence interval is thus $t_{0.975, 7597} = 1.96$.

For example, the 95% CI for the coefficient of Neighbourhood Cohesion is calculated as follows[2]:

$$\begin{aligned}CI_{0.95} &= 0.243 \pm 0.017 \times 1.96 \\ &= [0.210, 0.276]\end{aligned}$$

We can interpret this result (informally) by saying that we are 95% confident that the interval from 0.210 to 0.276 contains the true coefficient of Neighbourhood Cohesion, controlling for all other variables in the model. The confidence interval gives us a probable range of values of the coefficient that are compatible with our data.

Hypothesis test for a single coefficient

We can test hypotheses about a single slope coefficient from a multiple regression model as follows. Let's say we wish to test a hypothesis about the slope coefficient associated with a predictor X_k. This slope coefficient is called β_k, and its estimate from a sample, $\hat{\beta}_k$. It can be shown mathematically that, if all model assumptions hold, the statistic $t = \dfrac{\hat{\beta}_k - \beta_k}{\hat{SE}_k}$ follows a t-distribution with $n - p - 1$ df. The parameter β_k is

---

[2] A slight difference between the hand calculation and the result reported comes about because I have used more decimal points than I show.

MULTIPLE LINEAR REGRESSION: INFERENCE, ASSUMPTIONS AND STANDARDISATION | 129

of course unknown, but we can test hypotheses about it. In practice, it is often of interest to test the null hypothesis that $\beta_k = 0$, which would indicate that the predictor X_k has no relationship with the outcome variable (controlling for other variables in the model). If our hypothesis is that $\beta_k = 0$, the test statistic becomes simply

$$t = \frac{\hat{\beta}_k}{\hat{SE}_k}$$

We evaluate this test statistic against a t-distribution with degrees of freedom equal to $n - p - 1$. We will denote this distribution as t_{n-p-1}.

For example, for Model 5.1 (see Table 5.1), the test for the coefficient of Neighbourhood Cohesion gives[3]:

$$t = \frac{0.243}{0.017} = 14.45$$

The degrees of freedom are $n - p - 1 = 7603 - 5 - 1 = 7597$. In a t_{7597}-distribution, the probability to obtain $t = 14.45$ or a result more different from zero is vanishingly small ($p = 0.000$ to three decimal points). So there is strong evidence against the null hypothesis, and we are justified in concluding that Neighbourhood Cohesion is associated with Mental Wellbeing, in the presence of the other variables in Model 5.1.

Example application of the t-test for a single coefficient

Let's apply the t-test of the previous section to address a practical modelling question. One purpose of this test might be to help us decide whether to include an additional variable in our model, or not. We might do this by testing the null hypothesis that a coefficient is equal to zero. Say, for example, we wanted to explore whether the interaction NC × SUPP would improve our prediction of Mental Wellbeing, in the presence of all the other variables of Model 5.1. Then we could estimate a new model, which includes all the predictors of Model 5.1, plus the interaction NC × SUPP. Let's call this Model 5.2.

---

[3] If you check the calculation by hand, you will notice that 0.243/0.017 = 14.29412, rather than 14.45, as stated. The difference comes about because I have used more decimal points in the calculation than I show. The coefficient estimate is 0.2431095 to seven decimal points, and the standard error estimate is 0.01682358, to seven decimal points. Dividing these two numbers gives the result shown in the text.

Model 5.2:

$$MWB_i = \beta_0 + \beta_1 NC_i + \beta_2 SUPP_i + \beta_3 SocPart_i + \beta_4 Limill_i + \beta_5 SocPart_i \times Limill_i + \beta_6 NC_i \times SUPP_i \; \varepsilon_i$$

The results of estimating Model 5.2 using the NCDS data are shown in Table 5.2. Our null hypothesis is that the slope coefficient β_6 for the interaction NC × SUPP is zero, when controlling for all other variables in the model. We might write this as H_0: $\beta_6 = 0$. The t-test is conducted as follows[4]:

- Estimated coefficient for the interaction, $\hat{\beta}_6 = -0.009595$.
- Estimated standard error, $\widehat{SE}_{\hat{\beta}_6} = 0.005943$.
- Thus, $t = \dfrac{\hat{\beta}_6}{\widehat{SE}_{\hat{\beta}_6}} = 1.615$.

The t-statistic is evaluated using a t-distribution with $df = n - p - 1 = 7603 - 6 - 1 = 7596$ (since there are six predictors in this model). In this distribution, $t = 1.615$ yields a two-sided p-value of $p = 0.106$. This p-value is quite large, so from this analysis there is weak evidence for the idea that the interaction NC × SUPP improves the prediction of Mental Wellbeing, when controlling for the other variables contained in Model 4.3.

Table 5.2 Estimated coefficients for a regression of Mental Wellbeing on four predictors and two interactions (Model 5.2)

	Estimate	SE	95% CI	t	p
Intercept	23.595	1.150			
Neighbourhood Cohesion (NC)	0.330	0.056	[0.219, 0.440]	5.854	0.000
Social Support (SUPP)	0.747	0.126	[0.501, 0.993]	5.945	0.000
Social Participation (SocPart)	0.211	0.043	[0.126, 0.296]	4.854	0.000
Limiting Illness (Limill)	−4.834	0.280	[−5.383, −4.284]	−17.239	0.000
Interaction: SocPart × Limill	0.262	0.109	[0.048, 0.476]	2.404	0.016
Interaction: NC × SUPP	−0.010	0.006	[−0.021, 0.002]	−1.615	0.106

Note. N = 7603. Data were taken from the National Child Development Study, 2008 sweep. SE = standard error; CI = confidence interval.

Do we need to conduct a hypothesis test for every coefficient?

In their default output from a multiple regression, statistical software packages usually display a p-value for a t-test of every coefficient, where the null hypothesis in

---

[4] In the text below I give the coefficient and its standard error to six decimal points, to illustrate the hand calculation of t_{obs}. In Table 5.2, they are rounded to three decimal points.

each case is that the coefficient is equal to zero in the presence of all other predictors. Thus you might often see the results of fitting a multiple regression model displayed as in Table 5.2, which shows the results of *t*-tests for all slope coefficients at a glance. Note that the *p*-value for each *t*-test is given as if only one test was conducted. That is, there is no adjustment for conducting multiple hypothesis tests.

It is not always useful to conduct this default statistical test for every coefficient in a model, because we don't always have a reason to be interested in evaluating the hypothesis that the coefficient is zero for each variable in a model. I might have a theoretical reason to believe that a predictor X_k is important in my model – for example, because it is a plausible potential confounder for the relationship between my outcome and some other predictor of interest. In such a case, I might well decide to include X_k in my model on theoretical grounds, without consulting a hypothesis test. (And I might thus wish to ignore the results of the *t*-test for the slope coefficient of X_k, even if my software displays this by default.)

It is important to be mindful that a large *p*-value (absence of 'statistical significance') for a slope coefficient β_k does not constitute evidence that there is no relationship between X_k and Y. For example, in small samples a large *p*-value might indicate insufficient statistical power to detect an important relationship, rather than being an indication of 'no relationship'. In general, hypothesis tests should not be the only means by which I decide on which variables to include in my model. The practice of displaying a test for every coefficient is a consequence of the ease with which software programs conduct such tests, and it is liable to tempt researchers into using statistical hypothesis tests as a matter of routine and without thought. *The SAGE Quantitative Research Kit*, Volume 8, has more to say about the overuse of hypothesis tests in current research practice.

The analysis of variance table and the *F*-test of model fit

We will now go beyond inference about individual coefficients and consider inferences about multiple regression models as a whole. This section will consider the evaluation of a single model of interest to gauge whether there is evidence that a model makes any contribution to the prediction of the outcome at all. The comparison of two or more models of interest is discussed in the next section.

Let's consider the overall evaluation of a multiple regression model that has been fitted to a data set. Just as in simple linear regression (Chapter 2), in multiple linear regression, too, we can partition the total variation of the outcome in a given data set into two parts: (1) the variation accounted for by the regression model and (2) the residual variation. The variance terms for a regression are customarily summarised in an analysis of variance (ANOVA) table, as in Table 5.3.

Table 5.3 Analysis of variance table for linear regression

	Sum of Squares (SS)	Degrees of Freedom (df)	Mean Square (MS)
Regression	$SS_{Reg} = \sum(\hat{Y}_i - \bar{Y})^2$	$df_{Reg} = p$	$MS_{Reg} = SS_{Reg} / p$
Residual	$SS_{Res} = \sum(Y_i - \hat{Y}_i)^2$	$df_{Res} = n - p - 1$	$MS_{Res} = SS_{Res} / (n - p - 1)$
Total	$SS_{Tot} = \sum(Y_i - \bar{Y})^2$	$df_{Tot} = n - 1$	$MS_{Tot} = SS_{Tot} / (n - 1)$

Note. p = number of predictors in the model; n = sample size.

The regression, residual and total sum of squares are defined in the same way as in Chapter 2, only that this time, of course, the predicted values are derived from a regression equation based on more than one predictor. The degrees of freedom will be important for hypothesis testing and are calculated using the number of predictors in the model, p, and the sample size, n. The mean squares are equal to the sums of squares divided by their respective degrees of freedom.

F-test of model fit

In some situations, it might be of interest to investigate if a given model has any predictive value at all. One customary way of doing this is to conduct a test of the null hypothesis that *none* of the predictors is related to the outcome. This hypothesis test is based on the F-statistic, which is calculated from the mean squares (see Table 5.3) as follows:

$$F = \frac{MS_{Reg}}{MS_{Res}}$$

The null and alternative hypotheses of this F-test run as follows:

- Null hypothesis: *All* slope coefficients are equal to zero. Or (equivalently), none of the model predictors is related to the outcome.
- Alternative hypothesis: *At least one* of the slope coefficients is different from zero. Or (equivalently), at least one of the predictor variables is related to the outcome.

Intuitively we can say: If, in a given data set, a model explains a large proportion of the total variance relative to the unexplained variance, then MS_{Reg} will be large relative to MS_{Res}, and consequently $F = MS_{Reg} / MS_{Res}$ will be large. If, conversely, a model explains just a small proportion of the variance, then MS_{Reg} will be small relative to MS_{Res}, and consequently the F-statistic will be small. So a large F-statistic constitutes evidence against the null hypothesis. But what is 'large'? To gauge this, we need to know the sampling distribution of the F-statistic (i.e. we need to know how the F-statistic would be distributed across a large number of random samples).

MULTIPLE LINEAR REGRESSION: INFERENCE, ASSUMPTIONS AND STANDARDISATION | 133

If the null hypothesis is true, the sampling distribution of the F-statistic follows a characteristic shape, which is called the F-distribution, also known as the *Fisher distribution*. Fisher distributions are a family of distributions that are distinguished by their degrees of freedom, similar to the t-distribution family. Unlike t-distributions, however, Fisher distributions have two degree of freedom terms, which we will call df_1 and df_2. For the F-test of model fit, these two degree of freedom terms are

- $df_1 = df_{Reg} = p$ and
- $df_2 = df_{Res} = n - p - 1$,

where p is the number of predictors and n is the sample size (compare also Table 5.3).

Figure 5.1 shows the distribution of the F-statistic under the null hypothesis, with the degrees of freedom from Model 5.1 (see the section 'Inference About Coefficients'), which regresses Mental Wellbeing on five predictors, with sample size $n = 7603$. Thus, we have $df_1 = 5$ and $df_2 = 7597$.

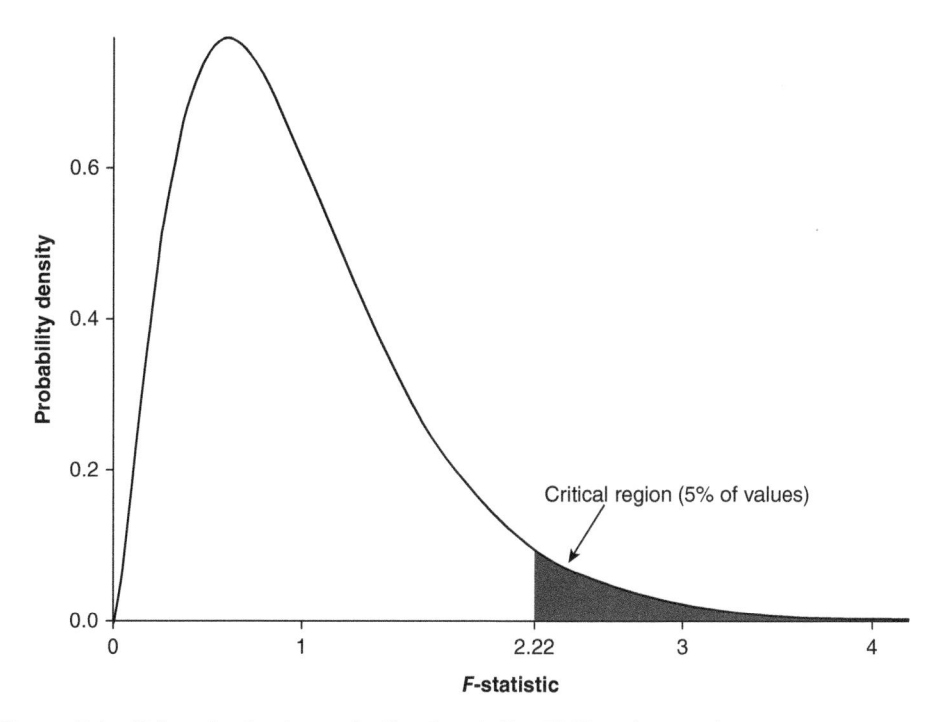

Figure 5.1 Fisher distribution with $df_1 = 5$ and $df_2 = 7597$, with critical region

Note. The critical region for a significance level of 0.05 is shaded in grey (critical value 2.22).

F-distributions have the following properties:

- *The F-statistic can never be negative.* This is easy to see: the *F*-statistic is the ratio of two variances, and variances can never be negative.
- *The right tail of the F-distribution asymptotically approaches the probability density value zero.* That is, large values of *F* become increasingly less probable, but their probability will never reach zero.

For a given observed *F*-statistic, we can calculate the probability of obtaining this statistic or a larger one in a random sample, if the null hypothesis was true. In other words, we can calculate a *p*-value. The shaded area in Figure 5.1 marks the critical region for a hypothesis test at the 5% significance level. The critical value for such an *F*-test with degrees of freedom $df_1 = 5$ and $df_2 = 7597$ is $F_{crit} = 2.22$. If the null hypothesis is true, the probability of obtaining an *F*-statistic of 2.22 or larger in a random sample is 0.05. So if we use the conventional 5% level of significance, we would interpret an *F*-statistic equal to or larger than 2.22 as evidence against the null hypothesis.

Standard software packages will usually display an ANOVA table as part of the results output of a regression analysis. Table 5.4 illustrates how these results are often presented, using Model 5.1 as an example. The *F*-statistic here is 231.1, which gives a very small *p*-value. So there is strong statistical evidence from the NCDS data that at least one predictor in Model 5.1 makes a contribution to the prediction of mental wellbeing. On the other hand, if we conduct the *F*-test of model fit and obtain a large *p*-value, this means that there is little evidence from our data that any of the predictors included in our model is related to the outcome.

Table 5.4 Analysis of variance table for a multiple regression predicting Mental Wellbeing (Model 5.1)

	Sum of Squares	df	Mean Square	F	p
Regression	66,032.35	5	13,206.47	231.13	0.000
Residual	434,080.41	7597	57.14		
Total	500,112.76	7602			

Note. *N* = 7603. Data were taken from the National Child Development Study, 2008 sweep. Outcome: Mental Wellbeing. Predictors: Neighbourhood Cohesion, Social Support, Social Participation, Limiting Illness, Interaction *SocPart* × *Limill*.

In many social science applications, the *F*-test of model fit does not answer the questions we are most interested in. We are not often interested in comparing a model with some predictors to a null model. Usually we would rather like to compare different theoretically plausible models with one another. That is the issue we consider next.

Model building and model comparison

We will now turn to the topic of model comparisons. In the section 'Inference About Coefficients', we considered the t-test of a coefficient and saw that this is one technique that can help us decide whether to include or not include a given predictor in a model. However, we can go further and systematically compare different models with one another, to see which model is most compatible with our data set. The models that we compare in this way may differ by one or several predictors.

In general, a good statistical model satisfies two criteria:

1. *Model fit:* good prediction of the outcome and adequate representation of the shape of the relationships between each predictor and the outcome
2. *Parsimony:* all else being equal, a simpler model is preferred to a more complex one

Model fit should be an obvious criterion for the quality of the model, but why do we prefer a parsimonious model to a complex one? There are philosophical arguments for parsimony in model selection, which are sometimes discussed under the name 'Occam's razor': this advises us, out of several models that make the same predictions, to select the one that provides the simplest explanation. In the context of applied statistical modelling, there may also be good practical reasons for parsimony. For example, think of a model that a doctor might use to predict the risk of serious illness for a patient. The predicted risk might inform decisions such as whether it is safe to discharge the patient from hospital, or not. A simple model with few variables may be preferable if it predicts the risk as well as a more complicated model that relies on many measurements, which take time to conduct and may distract from other important aspects of medical care.

In general, the ideal is to make the model as complex as necessary, but as simple as possible. Sometimes we may have to decide whether the gain in prediction we obtain by adding another predictor to a model is worth the expense of a larger model.

Nested and non-nested models

Let's imagine an analyst who has developed two different models for the prediction of an outcome. Both models predict the same outcome, and they were developed on the same data set. Then a fundamental question is whether the models are *nested* or not. The answer to this question decides which methods of model comparison our analyst can use.

Consider two models, Model A and Model B, where Model B is the larger model (with more parameters). If we can turn Model B into Model A by imposing *constraints* on one or more of the parameters of Model B, then the two models are nested. A typical constraint is that we set some of the parameters of the larger model B to zero.[5] For example, consider a case where Model B contains all the predictors that also feature in Model A, but in addition Model B contains one or more predictors that are not part of Model A. Thus, we can turn Model B into Model A by setting to zero the slope parameters relating to the variables unique to Model B. For an example, see Box 5.1. If two models are nested, we can use hypothesis tests to aid us in deciding which model we might prefer.

When we cannot turn one model into another by imposing parameter constraints, then the models are said to be non-nested. This typically occurs if both models contain at least one predictor not contained in the other. Non-nested models cannot be compared using hypothesis tests covered in this book, but other statistics are available. These are discussed further below in the section 'Adjusted R^2 Statistic'.

Box 5.1

Nested and Non-Nested Models

Consider the following three models. Which pairs of models are nested?

Model A: $Y_i = \beta_0 + \beta_1 X_{1i} + \epsilon_i$

Model B: $Y_i = \beta_0 + \beta_1 X_{1i} + \beta_2 X_{2i} + \epsilon_i$

Model C: $Y_i = \beta_0 + \beta_1 X_{1i} + \beta_3 X_{3i} + \beta_4 X_{4i} + \epsilon_i$

- Model A is nested within Model B, because if we set the parameter β_2 in Model B to zero, the two models are identical.
- Similarly, Model A is also nested within Model C, because we can turn Model C into Model A by setting $\beta_3 = 0$ and $\beta_4 = 0$.
- However, Models B and C are not nested, because each contains at least one parameter that the other does not have: Model C does not contain a parameter for variable X_2, while Model B does not contain parameters for X_3 and X_4. So there is no way that we can turn one of these models into the other by imposing constraints on only one of them.

---

[5]There are other types of constraints, but I shall stick with this simple example, which covers the most common practical application in social science research.

Comparing nested models: F-test of difference in fit

In linear regression, we can compare nested models using an *F*-test of difference in fit. Let's consider, as an example, the question whether highest qualification improves the prediction of Mental Wellbeing, when controlling for the predictors contained in Model 5.1. Recall that highest qualification is represented by five dummy variables. The *t*-tests of individual coefficients associated with each of the five dummy variables would give us evidence about the relative wellbeing of people in two particular categories of highest qualification, but would not allow us to evaluate the relationship between highest qualification and our outcome as a whole. To achieve the latter purpose, we can compare two nested models: Model 5.1 (without highest qualification) is the smaller model, and will be compared to a model that contains all the predictors of Model 5.1, and additionally the five dummy variables representing qualification levels. We will call the model with highest qualification Model 5.3.

Model 5.1 is the smaller of the two models. It is represented by the equation

$$MWB = \beta_0 + \beta_1 NC_i + \beta_2 SUPP_i + \beta_3 SocPart_i + \beta_4 Limill_i + \beta_5 Limill_i \times SocPart_i + \epsilon_i$$

Model 5.3 is the larger model, and contains five additional predictor variables:

Model 5.3:

$$MWB = \beta_0 + \beta_1 NC_i + \beta_2 SUPP_i + \beta_3 SocPart_i + \beta_4 Limill_i + \beta_5 Limill_i \times SocPart_i + \beta_6 NVQ1_i \\ + \beta_7 NVQ2_i + \beta_8 NVQ3_i + \beta_9 NVQ4_i + \beta_{10} NVQ5_i + \epsilon_i$$

We can turn Model 5.3 into Model 5.1 by setting $\beta_6 = \beta_7 = \beta_8 = \beta_9 = \beta_{10} = 0$. So the two models are nested.

The *F*-test of difference in fit assesses the null hypothesis that *all* of the additional parameters in the larger model are zero. In our example, this would imply that *none* of the five dummy variables representing highest qualification improves the prediction of Mental Wellbeing, after taking all other variables in the model into account. The alternative hypothesis is that *at least one* of the additional parameters is not zero. In our example, this would imply that at least one of the dummy variables has a coefficient that differs from zero, after taking all other variables in the model into account.

The *F*-test of difference in fit assesses the difference in regression sum of squares between the two models, taking into account the difference in regression degrees of freedom. Intuitively, we might say that the *F*-test assesses whether the additional reduction in error achieved by the larger model, compared to the smaller model, in a given data set constitutes evidence that the larger model would yield a better prediction in the population. The *F*-statistic is calculated as follows:

$$F = \frac{(SS_{Res,S} - SS_{Res,L}) / (df_{Res,S} - df_{Res,L})}{MS_{Res,L}}$$

where

- $SS_{Res,L}$, $df_{Res,L}$ and $MS_{Res,L}$ are the residual sum of squares, degrees of freedom and mean square of the larger model, respectively, and
- $SS_{Res,S}$ and $df_{Res,S}$ are the residual sum of squares and degrees of freedom of the smaller model, respectively.

Expressed in words, the equation above states that F is calculated as

$$F = \frac{\text{Difference in regression SS between the two models / Difference in df}}{\text{Residual MS for larger model}}$$

Results for this type of F-test are often displayed in a table such as Table 5.5, which shows the results of calculations from comparing Model 5.1 (with five predictors) to Model 5.3 (with 10 predictors).

Table 5.5 Model comparison of Models 5.1 and 5.3

	SS_{Res}	Diff. in SS_{Res}	df_{Res}	Diff. in df_{Res}	F	df	p
Model 5.1 (without hqual)	434080.4		7597				
Model 5.3 (with hqual dummies)	428968.8	5111.6	7592	5	18.1	5, 7592	0.000

Note. hqual = Highest Qualification. Model 5.1 predictors: Neighbourhood Cohesion, Social Support, Limiting Illness, Social Participation, Limill × SocPart. Model 5.3 predictors: Model 5.1 + NVQ1, NVQ2, NVQ3, NVQ4 and NVQ5. Diff. = difference; df = degrees of freedom.

The F-statistic is calculated from the numbers in Table 5.5 as follows:

$$F = \frac{(434080.4 - 428968.8)/(7597 - 7592)}{428968.8/7592} = \frac{5111.6/5}{56.5} = 18.1$$

If the smaller model is true (in the population), then this F-statistic follows a Fisher distribution with $df_1 = 5$ and $df_2 = 7592$. In this distribution, the probability of obtaining an F-statistic equal to or larger than 18.1 is very small ($p = 0.000$ to three decimal points). We can regard this as statistical evidence that the larger model provides a better prediction of the outcome than the smaller model does. In other words, there is strong evidence that highest qualification improves the prediction of Mental Well-being, when also controlling for the other variables.

Like all statistical significance tests, the F-test has limitations as a method for model comparison. If the sample size is small, the test may not be powerful enough to detect a real benefit of the larger model. On the other hand, if the sample size is very large, the F-test may be so powerful that it may signal a 'statistically significant difference' between the models, even if the real difference is negligible in size. Finally, the p-value calculated from the F-statistic is only valid if all underlying assumptions are satisfied – which includes all the assumptions discussed in Chapter 3.

MULTIPLE LINEAR REGRESSION: INFERENCE, ASSUMPTIONS AND STANDARDISATION | 139

The *F*-test is only valid for the comparison of nested models. To assess the relative merits of non-nested models, we need to use other methods. One such method is the so-called adjusted R^2 statistic, which we will look at next. Further methods for the comparison of non-nested models are introduced in *The SAGE Quantitative Research Kit, Volume 8*.

Adjusted R^2 statistic

Recall from Chapter 4 that we can measure the prediction quality in linear regression via the R^2 statistic. This is the proportional reduction in the residual sum of squares – an estimate of the proportional reduction of error that the predictor allows us to achieve. The R^2 statistic can be calculated as follows:

$$R^2 = 1 - \frac{SS_{Residual}}{SS_{Total}}$$

The R^2 statistic is a standardised measure of the quality of the prediction. There are two reasons, however, why it is not advisable to use R^2 for model comparison:

1. If we compare two models that are nested, then the larger model will never have a smaller R^2 than the smaller model, for a given data set. In other words, adding a predictor to a model can never make our prediction of the outcome in the same data set worse. So if we used R^2 for model comparison, we would always decide in favour of the larger model.
2. R^2 measures only one aspect of model quality, namely, the fit of the model. It fails to take account of parsimony.

A measure of model quality that avoids these two disadvantages of R^2 is the *adjusted* R^2. The *adjusted* R^2 statistic is given by

$$Adj.R^2 = 1 - \frac{MS_{Residual}}{MS_{Total}}$$

Thus, while the (unadjusted) R^2 uses the sums of squares (*SS*) to calculate the reduction in error, the adjusted R^2 uses the mean squares (*MS*). Recall that $MS = \frac{SS}{df}$. The *adjusted* R^2 is thus adjusting for the degrees of freedom of the *SS*. We can also write the formula of the *adjusted* R^2 as follows (as before, let's call the number of predictors in the model *p* and the sample size *n*):

$$Adj.R^2 = 1 - \frac{SS_{Residual} / df_{Residual}}{SS_{Total} / df_{Total}}$$

$$= 1 - \frac{SS_{Residual} / (n - p - 1)}{SS_{Total} / (n - 1)}$$

$$= 1 - \frac{SS_{Residual}}{SS_{Total}} \times \frac{n - 1}{n - p - 1}$$

The adjustment, $\frac{n-1}{n-p-1}$, has the effect of making the *adjusted* R^2 smaller than the unadjusted R^2. The size of the difference between the two measures depends on the number of predictors p and the sample size n: the greater p, the larger the difference between R^2 and *adjusted* R^2, other things being equal. And the larger n, the smaller the difference between R^2 and *adjusted* R^2.

The *adjusted* R^2 statistic balances model fit and parsimony. Model fit is taken into account via the residual variation; parsimony is taken into account via the number of parameters in the model. The number of parameters acts as a penalty for larger models.

Application of *adjusted* R^2

The *adjusted* R^2 statistic may be used to compare nested as well as non-nested models. As an example, let's once again compare Models 5.1 and 5.3. Table 5.6 gives the ANOVA table for both models.

Table 5.6 Analysis of variance table for Models 5.1 and 5.3

	Sum of Squares	df	Mean Square
Model 5.1 (without hqual)			
Regression	66032.35	5	13206.47
Residual	434080.41	7597	57.14
Total	500112.76	7602	65.79
Model 5.3 (including hqual)			
Regression	71143.92	10	7114.39
Residual	428968.84	7592	56.50
Total	500112.76	7602	65.79

Note. hqual = Highest Qualification; df = degrees of freedom.

From this information, we can calculate R^2 and *adjusted* R^2. For Model 5.1, we have

$$R^2 = 1 - \frac{SS_{Res}}{SS_{Tot}} = 1 - \frac{434080.41}{500112.76} = 0.1320$$

$$Adj.\ R^2 = 1 - \frac{MS_{Res}}{MS_{Tot}} = 1 - \frac{57.14}{65.79} = 0.1315$$

And for Model 5.3,

$$R^2 = 1 - \frac{428968.84}{500112.76} = 0.1423$$

$$Adj.\ R^2 = 1 - \frac{56.50}{65.79} = 0.1411$$

The *adjusted* R^2 statistic of Model 5.3 is larger than that of Model 5.1. This confirms the conclusion that we drew from the *F*-test of model comparison: the *Highest Qualification* dummies provide additional predictive power, after all the other variables in the model have been taken into account.[6]

Assumptions and estimation problems

In this chapter so far, we have been proceeding with estimating models and testing hypotheses about them without asking whether the assumptions underlying the models are satisfied. However, it is important to realise that all the assumptions that we made in simple linear regression also apply to multiple linear regression, and the methods for detecting violations of assumptions introduced in Chapter 3 should all be used in multiple regression as well. Later in this section, we consider regression diagnostics for Model 5.3. Before we get to this, however, there is another issue we must look at, which was not relevant to simple linear regression, because it can only rear its head once there are several predictors in the model. This is the issue of collinearity.

Collinearity and multicollinearity

One problem that the estimation of a multiple regression model may encounter is collinearity. Collinearity occurs when one or more predictor variables are highly correlated with one another, such that they are perfectly or almost perfectly predictable from one or more other predictors. Examples of how collinearity may occur are as follows:

a. You have mistakenly used the same predictor twice: for example, you may have 'height' in your data set twice, once measured in metres and once measured in inches, say. The two height variables are, of course, perfectly correlated with one another. In such a case, we say that the two variables are 'perfectly collinear'.
b. You use two predictors that are very strongly (although not perfectly) correlated. For example, one of your predictors may be 'salary', while another may be 'total income last year'. These two variables are likely to be highly correlated, because for many people their salary represents a substantial part, or even all, of their total income. In such a case, we say that the two variables are 'highly collinear'.

---

[6]You may have noticed that in both models the difference between R^2 and *Adj.* R^2 is small. The reason for the small difference is that the sample size is very large compared to the number of parameters. In analyses with smaller sample sizes, there may well be a considerable difference between R^2 and *Adj.* R^2.

c. Collinearity may also occur as a result of relationships involving more than two variables. This is sometimes called multicollinearity. Say, for example, you have conducted a survey and have asked your respondents a series of questions about how much they earn from different sources of income – from their employment, self-employment, interest on investments and so on. You may then calculate 'total income' as the sum of all these different incomes. Now, suppose you were to estimate a regression and use as predictors all the individual sources of income as well as the total income. Then 'total income' can be calculated exactly from these other variables. In this case, we speak of 'perfect multicollinearity'.

When there is perfect collinearity or multicollinearity, such as in examples (a) and (c), the model estimation will break down: if you were to try to apply the method of least squares by hand and do the calculations, you would notice that the equations have no unique solution. A computer program faced with perfect collinearity among model predictors will either return an error or automatically omit one of the variables that cause collinearity.

When predictors are very highly correlated, even though not perfectly collinear, the model estimation may be mathematically possible, but the results might be unstable. 'Unstable' here means that the coefficient estimates would be liable to change drastically in response to small changes in the data. This can sometimes be recognised if, after estimation, some coefficients turn out to have very large standard errors.

In practice, both perfect and high collinearity pose a problem, and we should try to avoid estimating a model that features collinear predictors. One way to avoid problems with collinearity is to carefully think about your predictors before you estimate your model and make sure each predictor measures a unique and important concept. In other words, avoid doing the sorts of things described in examples (a), (b) and (c) above. However, in regression models with many predictors, collinearity can occur despite careful prior thought. It is therefore useful to have formal measures for detecting potential collinearity in a model we have estimated. This is the issue we turn to next.

Diagnosing collinearity

A statistic that is commonly calculated to assess multicollinearity is the *variance inflation factor (VIF)*. We can calculate a *VIF* for each predictor variable. The *VIF* of a predictor is an estimate of how much the standard error of the slope coefficient of that predictor is increased due to multicollinearity. The *VIF* is estimated by

$$VIF_k = \frac{1}{1 - R_k^2}$$

where VIF_k is the variance inflation factor of the *k*th predictor, and R_k^2 is the coefficient of determination from a regression of the *k*th predictor on all other predictors in the regression model we are evaluating. For example, to calculate VIF_{NC}, the variance inflation factor of Neighbourhood Cohesion (NC) in Model 5.3, we use the R^2 from a regression of *NC* on all other predictors contained in Model 5.3. In practice, statistical software packages have functions that automatically calculate the *VIF*s for all predictors in a model, saving you the work of going through the above steps. Some programs instead (or in addition) display the *tolerance*, which is simply the inverse of the *VIF*:

$$Tolerance_k = \frac{1}{VIF_k} = 1 - R_k^2$$

A rule of thumb is that $VIF \geq 10$ (or equivalently, $Tolerance \leq 0.1$) indicates too much multicollinearity. Looking at the definitions of *VIF* and tolerance above, and applying a little algebra, makes clear that this rule implies that the R^2 from a regression of one predictor on all the others should be smaller than 0.9.

The *VIF*s and tolerances of all predictors in Model 5.3 are presented in Table 5.7. All *VIF*s are well under 10 (and consequently all tolerances are well above 0.1), so we have no cause for concern about multicollinearity. If we do find that two or more predictors seem to be collinear with one another, you may want to consider removing one or several of the offending predictors, such that a model without concerns about multicollinearity results. This will, of course, change your model and your interpretation of the results, since you are now not anymore able to control for the predictor you have removed. To make a decision in practice, you may have to carefully weigh the advantages and disadvantages of removing or retaining a predictor.

Table 5.7 Multicollinearity diagnostics for Model 5.3

Predictor	VIF	Tolerance
Neighbourhood Cohesion (NC)	1.09	0.92
Social Support (SUPP)	1.10	0.91
Social Participation (SocPart)	1.31	0.76
Limiting Illness (Limill)	1.48	0.68
SocPart × Limill	1.60	0.63
Highest Qualification:		
NVQ1	1.88	0.53
NVQ2	2.69	0.37
NVQ3	2.32	0.43
NVQ4	3.07	0.33
NVQ5	1.45	0.69

Note. NVQ = National Vocational Qualification; *VIF* = variance inflation factor.

In Table 5.7, note that the *VIFs* are highest for the dummy variables that indicate qualification levels. This is partly due to the fact that these dummy variables are by definition negatively correlated with one another: if one qualification dummy has the value 1, all the others must by definition have the value 0. Similarly, the interaction *SocPart* × *Limill* is by definition positively correlated with both *SocPart* and *Limill*, and thus its *VIF* is large relative to the *VIFs* of most other variables.

Regression diagnostics

All assumptions we made in the simple linear regression model apply to multiple regression also, and the methods for investigating standardised residuals to diagnose potential problems with the model, which we considered in Chapter 3, apply in the same way. These procedures are even more important in multiple linear regression, because the multivariate data and the model predictions can't be as easily visualised as the data and results from a simple linear regression. For example, Model 5.3 features three numeric predictors, and thus a full visualisation of the data and model predictions would require that we use at least four-dimensional space.

To illustrate the investigation of multiple regression assumptions, let's consider the residual diagnostics for Model 5.3. This is the regression of Mental Wellbeing on Neighbourhood Cohesion, Social Support, Highest Qualification, Social Participation, Limiting Illness and the interaction of Social Participation and Limiting Illness.

Normality. To investigate the assumption of normality of errors, we inspect a normal q–q plot of the standardised residuals from Model 5.3. This is shown in Figure 5.2. The plot suggests that the standardised residuals are approximately normally distributed, although there are a few more large negative standardised residuals than expected. This indicates a slight negative skew. A slight negative skew is also visible in the sample distribution of Mental Wellbeing, which is illustrated in Chapter 4, Figure 4.6. So it seems that the negative skew in our outcome variable has not been entirely accounted for by the predictors in Model 5.3 and is thus still visible in the standardised residuals.

Linearity and homoscedasticity. Next, we investigate homoscedasticity and linearity. We do this by looking at a spread-level plot such as Figure 5.3. There is an indication of mild heteroscedasticity: the spread of values is largest for predicted values between about 28 and 35, and narrows slightly towards the left and right edges of the plot. This suggests a slight tendency for the residual variance to get smaller for individuals with either very low or very high predicted values of mental wellbeing. But the differences in variation are very subtle here, and do not indicate a serious violation of the homoscedasticity assumption.

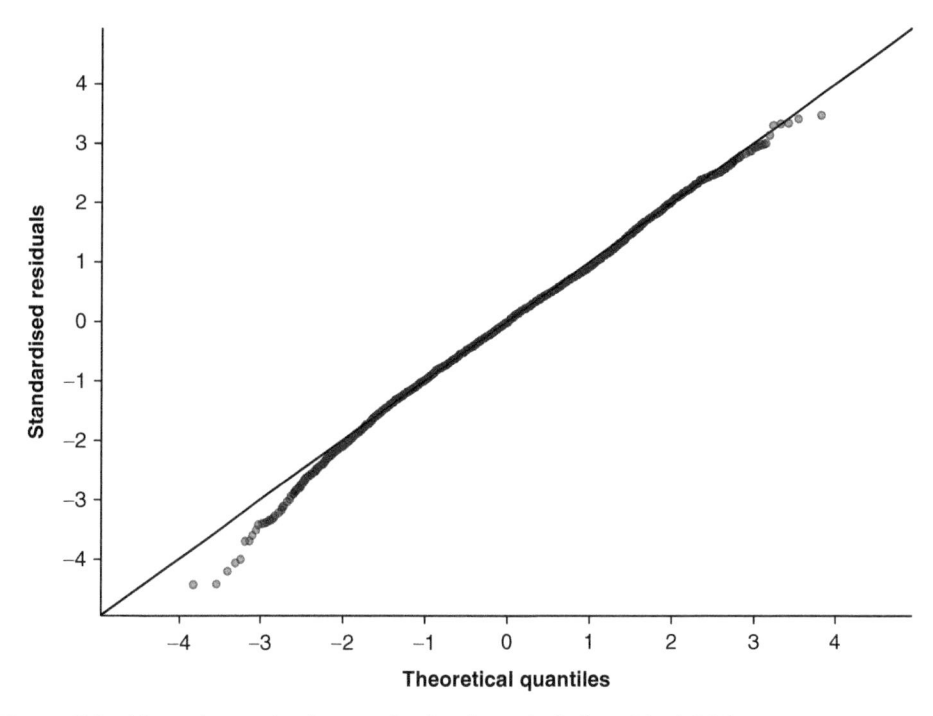

Figure 5.2 Normal q–q plot for standardised residuals from Model 5.3

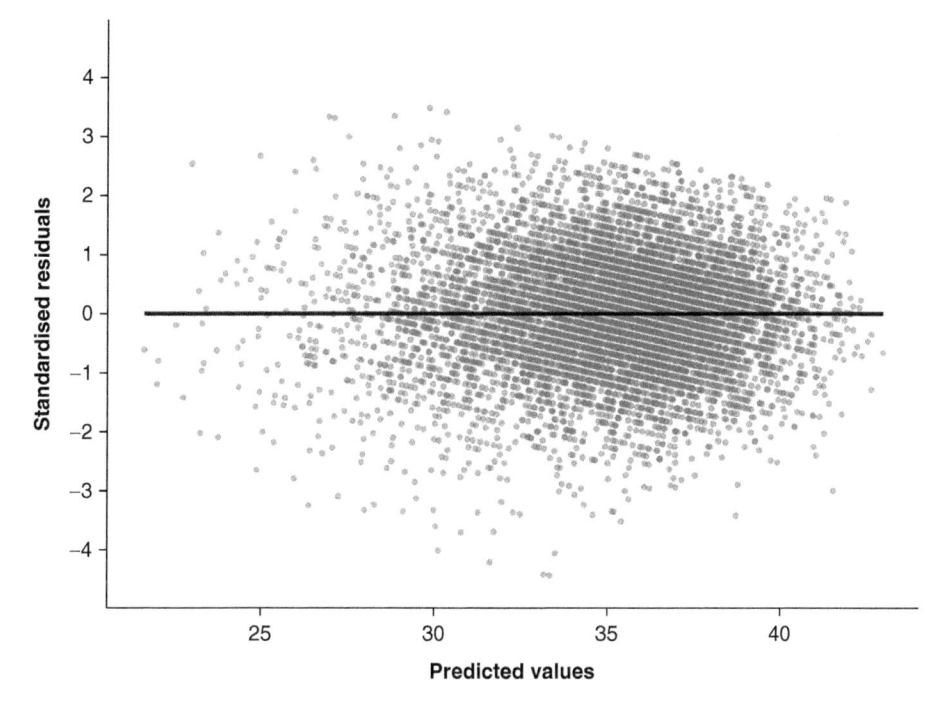

Figure 5.3 Spread-level plot of standardised residuals against predicted values from Model 5.3

There is no suggestion of non-linearity in Figure 5.3. If there was a strong non-linear relationship between the outcome and one or more of the predictors, this would be likely to show as a pattern (e.g. a curve – see Chapter 3).

Absence of outliers. Next we consider whether there is evidence for outliers in this sample. Table 5.8 shows the largest negative and positive residuals from Model 5.3. This confirms the presence of some large negative residuals, which we already detected in the normal q–q plot (see Figure 5.2). If our errors were perfectly normally distributed, we would expect standardised residuals larger than |4| fewer than once in every 10,000 cases. So to have five large negative standardised residuals with values below –4 in a sample of 7603 participants indicates a weakness in the model.

Table 5.8 The largest standardised residuals from Model 5.3

Large Negative	Large Positive
−4.44	3.48
−4.42	3.42
−4.21	3.35
−4.06	3.34
−4.01	3.32

Recall that negative residuals indicate observed outcome values that are smaller than predicted by the model. Thus the presence of large negative standardised residuals could mean that the model does not do a good job at predicting some low values of wellbeing.

Absence of influential observations. As we saw in Chapters 2 and 3, in simple linear regression it is relatively easy to identify influential observations from a scatter plot of the outcome and the predictor. In multiple regression, however, this is generally not the case, because multivariate relationships (between two or more predictors and the outcome) are difficult to visualise. Therefore, in multiple regression the Cook's distance becomes an important diagnostic tool for detecting influential observations. The Cook's distance is formally defined in Chapter 3. You can think of the Cook's distance of an observation as a measure of how much the regression coefficient estimates would change if that observation was deleted from the data set. Recall that the Cook's distance is calculated from two quantities: the size of the standardised residual and the leverage. A large (positive or negative) standardised residual indicates that an observation's outcome value is very different from the model prediction. A large leverage indicates that an observation has predictor values that are very different from the predictor means. A large Cook's distance, then, results if an observation is untypical in both its outcome and predictor values. Such untypical observations exert a larger influence on the coefficient estimates than a single observation that is more 'typical' in its outcome and predictor values (and therefore would have a small Cook's distance).

To investigate whether our model estimates are strongly influenced by a small number of observations, we inspect the observations with the largest Cook's distances. If we are concerned that our regression estimates might be strongly influenced by one or a few observations, we might re-estimate our model with those observations deleted to gauge whether this changes the results appreciably.

In our example, the largest Cook's distance is 0.011. This belongs to a respondent with the following characteristics:

a. They have very high values on social support and social participation, live in an area with above-average neighbourhood cohesion, and report a limiting illness and an NVQ level 4 education. These values are 'untypical' (in the sense that they are rarer than other values and, for continuous variables, are far away from the mean), and thus make for a relatively high leverage.
b. They report relatively low mental wellbeing, despite having many of the characteristics generally associated with high mental wellbeing (high social support, high social participation and so forth). Thus they have a large negative standardised residual.

There is no indication that any of these values are mistakes (as might result, e.g., from mistakes in data entry or coding) or that they are so unusual that the respondent might be considered to be, in some sense, outside of our population of interest. Nonetheless, I checked whether the estimates for Model 5.3 are strongly influenced by the inclusion of this observation. It turns out that upon deleting this respondent from the data set and re-estimating the model, the coefficient estimates are almost the same as before. So there is no reason to think that the conclusions are strongly influenced by including this respondent, and therefore there is no reason to exclude them.

In general, influential observations often result either from mistakes, or occur in data sets that contain variables that have potentially high maxima or minima, or that are not bounded at all, such as income, wealth, number of days spent in hospital, and so on. In such a data set, a billionaire or a person who has spent a year in hospital might well constitute an influential observation.

Consider, in contrast, the variables contained in Model 5.3. All the numeric variables are calculated from questionnaire scales and have imposed bounds. For example, the Social Participation Index has an imposed range from 0 to 10. Such a variable cannot, by definition, generate the sort of extreme outliers that might occur in a variable such as wealth. So, given the types of variables included in Model 5.3, it is in fact unlikely to find an extremely influential observation that would seriously distort our regression analysis, especially when the sample size is large.

Conclusion. We have investigated the assumptions of multiple linear regression. We found no evidence for strongly influential observations and no evidence for non-linearity. There was some evidence for slight heteroscedasticity, but the violation of the homoscedasticity assumption is probably too small to matter much. The standardised residuals follow a normal distribution pretty well, with the exception of the left tail, where we find a slightly larger number of large negative residuals than we would expect. It is thus possible that the model does not adequately predict the mental wellbeing of a small proportion of the population who report low mental wellbeing. However, this affects only a few cases in the sample, and overall the model assumptions appear to be met reasonably well. On balance, these results suggest that we can trust confidence intervals and hypothesis tests about coefficients from this model. However, as researchers we might be interested in finding out whether there are other variables, which we haven't yet considered as predictors for our model, that might explain some of the low values of mental wellbeing that we find in some respondents, and which show in our analysis as large negative standardised residuals.

Standardisation

There is one more technique that we should consider before concluding this chapter. This is the **standardisation** of coefficients. Standardisation does not change the model itself but can help us interpret the effects of predictors on the outcome. This is achieved by rendering the coefficient estimates independent of the scales on which our variables are measured.

Let's consider again Model 5.3, which predicts Mental Wellbeing by Neighbourhood Cohesion, Highest Qualification, Social Support, Social Participation and Limiting Illness, and allows for an interaction between Social Participation and Limiting Illness. The coefficient estimates from that model were shown in Chapter 4, but Table 5.9 shows them again for convenience.

The slope coefficients have to be interpreted with reference to the scales of the variables. For example, the estimate 0.247 for the slope of Neighbourhood Cohesion means: for a difference of 1 point on Neighbourhood Cohesion, the predicted difference in Mental Wellbeing is 0.247 points, controlling for the other predictors. But what do '0.247 points' on Mental Wellbeing mean? It is not straightforward to translate this coefficient into a meaningful interpretation, because few of us have an intuitive understanding of how much difference 0.247 points make to a person's mental wellbeing. Slope coefficients are easier to interpret when the scales of the variables involved (both the predictor and the outcome) are in themselves meaningful.

MULTIPLE LINEAR REGRESSION: INFERENCE, ASSUMPTIONS AND STANDARDISATION

Table 5.9 Estimates from a linear regression predicting Mental Wellbeing (Model 5.3)

	Estimate	SE	95% CI
Intercept	24.118	0.490	
Neighbourhood Cohesion	0.247	0.017	[0.214, 0.280]
Social Support	0.533	0.036	[0.464, 0.603]
Social Participation	0.107	0.045	[0.019, 0.194]
Limiting Illness	−4.628	0.280	[−5.178, −4.079]
Interaction: SocPart × Limill	0.259	0.109	[0.047, 0.472]
Highest Qualification:			
NVQ1	0.124	0.380	[−0.621, 0.869]
NVQ2	1.243	0.325	[0.606, 1.881]
NVQ3	1.499	0.348	[0.817, 2.181]
NVQ4	2.186	0.323	[1.553, 2.819]
NVQ5	3.288	0.499	[2.310, 4.267]

Note. $N = 7603$. Data were taken from the National Child Development Study, 2008 sweep. Residual standard error = 7.52. $R^2 = 0.14$. SE = standard error; CI = confidence interval; NVQ = National Vocational Qualification.

For example, consider again Galton's regression of child's height on parental height in Chapter 2. There we saw that the slope coefficient (which is equal to about 0.6) was interpreted on the scale of inches, which is a natural measurement for heights (in the Anglophone world): a difference of 1 inch in parental height is associated with a difference of about 0.6 inches in the child's height. This is interpretable, because we have an intuitive understanding of what an inch is.

In social science we often encounter variables that are measured on scales that are essentially arbitrary. This is true for variables that represent sums of answers to survey questions, such as the Neighbourhood Cohesion Scale or the Mental Wellbeing Scale. There is no intuitive or substantively interesting interpretation of a '1-point difference' on either of these scales. Thus, it is not intuitively clear how a slope of 0.247 might be interpreted. Is this a weak effect or a strong effect? Without further information, we cannot say.

Furthermore, because the scales are arbitrary, the coefficient estimates cannot be used to compare different predictors with respect to their relative importance. For example, although the coefficient for Neighbourhood Cohesion is 0.247, and the coefficient for Social Support is 0.533 (more than twice as large), we *cannot* use this to justify a statement such as 'social support is more important than neighbourhood cohesion in the prediction of mental wellbeing'. These coefficients on their own give us no information about the relative importance of different predictors, because the value of each coefficient depends on the scale on which the variables are measured.

This is where standardisation can help us. Standardisation renders our slope coefficients independent of the scale on which the variables are measured. The most intuitive way to obtain **standardised coefficients** is to use standardised variables in the estimation of the regression model. A standardised variable has a mean of zero and a standard deviation (SD) of 1. We can standardise a variable X by using the following formula:

$$Z = \frac{X - \bar{X}}{s_x}$$

where $\bar{X}$ is the sample mean of X, s_x is the sample standard deviation of X, and Z denotes the standardised version of X. This is a type of variable transformation and is also often called **z-standardisation**.

Standardisation of coefficients in a regression model can be of different types, depending on whether we standardise the predictors, the outcome or both.

- **x-standardisation** of a coefficient results from standardising a numeric predictor in a regression model. The interpretation of an x-standardised coefficient in linear regression is 'the predicted unit difference in Y for a 1 standard deviation (SD) difference in X'.
- Standardising the outcome of a linear regression model leads to **y-standardisation** of coefficients. The y-standardised slope coefficients are to be interpreted as 'the predicted difference in standard deviations in Y, for a unit difference in X'.
- Finally, **xy-standardisation** is achieved by standardising both the numeric predictor and the outcome. Slope coefficients then indicate the predicted difference in standard deviations of Y for a 1 SD difference in X.

Let's look at examples of standardised coefficients. Table 5.10 displays four sets of coefficient estimates from Model 5.3: unstandardised, x-standardised, y-standardised and xy-standardised. I designed this table to illustrate the technique of standardisation for the purpose of this textbook. I would not usually report the results of a regression model in this way, but instead would usually choose to display just one type of coefficient (or two types at most).

The coefficient of Neighbourhood Cohesion, for example, is to be interpreted as follows in the four different columns:

1. *Unstandardised:* for a 1-point difference in Neighbourhood Cohesion, and keeping all other predictors constant, the predicted difference in Mental Wellbeing is 0.247 points.
2. *x-standardised:* for a 1-SD difference in Neighbourhood Cohesion, keeping all other predictors constant, the predicted difference in Mental Wellbeing is 1.326 points.
3. *y-standardised:* for a 1-point difference in Neighbourhood Cohesion, keeping all other variables constant, the predicted difference in Mental Wellbeing is 0.030 *SDs*.
4. *xy-standardised:* for a 1-SD difference in Neighbourhood Cohesion, keeping all other predictors constant, the predicted difference in Mental Wellbeing is 0.164 *SDs*.

Table 5.10 Unstandardised and standardised coefficient estimates from Model 5.3

	Coefficient Estimates			
	Unstandardised	x-Standardised	y-Standardised	xy-Standardised
Intercept	24.118	34.270	−1.341	−0.089
Neighbourhood Cohesion (NC)	0.247	1.326	0.030	0.164
Social Support (SUPP)	0.533	1.356	0.065	0.167
Social Participation (SocPart)	0.107	0.236	0.013	0.029
Limiting Illness (LimIll)[a]	−4.628	−4.191	−0.571	−0.517
SocPart × LimIll[b]	0.259	0.573	0.032	0.071
Highest Qualification:				
NVQ1[c]	0.124	0.124	0.015	0.015
NVQ2[c]	1.243	1.243	0.153	0.153
NVQ3[c]	1.499	1.499	0.185	0.185
NVQ4[c]	2.186	2.186	0.270	0.270
NVQ5[c]	3.288	3.288	0.405	0.405

[a]Limiting Illness is a dummy variable and was not standardised.
[b]Interaction: *SocPart* × *LimIll*: This was calculated using the standardised version of *SocPart* in x-standardisation and xy-standardisation.
[c]Dummy variables relating to categories of Highest Qualification are not standardised.

Standardisation and dummy predictors

An x-standardised or xy-standardised coefficient for a dummy variable does not have a useful interpretation. Literally, such a coefficient would have to be interpreted as 'the predicted change in Y for a one standard deviation difference in the dummy variable'. But a dummy can only assume the values 0 or 1, and the population standard deviation of such a variable can at most be 0.5. So by definition, two respondents can never be 1 SD apart on a dummy variable.[7] I therefore do not recommend x-standardisation or xy-standardisation of coefficients for dummy variables. In Table 5.10, the coefficients for Limiting Illness and the NVQ dummies are therefore not x-standardised.

Standardisation and interactions

Notice that the NVQ dummy coefficients are the same in the unstandardised and the x-standardised columns. This is because the standardisation of some predictors in a model does not affect the size of the coefficients of other (unstandardised) predictors, as long as these unstandardised predictors are not involved in an interaction.

---

[7]Note that nonetheless some software packages, when you use them to calculate standardised coefficients, will by default give you xy-standardised coefficients for all predictors, including dummies.

However, the coefficient for Limiting Illness does differ between the unstandardised and *x*-standardised columns. The reason is that Limiting Illness is part of an interaction with a numeric variable, Social Participation, and that Social Participation has of course been standardised in the *x*-standardised column. The interpretation of the coefficient for Limiting Illness thus differs between the unstandardised and the *x*-standardised columns:

- Unstandardised column: *Among people with a score of zero on Social Participation,* those with a limiting illness have a predicted Mental Wellbeing score that is 4.628 points lower than those without.
- *x*-standardised column: *Among people with a Social Participation score equal to the sample mean* (i.e. with a score of zero on *standardised* Social Participation), those with a limiting illness have a predicted Mental Wellbeing score that is 4.191 points lower than those without.

Comparing coefficients of different predictors

Using *x*- or *xy*-standardisation, it is possible to compare the sizes of coefficients for numeric predictors. A larger (positive or negative) *x*-standardised or *xy*-standardised coefficient indicates a stronger effect, or relationship. For example, the *xy*-standardised coefficients for Neighbourhood Cohesion and Social Support are almost identical (0.164 and 0.167, respectively), suggesting that both predictors have about equally strong associations with the outcome, according to this model. Note that the unstandardised coefficients of these two predictors differ considerably. This illustrates the relevance of using (*x*- or *xy*-) standardised coefficients when the aim is to gauge the relative importance of different numeric predictors.

If a predictor is involved in an interaction, we need to be a little careful, because in the presence of an interaction, the importance of one variable depends on the values of another. Thus, in our example, the coefficient for Social Participation must be interpreted in relation to the interaction with Limiting Illness, because the slope of Social Participation depends on the value of Limiting Illness. The *xy*-standardised coefficient for Social Participation (0.029) estimates the slope for people without a limiting illness. For those with a limiting illness, the estimated slope is 0.029 + 0.071 = 0.100. So social participation is a more important predictor of mental wellbeing among those with a limiting illness than among those without.

Some final comments on standardisation

Standardisation does not affect model fit or model quality: R^2 and *Adjusted* R^2 are identical regardless of whether I employ standardisation or not. Predictions and residuals are also the same, although of course they will be on the scale on the standardised outcome, if y- or xy-standardisation is used.

When researchers and software packages refer to standardised coefficients, they typically mean xy-standardisation, although this is often not explicitly stated. Such xy-standardised coefficients are called 'beta coefficients' in some software packages. Note also that software packages and researchers may well report standardised slope coefficients for dummy variables. As I said, I do not think that this is helpful for interpretation, although it does no harm to the model estimation.

There are no hard-and-fast rules regarding whether you should report unstandardised or standardised coefficients. The choice should be informed by the aims of your analysis:

- If you wish to compare coefficients of numeric predictors, then x- or xy-standardisation ensures that you put the numeric predictors on an equal footing with one another.
- If some or all of your variables are on arbitrary scales, then standardisation can make the coefficients more interpretable. This applies to most variables derived from sums of responses to a set of survey questions (e.g. Likert scales).
- On the other hand, if your variables are on substantially meaningful scales (e.g. inches for height, kilogram for weight, pounds for income, years for age), then standardisation may make the meaning of coefficients more opaque, and the unstandardised coefficients may be more readily interpretable.

Chapter Summary

- You might consider linear regression when the outcome of your analysis is a numeric variable that is either continuous (e.g. height) or can be treated as if it was continuous (e.g. the mental wellbeing score that features in the examples of this chapter). Although the outcome does not necessarily have to be normally distributed for linear regression to be appropriate, the errors of the regression model (which we estimate by standardised residuals) should be.
- In social science practice, it is seldom the case that normal errors result when the outcome distribution is very different from normal.
- Non-normality of errors can be tolerated in large samples – or more precisely, when the sample size is large relative to the number of predictors in the model. This is because, when the sample size is large, the coefficient estimates from a linear regression will tend to approximately follow a normal distribution, even if the errors are not normally distributed. In large samples, t-tests and confidence intervals about coefficients, as well as F-tests of model comparisons, will yield valid results even if the error distribution is decidedly non-normal. For an illustration and further explanation, see for example Lumley et al. (2002).

Further Reading

Krzanowski, W. J. (1998). *An introduction to statistical modelling.* Wiley.

Krzanowski's book teaches the theory of multiple regression in more mathematical depth than the book you are reading now.

Tabachnick, B. G., & Fidell, L. S. (2014). *Using multivariate statistics* (6th ed.). Pearson.

This book includes a chapter on multiple regression that contains a thorough discussion of regression diagnostics as well as helpful examples of how to use software to conduct a regression analysis.

6
WHERE TO GO FROM HERE

Chapter Overview

Regression models for non-normal error distributions 156
Factorial design experiments: analysis of variance 157
Beyond modelling the mean: quantile regression 158
Identifying an appropriate transformation: fractional polynomials.......... 158
Extreme non-linearity: generalised additive models 159
Dependency in data: multilevel models (mixed effects models,
hierarchical models) 159
Missing values: multiple imputation and other methods........................ 159
Bayesian statistical models.. 160
Causality 160
Measurement models: factor analysis and structural equations 161

The first five chapters of this book have set up a foundation for understanding statistical models. They have discussed what a statistical model is, introduced linear regression as a relatively simple kind of model, and given examples of how statistical models may be applied within a research investigation. Using linear regression as an illustrative case, we have considered important principles of statistical modelling, as well as techniques for the application of these principles. Thus, we have considered assumptions that data need to meet for inferences from a linear regression to be valid, and we have discussed techniques for evaluating the plausibility of these assumptions. We have also considered indicators of model fit and predictive power (e.g. the R^2 statistic), methods for comparing models with one another (the F test and the *adjusted* R^2 statistic), and the interpretation of slope coefficients for predictors, including complicated cases involving interactions and transformed predictor variables.

This final chapter suggests some ways in which you could deepen and widen your knowledge of regression and other statistical models. Like a guidepost that points to multiple directions, the next few pages indicate paths you could take if you come across data for which linear regression isn't a suitable model, if you are faced with decisions or problems that this book alone does not help you solve, or if you are simply hungry for more information.

Regression models for non-normal error distributions

As we have seen, linear regression is a model for a numeric (ideally: continuous) outcome that (ideally) follows a normal distribution contingent on a set of predictor variables. This is an important model and is frequently applied in the social sciences and beyond. But there are many types of outcome variables that are either not numeric, or are numeric but unlikely to have a normal distribution of errors in a linear model. For example, outcomes might be categorical, might represent discrete counts, or might be continuous variables with distributions very different from normal. In these cases, linear regression is often not an appropriate model.

Categorical variables can be of three types:

1. **Dichotomous** or **binary**: having two categories, such as ill or healthy
2. **Nominal**: with unordered categories, such as party voted for at the last election
3. **Ordinal**: with ordered categories, such as highest qualification

Categorical outcomes are often modelled using logistic regression, a family of models that aims to predict the probability of being in a certain outcome category (e.g. the probability of illness, the probability of voting for a certain political party, or the probability of obtaining a university degree). Logistic regression models for dichotomous, nominal and ordinal outcomes are discussed in *The SAGE Quantitative Research Kit*, Volume 8.

Count outcomes are variables that represent discrete counts. Examples are the number of times a person went to see a doctor in the past year, the number of crimes recorded in an area in a month, or the number of cycle accidents in a city. Two common models for count outcomes are Poisson regression and negative binomial regression. Both of these explicitly take into account that count outcomes cannot be negative (a person can't visit the hospital −2 times) and always have whole number values (there can be 10 accidents or 11 accidents, but not 10.48 accidents). Both Poisson and negative binomial regression are discussed in *The SAGE Quantitative Research Kit*, Volume 8, alongside several other models for count outcomes that deal with different situations often encountered in practice.

Other types of regression include models for variables that are continuous, but don't result in a normal distribution of errors. For example, gamma regression is a model for continuous outcomes that follow a gamma distribution, rather than a normal distribution. The gamma distribution is a probability distribution for a non-negative continuous variable. Unlike the normal distribution, the gamma distribution can be skewed, and so gamma regression might be a model to consider when the interest is in modelling a skewed outcome variable that cannot take negative values, such as waiting times or costs.

All these models – linear regression, the three types of logistic regression, as well as Poisson and gamma regression – are members of a large family called *generalised linear models (GLM[1])*. All GLMs relate an outcome to a linear combination of predictor variables, but they differ in whether and how the outcome is transformed, and in the distribution of errors assumed for the outcome. A good place to learn about GLMs is Chapter 5 in Krzanowski (1998).

Factorial design experiments: analysis of variance

Another special case of the generalised linear model (GLM) is a procedure known as analysis of variance (ANOVA). This is often taught in introductory statistics courses as a generalisation of the *t*-test for independent samples. While the *t*-test compares the means of two groups, ANOVA allows you to analytically compare the means of three or more groups. ANOVA is typically used to analyse data originating from laboratory or field experiments, where multiple experimental conditions (called 'factors') are being tested. Mathematically, ANOVA is equivalent to a linear regression where the predictors are all categorical, and where the predictors may be allowed to interact. However, ANOVA has a separate analytic tradition from regression and is associated

---

[1]Negative binomial regression has several variants, some of which belong to the family of generalised linear models, while others do not.

with specialised methods to deal with research questions frequently associated with designed experiments. Most introductory statistics textbooks for psychologists cover ANOVA. An excellent such book is Howell (2010).

Beyond modelling the mean: quantile regression

Linear regression is concerned with predicting the *mean* of the outcome variable. In our examples, we have predicted the mean height of people conditional on their parents' heights, the mean mental wellbeing score of a person conditional on their perception of social cohesion in their neighbourhood, the mean life expectancy of countries given their GDP, and so forth. But what if we're not interested so much in the mean of a distribution, but in other statistics – for example, the median, or the 5th percentile, or the 75th percentile? These are called the *quantiles* of a distribution, and a method for modelling them is *quantile regression*. One of the advantages of quantile regression is that it does not require us to assume a particular probability distribution associated with the outcome, so it generally relies on fewer statistical assumptions than linear regression and other types of GLMs. A good place to learn about quantile regression is in publications by Roger Koenker (Koenker, 2005, 2019; Koenker & Hallock, 2001).

Identifying an appropriate transformation: fractional polynomials

In the practice of statistical data analysis, it is common to find non-linear relationships between predictor and outcome variables. Chapter 3 has introduced the technique of variable transformation, which can be used to try to achieve adequate models for non-linear relationships. In practice, it is sometimes difficult and often laboursome to find suitable transformations, especially when the data set contains many predictors that potentially need to be transformed.

A statistical technique for identifying suitable transformations is the use of *fractional polynomials*. This works by assessing a range of potential transformations and choosing the one that achieves the best fit to the data at hand. Fractional polynomials can be applied in the context of bivariate relationships, as well as in the context of models with many predictors. The procedure can be automated, such that many different transformations can be assessed via a single command in statistical software. At the time that I am writing this, I am not aware of an easy-to-read introduction to fractional polynomials. Possibly the most accessible is Royston and Sauerbrei (2008).

Extreme non-linearity: generalised additive models

Sometimes you may find that the relationship between two variables is characterised by extreme non-linearity, which is not easily accommodated by variable transformations. This frequently occurs, for example, when monitoring a trend over time: the relationship between 'time' and the outcome of interest is often neither linear nor non-linear in an easily describable fashion. In such a situation, generalised additive models (GAM) may be worth considering. They essentially represent a principled attempt to fit a smoothed curve to data that are assumed to come from a complex non-linear relationship between two or more variables. A good place to learn about GAMs is the book by Simon Wood (2006).

Dependency in data: multilevel models (mixed effects models, hierarchical models)

As we saw in Chapter 3, one important assumption of linear regression (and, in fact, of all GLMs) is that observations are independent from one another. However, social science data frequently do not meet this assumption. For example, a study of academic achievement might have sampled 10,000 students from 150 schools. Students in the same school are likely to have some things in common: many of them have the same teachers, and this might be related to their academic achievement. Such data sets are said to have a *dependent* data structure. Synonymous names for dependent data structures are nested, clustered, or hierarchical data structures. Other examples of data that are likely to feature dependency are patients clustered in hospitals and voters clustered in electoral districts. Models that ignore dependency in the data run the risk of misestimating the standard errors of their coefficients, among other disadvantages. One class of models suitable for dependent data are multilevel models (also called mixed effects models, or hierarchical models). They have the advantage of being able to account for outcome variation at different levels of the clustered data structure: for example, a multilevel model might separate how much of the variation between school pupil's academic achievement is due to the quality of their school, and how much is due to their individual or family characteristics. Good places to start learning about these are *The SAGE Quantitative Research Kit*, Volume 9, the books by Sophia Rabe-Hesketh and Anders Skrondal (2012a, 2012b), and the online learning platform LEMMA (Centre for Multilevel Modeling, n.d.).

Missing values: multiple imputation and other methods

All the data analysis examples in this book have used complete data sets, where every case e.g. (every person, every country) had complete information on all the variables we used in our models. In reality, data often aren't like that. Many data sets have missing values. Some survey respondents do not answer all the questions we ask them, some cohort members drop out of longitudinal studies, hospital records about patients are incomplete, and some area statistics have not been collected or only unreliably so. A variety of methods for dealing with missing values have been developed, including inverse probability weighting and multiple imputation, among others.

Multiple imputation (MI) involves building a statistical model for substituting plausible values for the missing pieces of information. MI is a complex procedure with several steps. One of these steps typically uses linear regression or another GLM to predict what the missing values would have been if we had been able to observe them. This is an example of how elementary statistical models, such as linear regression, can also be used as elements within more complex procedures. A thorough treatment of analysis of data with missing values is provided in the book by Carpenter and Kenward (2013).

Bayesian statistical models

The way I have presented regression models in this book is rooted in the frequentist tradition of statistics. This refers to the philosophical stance that defines a probability as a hypothetical relative frequency. For example, a frequentist interpretation of a *p*-value is that it is the proportion of times I would obtain the observed result or a more extreme one, under the assumption that the null hypothesis is correct, if I was able to conduct an infinite number of studies. An alternative perspective on statistical models and the investigation of research hypotheses is presented by the Bayesian tradition. The idea of Bayesian statistics is to systematically assess and quantify the state of the evidence (or plausibility) of different models and parameter values *prior* to investigating a new data set. Modelling of a new data set then has the aim of updating prior beliefs in the light of the new evidence. An excellent introduction to Bayesian statistics is Gelman et al. (2013).

Causality

On various occasions in this book, when interpreting the results of a fitted model, I have pointed out that the results in themselves do not prove the causal hypothesis that the model was designed to investigate. For example, in Chapters 4 and 5 we saw that Elliott et al. (2014) found statistical evidence for an association between self-reported neighbourhood cohesion and mental wellbeing. However, this in itself does not tell us whether neighbourhood cohesion promotes mental wellbeing, whether mental wellbeing affects the perception of neighbourhood cohesion, whether there is a third variable that is not controlled for in the model and that causes the association, or whether all these possibilities are involved in combination.

Outside of designed experiments, causal relationships are usually difficult to disentangle, and often it requires several studies, possibly looking at the same question with different data sets and different methods, to establish a plausible argument for causality. However, there are statistical approaches to the analysis of causal relationships in non-experimental data, and *The SAGE Quantitative Research Kit*, Volume 10, is devoted to this topic.

Measurement models: factor analysis and structural equations

One assumption of linear regression is that all predictor variables are measured without error. (There is no error term associated with the *X*-variables in these models.) In social science, this assumption may not always be realistic. In particular, consider variables that measure concepts that cannot be observed directly, such as attitudes, personality characteristics, mental wellbeing, and so forth. It is often not plausible that a single survey question can be a perfect measure of, say, a person's attitude to migration, whether they are an introvert or an extravert, or the quality of their mental health. That is why in social research practice, such concepts are often measured by several variables rather than just a single one. A concept that cannot be observed directly, but only indirectly via observed indicators, is called a latent variable.

Factor analysis is a statistical model for deriving measurements of latent variables from a set of observed variables. These measurements, called 'factors', are theorised to be free from the measurement errors associated with the observed variables. Factors can be used in further analyses as variables in their own right.

Going even further, structural equation models can combine, in a single modelling procedure, elements of factor analysis and regression. Using structural equations, it is possible, for example, to construct a regression model where not only the outcome but also the observed predictors are modelled as being subject to measurement error. More advanced types of structural equation models are able to combine features of factor analysis with features of causal modelling, such as path analysis. An introduction to factor analysis and structural equations can be found in *The SAGE Quantitative Research Kit*, Volume 9.

Final Comments

Statistical models are used in all areas of human knowledge and are involved in many applications of science, such as weather forecasts, medical diagnostics and prognosis, and insurance. In this book, I have pointed out that all inferential statistics – that is, all use of statistics that aims to generalise from a sample to a population, or from a data set at hand to an underlying process in the real world – are based on statistical models. In Chapter 1, we have seen that even the humble *t*-test is a comparison of two statistical models.

At the time of writing this book, many scientists and non-scientists are discussing the possibilities that the increasing availability of large data sets affords the sciences and technology. This is an important topic, and *The SAGE Quantitative Research Kit*, Volume 11, is devoted to methods for the analysis of such 'Big Data' to address social science research questions. Sometimes the view is taken that in the age of Big Data, statistical models become less relevant, and model-free pattern search techniques associated with machine learning will replace statistical models as the most important analytic tools. Although machine learning algorithms have proved enormously powerful in some applications (e.g. consider online search engines), and will doubtless continue to increase in sophistication and use, my bet is that the ubiquity of data will make statistical models become more important, not less.

A lot of data means a lot of noise, a lot of random variation that does not relate to any scientifically or practically interesting effects. As researchers, amid all this noise we aim to distinguish the signal: the effect, visible in the data, of a process that operates in the world. In order to do so, we need techniques that can separate systematic effects from random error. That is the essence of what statistical models are designed to do. So the study of statistical models is useful not only for the purposes of analysing data and for getting your head around the statistical sections of scientific research reports, but also for understanding the scientific insights and technologies that shape our world.

GLOSSARY

Binary variable: See *Dichotomous variable*.

Categorical variable: A categorical variable is one whose values are categories, rather than numbers. The categories may be ordered or unordered. For example, *country of birth* is an unordered categorical variable, while *highest qualification* is ordered. Unordered categorical variables are also often referred to as nominal variables, while ordered categorical variables are often called ordinal variables. A variable that has precisely two categories is called a dichotomous or binary variable.

Centring: Centring is a type of variable transformation that defines the transformed variable to be equal to the original variable minus a constant number c. That is, $trans(x) = X - c$. This is called centring X on c. Centring on X implies that $trans(X) = 0$ whenever $X = c$, and that $trans(X)$ records the positive and negative deviations of the values of X from c. Typically, variables are centred around their mean or their median, or a rounded number close to the mean or median. This is called mean-centring. In the context of regression models, centring of predictors sometimes has the advantage of making the intercept of the model meaningful in cases where X never takes the value 0. Another purpose of centring is to reduce collinearity when using both a predictor and its square transformation in a model. If X is a variable that has only positive values (e.g. age), and I wish to use both X and X^2 as predictors, then I will find that X and X^2 are highly correlated. If I instead mean-centre X and use $trans_1(X) = X - \bar{X}$ and $trans_2(X) = (X - \bar{X})^2$ as my predictors, the collinearity will be much reduced.

Coefficient: A coefficient is a number by which a variable or a constant is multiplied within an equation. For example, in the fitted statistical model equation, $\hat{Y}_i = 0.5 + 3X_i$, the numbers 0.5 and 3 are coefficients. In this case, the coefficient 0.5 represents the intercept, and the coefficient 3 represents the slope. The intercept is called a constant coefficient, since it is not multiplied with a variable. (You can think of it as being multiplied by 1.) In statistical modelling, we use data to estimate the coefficients of a statistical model. The true coefficients, which we usually do not know, are called parameters. Our aim in statistical analysis is to estimate these parameters. A typical table showing the results of a statistical model reports coefficient estimates – that is, estimates of the intercept and slopes of our statistical model. The term *coefficient* is also used more generally to indicate a statistical measure, as in 'correlation coefficient', 'Gini coefficient', 'coefficient of determination' and so on.

Coefficient of determination: See *R-squared*.

Confounder, confounding: A confounder is a variable that is related to both the predictor and the outcome, and thus causes an association between the predictor and the outcome. An association between a predictor and an outcome is called 'spurious' if it is entirely caused by one or several confounders, while there is no causal relationship between the predictor and the outcome.

Continuous variable: A continuous variable is a numeric variable that can take any value within its possible range. For example, age is a continuous variable: a person can be 28 years old, 28.4 years old or even 28.397853 years old. Age changes every day, every minute, every second, every millisecond; so our measurement of age is limited only by how precise we can or wish to be. Contrast this with a discrete variable, which can only take particular values within its range (e.g. 1, 2, 3, ...). In practice, continuous variables such as age are often measured with a moderate degree of precision that makes them look like discrete variables in a data set. For example, age might be measured in whole years, but conceptually we still think of it as continuous. A borderline case is psychometric scales and other similar summary measures, such as the Mental Wellbeing Scale that is used as an outcome variable in Chapter 4 of this book. Because of the way it is calculated from numeric scores given to the responses to 14 survey questions, the Mental Wellbeing Scale can only take the discrete values 0, 1, 2, ..., 56. Nonetheless, most analysts think of these numbers as discrete measurements of a continuous variable, in the same way that 'age in years' is a discrete measurement of continuous age.

Correlation: The term *correlation* generally denotes a relationship between two things, or an interdependence of two things. In statistics, correlation has a very precise meaning, referring to the linear association between two numerical variables. The degree of correlation is measured by Pearson's product moment coefficient, also called correlation coefficient, Pearson's *r* or simply *r*. Pearson's *r* can take values between −1 and +1, where −1 indicates a perfect negative linear relationship, +1 indicates a perfect positive linear relationship, and 0 indicates absence of a linear relationship. When the true relationship between two variables is non-linear, Pearson's *r* will be an inadequate measure of the strength of that relationship. For example, it is possible for Pearson's *r* to be very small or even zero in a case where two variables have a strong curvilinear relationship.

Dichotomous variable: A dichotomous variable is one that has exactly two values. A synonym for dichotomous is binary.

Discrete variable: A discrete variable is a numeric variable that can only take particular, 'discrete' values. For example, count variables are discrete variables; they can take the values 0, 1, 2, 3 and so on. Number of children is a discrete variable: you can have zero children, one child, or seven children, but not 1.5 children. This is in contrast to a continuous variable, which can take any value within its range.

Dummy variable: A dummy variable is a binary variable whose only two possible values are 0 and 1. Dummy variables are used as a device for representing categorical predictors in a statistical model. Take the variable smoking status with three categories: 'never smoked', 'ex-smoker' and 'current smoker'. This might be represented by two dummy variables: one dummy identifies current smokers by having the value 1 for current smokers and the value 0 for all others; a second dummy identifies ex-smokers in the analogous way. The remaining category, 'never smoked', is called the reference category. In general, to represent a categorical predictor with k categories, we need $k - 1$ dummy variables. Dummy variables are also called indicator variables in the statistical literature.

Effect, effect size: In statistical modelling, the word *effect* is used to denote the relationship between a predictor, X, and an outcome, Y. This terminology sounds as if it implies a causal relationship, whereby X 'has an effect' on Y. However, the word *effect* is also sometimes used loosely in situations where a causal relationship cannot be demonstrated, such as in the analysis of cross-sectional surveys. The size of the effect, in either sense of the word, can be estimated by the slope coefficient of X in a model predicting Y. In some contexts, it is useful to transform the slope coefficient to facilitate interpretation of the size of the effect. Thus, in linear regression, sometimes standardised coefficients are used.

Error: The term *error* has a specific meaning in statistics. The error is the difference between a prediction from a true model and a true value. For example, consider the following statistical model:

$$Y_i = \beta_0 + \beta_1 X_i + \varepsilon_i$$

$$\varepsilon_i \sim NID(0, \sigma^2)$$

where the ε_i are the errors, and are equal to $\varepsilon_i = Y_i - (\beta_0 + \beta_1 X_i) = Y_i - \hat{Y}_i$.

All statistical models make assumptions about the distribution of the errors. For example, linear regression assumes that the errors are independent, homoscedastic and follow a normal distribution. Errors should be distinguished from residuals (see the Glossary entry on 'residuals'). Residuals can be considered estimates of the true errors.

Estimate: In statistics, an estimate is a number that has been calculated from data and is considered a measure of a parameter. For example, the mean height calculated from a random sample of 1000 people can be considered as an estimate of the mean height in the population from which the sample was drawn. Similarly, the slope coefficient of the regression of child's height on parents' average height, calculated by statistical software from data about 1000 families, is an estimate of the slope coefficient in the population. In mathematical notation, estimates are usually marked with a 'hat': for example, $\hat{\beta}$ (pronounced 'beta-hat') denotes an estimate of β.

Estimating a model: See *Fitting a model*.

Fitting a model: Fitting a model to a data set means using the data to estimate the model parameters. This is also called 'estimating a model'. For example, Francis Galton's model of the relationship between parents' heights and adult children's heights is *Child's height* = $\alpha + \beta \times$ *Parents' height*. He fitted this model to data on 928 child–parent pairs, and thereby obtained estimates of the parameters α and β.

Goodness of fit: The goodness of fit of a statistical model describes how close the observations from a data set are to the values predicted by the model. Various measures and techniques are used to assess goodness of fit, such as graphical exploration of residuals, the R^2 statistic in linear regression, and other techniques which may be different for different types of statistical models.

Heteroscedasticity: Heteroscedasticity means 'differences between variances'. The term is used to describe a situation where the variance of a variable differs across different groups in the data set. In regression modelling, we often consider how the variance of the errors (or the variance of the observed values) depends on the predicted mean. For example, in linear regression we assume homoscedasticity of errors, which is the opposite of heteroscedasticity.

Homoscedasticity: Homoscedasticity means 'equality of variances'. The term is used to describe a situation where the variance of a variable is the same across different groups in the data set. In regression modelling, we often consider whether the variance of the errors (or the variance of the observed values) depends on the predicted mean. For example, homoscedasticity is one of the assumptions of linear regression; that is, for statistical inference about linear regression coefficients to be valid, we must assume that the error variance is the same, regardless of the predicted mean.

Inference, inferential statistics: Inferential statistics is the art of using a sample to draw conclusions about a population, or using a data set to draw conclusions about a process. Tools of inferential statistics used in this book are confidence intervals and prediction intervals for inferential estimation and prediction, and statistical hypothesis tests for model comparison and investigating hypotheses about model parameters.

Intercept: The intercept of a regression equation is the predicted value of the outcome variable when all predictors are equal to zero. In simple linear regression, when the Y-axis is drawn at $X = 0$, the intercept is the height at which the regression line crosses the Y-axis.

Least squares: The method of least squares is a technique for finding the estimated coefficients of a linear regression model. The method finds the coefficient estimates that minimise the sum of the squared residuals of the outcome variable.

Leverage: The leverage is a measure of how far away an observation is from other observations in terms of its values on the predictor variables in a linear regression model. A high leverage indicates a relatively *un*typical observation within a data set. Observations with higher leverage have a higher influence on the estimated model coefficients than observations with lower leverage. A high leverage is therefore potentially indicative of an influential observation or outlier.

Logarithm: A logarithm is the answer to the question: b to the power of what gives n? For example, if $b = 2$ and $n = 8$, the question is, 2 to the power of what gives 8? The answer is 3, since $2^3 = 2 \times 2 \times 2 = 8$. This is written as $\log_2(8) = 3$. The number b is called the base of the logarithm, so in this example the base is 2. Of particular importance in mathematics and statistics is the logarithm to base e, where $e \approx 2.71828 \ldots$, also called Euler's number. A logarithm to the base e is called the natural logarithm. If the base is not specified, such as when writing $\log(4)$, then it is usually assumed that the natural logarithm is meant. This is the case in this book. In statistical modelling, logarithms are used in variable transformations. Log transformation of a predictor variable is sometimes used to deal with a non-linear relationship.

Mean-centring: *see centring.*

Nominal variable: A nominal variable is a categorical variable whose categories cannot be ranked, or ordered. Examples of nominal variables are country of birth, ethnicity, and choice of dish at a restaurant.

Numeric variable: A numeric variable is one whose values are numbers that represent meaningful measurements of some quantity. Numeric variables may be continuous or discrete.

Ordinal variable: An ordinal variable is a categorical variable whose categories have a natural order, or ranking. An equivalent term is *ordered variable*. An example of an ordinal variable is 'highest qualification', which might have the categories: 'no qualification', 'completed secondary school', 'high school/A-level', 'university degree or equivalent'.

Outcome, outcome variable: In this book, I use the term *outcome*, or *outcome variable*, to denote the variable that a statistical model aims to predict. Synonymous terms in this context are *dependent variable*, or *response*.

Parameter: A parameter is a quantifiable property of a population, or process. Examples of parameters are the mean height of all adult residents in Greenland, or the average effect of a medicine on human blood pressure. The value of a parameter tells us something interesting or important about the population or process – for example, whether a medicine tends to reduce or increase blood pressure, and by how much. In general, parameters are unknown, but they can be estimated from data. For example, a representative sample of Greenland residents might allow us to estimate the parameter 'average height of all Greenlanders'. A randomised placebo controlled trial might allow us to estimate the parameter 'average effect of a medicine on blood pressure over and above the placebo effect'.

Parameters also feature in statistical models. For example, the model

$$Y_i = \beta_0 + \beta_1 X_i + \varepsilon_i$$
$$\varepsilon_i \sim NID(0, \sigma^2)$$

contains the parameters β_0, β_1 and σ^2. These can be estimated from a data set that contains sample measurements of the variables X and Y.

Predicted value: The predicted value of a fitted regression model is the outcome value that, according to our model estimates, is most likely given the values of the predictors.

Predictor, predictor variable: In this book, I use the term *predictor*, or *predictor variable*, for a variable that is used in a statistical model to predict the outcome. Synonymous terms are *independent variable*, *explanatory variable* and *exposure*. The terms *covariate* (for continuous predictors) and *factor* (for categorical predictors) are also sometimes used.

R-squared: R-squared, usually written R^2, and also called the coefficient of determination, is a measure of the proportion of the outcome variance that is accounted for by a linear regression model. R^2 is calculated from the data on which the regression is estimated. R^2 tends to overestimate the proportion of the outcome variance that the same regression model would account for in a new data set. Therefore, it is often preferable to report the adjusted R^2-value, which corrects R^2 downwards (towards zero).

Residual: A residual is the difference between a prediction based on a fitted model and an observed value. This is in contrast to an error, which is the difference between a prediction based on a true model and a true value. A residual can be considered an estimate of the error. For example, in the fitted model

$$Y_i = \hat{\beta}_0 + \hat{\beta}_1 X_i + e_i$$

the residuals are $e_i = Y_i - (\hat{\beta}_0 + \hat{\beta}_1 X_i)$. The residuals represent the part of the outcome variation that the model does not account for. As such, 'explaining the residual variation', that is, trying to explain what we can't yet explain, is one of the ways in which researchers aim to make progress in science. Residuals are also used to investigate the plausibility of model assumptions about the errors. To this end, often transformations of residuals are used, such as standardised residuals or deviance residuals.

Slope: In regression models, a slope coefficient of a predictor variable (X) tells us by how much the outcome (Y) is predicted to differ for a 1-unit difference in X, keeping all predictor variables other than X constant.

Standardisation: See *standardised regression coefficient, standardised residual, z-standardisation.*

Standardised regression coefficient: In linear regression, a standardised coefficient is a slope estimate that is independent of the scale on which either the outcome (Y) or the predictor (X), or both are measured. There are three types of standardisation: x-standardisation, y-standardisation and xy-standardisation. When the type of standardisation is not specified, usually xy-standardisation is meant. Standardised slope coefficients express the effect of X on Y in terms of standard deviations (SD). An x-standardised slope measures the effect associated with a 1-SD difference in X on Y, where Y is measured in some unit (e.g. centimetres, inches, etc.). A y-standardised slope measures the effect associated with a 1-unit difference in X on Y, in terms of the standard deviation of Y. An xy-standardised slope measures the effect associated with a 1-SD difference in X on Y in terms of the standard deviation of Y. For example, an xy-standardised coefficient of 0.5 would mean that a 1-SD difference in X is associated with a 0.5-SD difference in Y.

Standardised residual: Standardised residuals are calculated from the (raw, unstandardised) residuals of a linear regression model by a transformation that ensures that their standard deviation is equal to 1. Standardised residuals are used in regression diagnostics to investigate the plausibility of the assumptions of a linear regression model.

Transformation: See *Variable transformation.*

Variable transformation: A variable transformation is an operation that assigns new values to a variable via a mathematical function. For example, the square transformation of a variable X is calculated as $trans(X) = X^2$. The logarithmic transformation defines $trans(X) = \log(X)$, and so forth. In general, $trans(X) = f(X)$, where

$f( )$ may in principle be any mathematical function. Transformations of predictors are used within regression models to enable modelling of non-linear relationships between a numeric predictor and an outcome.

z-Standardisation: Z-standardisation of a variable X means to transform X into a new variable Z by calculating $Z = \dfrac{X - \bar{X}}{s}$, where $\bar{X}$ is the sample mean of X, and s is the sample standard deviation of X. That is, we subtract from X its mean and divide the result by the standard deviation. The mean of a z-standardised variable is equal to 0, and its standard deviation is equal to 1.

Check out the next title in the collection *Regression Models for Categorical and Count Data*, for guidance on statistical models beyond linear regression.

REFERENCES

Anscombe, F. J. (1973). Graphs in statistical analysis. *The American Statistician, 27*(1), 17–21. https://doi.org/10.1080/00031305.1973.10478966

Bryan, J. (2017). *gapminder: Data from gapminder* [R package]. Retrieved June 28, 2020, from https://cran.r-project.org/package=gapminder

Carney, D. R., Cuddy, A. J. C., & Yap, A. J. (2010). Power posing. *Psychological Science, 21*(10), 1363–1368. https://doi.org/10.1177/0956797610383437

Carpenter, J. R., & Kenward, M. G. (2013). *Multiple imputation and its application.* Wiley. https://doi.org/10.1002/9781119942283

Centre for Multilevel Modeling. (n.d.). *LEMMA: Learning environment for multilevel methodology and applications.* www.cmm.bris.ac.uk/lemma/

Elliott, J., Gale, C. R., Parsons, S., & Kuh, D. (2014). Neighbourhood cohesion and mental wellbeing among older adults: A mixed methods approach. *Social Science & Medicine, 107*, 44–51. https://doi.org/10.1016/j.socscimed.2014.02.027

Galton, F. (1886). Regression towards mediocrity in hereditary stature. *Journal of the Anthropological Institute of Great Britain and Ireland, 15*, 246–263. https://doi.org/10.2307/2841583

Gelman, A., Carlin, J. B., Stern, H. S., Dunson, D. B., Vehtari, A., & Rubin, D. B. (2013) *Bayesian Data Analysis* (3rd ed.). CRC Press. http://www.stat.columbia.edu/~gelman/book/

Hamilton, L. C., & Saito, K. (2015). A four-party view of US environmental concern. *Environmental Politics, 24*(2), 212–227. https://doi.org/10.1080/09644016.2014.976485

Herrington, W., Staplin, N., Judge, P. K., Mafham, M., Emberson, J., Haynes, R., Wheeler, D. C., Walker, R., Tomson, C., Agodoa, L., Wiecek, A., Lewington, S., Reith, C. A., Landray, M. J., Baigent, C., & SHARP Collaborative Group. (2017). Evidence for reverse causality in the association between blood pressure and cardiovascular risk in patients with chronic kidney disease. *Hypertension, 69*(2), 314–322. https://doi.org/10.1161/HYPERTENSIONAHA.116.08386

Howell, D. C. (2010). *Statistical methods for psychology* (7th ed.). Cengage.

Jaccard, J., & Turrisi, R. (2003). *Interaction effects in multiple regression* (2nd ed.). Sage. https://doi.org/10.4135/9781412984522

Koenker, R. (2005). *Quantile regression.* Cambridge University Press. https://doi.org/10.1017/CBO9780511754098

Koenker, R. (2019, June 28). *Quantile regression in R: A vignette.* https://cran.r-project.org/web/packages/quantreg/vignettes/rq.pdf

Koenker, R., & Hallock, K. F. (2001). Quantile regression. *Journal of Economic Perspectives, 15*(4), 143–156. https://doi.org/10.1257/jep.15.4.143

Krzanowski, W. J. (1998). *An introduction to statistical modelling.* Wiley.

Langkjær-Bain, R. (2019). The troubling legacy of Francis Galton. *Significance, 16*(3), 16–21. https://doi.org/10.1111/j.1740-9713.2019.01275.x

Lumley, T., Diehr, P., Emerson, S., & Chen, L. (2002). The importance of the normality assumption in large public health data sets. *Annual Review of Public Health, 23*, 151–169. https://doi.org/10.1146/annurev.publhealth.23.100901.140546

Martorano, B., Natali, L., De Neubourg, C., & Bradshaw, J. (2014). Child well-being in advanced economies in the late 2000s. *Social Indicators Research, 118*(1), 247–283. https://doi.org/10.1007/s11205-013-0402-z

Pickett, K. E., & Wilkinson, R. G. (2007). Child wellbeing and income inequality in rich societies: Ecological cross sectional study. *British Medical Journal, 335*(7629), 1080–1084. https://doi.org/10.1136/bmj.39377.580162.55

Rabe-Hesketh, S., & Skrondal, A. (2012a). *Multilevel and longitudinal modeling using Stata: Vol. I. Continuous responses* (3rd ed.). Stata Press.

Rabe-Hesketh, S., & Skrondal, A. (2012b). *Multilevel and longitudinal modeling using Stata: Vol. II. Categorical responses, counts, and survival* (3rd ed.). Stata Press.

Ranehill, E., Dreber, A., Johannesson, M., Leiberg, S., Sul, S., & Weber, R. A. (2015). Assessing the robustness of power posing. *Psychological Science, 26*(5), 653–656. https://doi.org/10.1177/0956797614553946

Revelle, W. (2020). *How to: Use the psych package for factor analysis and data reduction.* http://personality-project.org/r/psych/HowTo/factor.pdf

Rowntree, D. (1981). *Statistics without tears. A primer for non-mathematicians.* Penguin.

Royston, P., & Sauerbrei, W. (2008). *Multivariate model-building: A pragmatic approach to regression analysis based on fractional polynomials for modelling continuous variables.* Wiley.

Silver, N. (2012). *The signal and the noise: The art and science of prediction.* Penguin.

Tabachnick, B. G., & Fidell, L. S. (2013). *Using multivariate statistics* (6th ed.). Pearson.

Todorov, T. (1993). *On human diversity: Nationalism, racism, and exoticism in French thought*. Harvard University Press.

UK Government. (n.d.). *What qualification levels mean*. Retrieved February 11, 2020, from www.gov.uk/what-different-qualification-levels-mean/list-of-qualification-levels

Ulmer, J. T., & Steffensmeier, D. (2015). The age and crime relationship: Social variation, social explanations. In K. M. Beaver, J. C. Barnes, & B. B. Boutwell (Eds.), *The nurture versus biosocial debate in criminology: On the origins of criminal behavior and criminality* (pp. 377–396). Sage. https://doi.org/10.4135/9781483349114.n24

Williams, R. (2015, February 15). *Suppressor effects*. www3.nd.edu/~rwilliam/stats2/l35.pdf

Wood, S. N. (2006). *Generalized additive models: An introduction with R*. Chapman & Hall.

INDEX

Page numbers in *italic* indicate figures and in **bold** indicate tables.

additive scales, *71*, 76
adjusted R^2-statistic, 139–41
analysis of variance (ANOVA), 157–8
analysis of variance (ANOVA) table, 131–2, **132**, 134, **134**, **140**
assumptions of linear regression, 52–70
  collinearity and multicollinearity, 141–4, **143**
  homoscedasticity of errors, 52–3, *54*, 61–4, *63*, 144–6, *145*
  independence of errors, 53, 70
  influential observations and outliers, 53, 64–70, *66*, *68*, *69*, *145*, 146–7, **146**
  linearity, 52, *54*, 61–4, *63*, 144–6, *145*
  for multiple linear regression, 141–8, **143**, *145*, **146**
  normality of errors, 52, *54*, 56–60, *58*, *59*, *60*, 61, 144, *145*
  predictors have no measurement errors, 53
  randomness of errors, 53
  see also variable transformations

Bayesian statistical models, 160
beta coefficients, 153
binary variables, 25, 156

Carney, D. R., 7, 14
categorical variables, 18, 156
  dummy variables for, 94, 117–22, **118**, *119*, **120**, **122**, 151
causality, 21, 89, 92, 93, 160–1
central limit theorem, 57
centring, 83
climate change, 105
clustering, 70
coefficient of determination *see* R^2-statistic
coefficients *see* intercept and slope
collinearity, 141–4, **143**
confidence intervals, 38–9, **38**, **127**, 128
confidence range for regression line, 39–41, *40*, 42
confounding variables, 88–90, *89*, *90*
continuous variables, 18, 157
Cook's distance, 67–8, *68*, *69*, 70, 146–7
correlation coefficients *see* Pearson correlation
count variables, 157

data subgroup selection, 46–7, *46*
degrees of freedom, 37, 128, 129, 132, **132**, 133, **134**, 137–8, **138**, 139, **140**
dependency, 70, 159
dependent variables *see* outcome variables
deterministic models, 2–3, 24
dichotomous variables, 25, 156
discrete variables, 18
Down syndrome, 89
dummy variables, 94, 117–22, **118**, *119*, **120**, **122**, 151

Edinburgh–Warwick Mental Wellbeing Scale, 99
Elliott, J. *see* mental wellbeing example
errors, 9, 54
  measurement errors, 14–15, 53
  proportional reduction of error, 31–2
  random variation and, 24–5
  residual standard error, 33, 97
  standard errors, 13, 35–6, 40–1, 126–8, **127**
estimating a model, 25–6, 27–9
eugenics, 20
Euler's number, 74, **75**
explanatory variables *see* predictor variables
exposure *see* predictor variables
extrapolation, 47–9, *48*

F-distribution, 133–4, *133*
F-test, 132–4, *133*, **134**, 137–9, **138**
factor analysis, 161
factorial design experiments, 157–8
Fisher distribution, 133–4, *133*
fitting a model, 25–6, 27–9
fractional polynomials, 158

Galton, Francis, 18, 20, 35
  see also inheritance of height example
gamma distribution, 157
gamma regression, 157
Gapminder Foundation *see* life expectancy and GDP example
GDP *see* life expectancy and GDP example
generalised additive models (GAM), 159

generalised linear models (GLMs), 157
Gini coefficient, 4–5, *4*
goodness of fit *see* model fit

Hamilton, L.C., 105
heredity *see* inheritance of height example
heteroscedasticity, 52–3
histograms, 58, *58, 59*
homoscedasticity of errors assumption, 52–3, *54*, 61–4, *63*, 144–6, *145*
hypothesis testing *see* *F*-test; *t*-test

independence of errors assumption, 53, 70
independent variables *see* predictor variables
inference, 35
   adjusted R^2-statistic, 139–41
   analysis of variance (ANOVA) table, 131–2, **132**, 134, **134**, **140**
   for coefficients in multiple regression, 126–31, **127**, **130**
   confidence intervals, 38–9, **38**, **127**, 128
   confidence range for regression line, 39–41, *40*, 42
   F-test, 132–4, *133*, **134**, 137–9, **138**
   model comparison in multiple regression, 135–41, **138**, **140**
   prediction intervals, 42–4, *43*
   standard errors, 13, 35–6, 40–1, 126–8, **127**
   see also *t*-test
inferential statistics, 38, **38**
influential observations and outliers, 45–6, *45*, 53, 64–70, **66**, *68*, *69*, *145*, 146–7, **146**
inheritance of height example, 18–20, **19**, *19*
   confidence intervals, 38–9, **38**
   confidence range for regression line, 39–41, *40*, 42
   errors of prediction and random variation, 24–5
   goodness of fit, 32–3
   histogram of standardised residuals, 58, *58*
   homoscedasticity assumption, 53, *54*
   influential observations and outliers, 64, 66, **66**, 67–9, *68*, *69*
   intercept and slope, 22, 24, 28–9
   interpretation of results, 33–5, *34*
   normal q–q plot of standardised residuals, 58–60, *60*
   normality assumption, 53, *54*
   prediction and prediction intervals, 42–4, *43*
   proportional reduction of error, 32
   R^2-statistic, 32–3
   regression line, 21–3, *22*, 24, 28–9
   residual standard error, 33
   residuals, 26–7, *27*, 28
   spread-level plot of standardised residuals, 61, *62*
   standard error, 35–6
   t-test, 36–9, **38**
interactions
   defined, 104–5
   standardisation and, 151–2
intercept and slope
   multiple linear regression, 96–7
   simple linear regression, 22, 23–4, *23*, 28–9
inverse transformations, 80, 83, 84

least squares, 28–9, 97
leverage, 55, 66–7

life expectancy and GDP example, 5, *6*, 15, 46–9, *46*, *48*
   see also logarithmic transformation of GDP example
linear relationships, 4–5, *4*
linearity assumption, 52, *54*, 61–4, *63*, 144–6, *145*
   see also logarithmic transformation of GDP example
log-normal distribution, 81
logarithmic transformation of GDP example, 71–9
   non-linear relationship of data, 71–3, *71*, **72**, *73*
   regression diagnostics, 73, *73*, 79, *79*
   transformation technique, 73–8, **75**, **76**, *76*, **77**, *78*
logarithmic transformations, 80–2, *81*, 83, 84
   see also logarithmic transformation of GDP example
logarithms, 74–5, **75**
logistic regression, 156, 157

masked relationships, *91*, 92
mean-centred variables, 83
mean squares, 132, **132**, **134**, 137–8, 139, 140, **140**
measurement errors, 14–15, 53
measurement models, 161
mental wellbeing example, 93–5, *94*
   adjusted R^2-statistic, 140–1
   analysis of variance (ANOVA) table, 134, **134**, **140**
   causality, 93, 116, 160–1
   confidence intervals, **127**, 128
   F-test, 137–8, **138**
   Fisher distribution, 133–4, *133*
   homoscedasticity assumption, 144–6, *145*
   influential observations and outliers, *145*, 146–7, **146**
   linearity assumption, 144–6, *145*
   model with dummy variables, 94, 118–22, *119*, **120**, **122**, 151
   model with one numeric and one dichotomous predictor, 98–107, *98*, *100*, **101**, *101*
   model with two numeric predictors, 107–13, *108*, **109**, *110*, *111*, **112**, *113*
   multicollinearity, 143–4, **143**
   normality assumption, 144, *145*
   regression diagnostics, 144–8, *145*, **146**
   standard errors, 127–8, **127**
   standardisation of coefficients, 148–52, **148–9**, **150–1**
   t-test, 129–30, **130**
   unadjusted and adjusted models, 113–17, **114–15**, *116*
   variance inflation factor (VIF), 143–4, **143**
mind–body connection *see* power pose example
missing values, 42, 159–60
mixed effects models, 70, 159
model comparison in multiple regression, 135–41, **138**, **140**
model fit
   multiple linear regression, 132–4, *133*, 135, 137–41, **138**, **140**
   simple linear regression, 29–33, *31*
multicollinearity, 141–4, **143**
multilevel models, 70, 159
multiple imputation, 159–60

multiple linear regression, 88–123, 126–53
  adjusted R²-statistic, 139–41
  analysis of variance (ANOVA) table, 131–2, **132**, 134, **134**, **140**
  assumptions, 141–8, **143**, *145*, **146**
  collinearity and multicollinearity, 141–4, **143**
  confidence intervals, **127**, 128
  confounding variables, 88–90, *89*, *90*
  dummy variables for categorical predictors, 94, 117–22, **118**, *119*, **120**, **122**, 151
  F-test, 132–4, *133*, **134**, 137–9, **138**
  general definition, 96–7
  inference about coefficients, 126–31, **127**, **130**
  influential observations and outliers, *145*, 146–7, **146**
  interactions defined, 104–5
  intercept and slope, 96–7
  masked relationships, *91*, *92*
  model comparison, 135–41, **138**, **140**
  model fit, 132–4, *133*, 135, 137–41, **138**, **140**
  model with one numeric and one dichotomous predictor, 98–107, *98*, *100*, **101**, *101*
  model with two numeric predictors, 107–13, *108*, **109**, *110*, *111*, **112**, *113*
  multivariate relationships, 93–5, *94*
  nested and non-nested models, 135–41, **138**, **140**
  purposes, 88
  R²-statistic, 97
  reference categories for dummy variables, 118, 119, 121, 122
  regression diagnostics, 144–8, *145*, **146**
  residual standard error, 97
  spurious relationships, 90, *90*
  standard errors, 126–8, **127**
  standardisation of coefficients, 148–53, **148–9**, **150–1**
  suppressor variables, 91–2, *91*
  t-test, 128–31, **130**
  unadjusted and adjusted models, 113–17, **114–15**, *116*
  variance inflation factor (VIF), 142–4, **143**
multiplicative scales, 74, 76–7, *76*

National Child Development Study (NCDS), UK *see* mental wellbeing example
natural logarithms, 74, **75**
negative binomial regression, 157
nested and non-nested models, 135–41, **138**, **140**
noise and signal, 14–15
nominal variables, 156
non-linear relationships, 5, *6*
  generalised additive models (GAM), 159
  see also logarithmic transformation of GDP example
non-normal error distributions, 156–7
normal distribution, 56–7, *57*, 64–5, *65*
normal quantile–quantile plots (q–q plots), 58–60, *60*, *61*, 144, *145*, 146
normality of errors assumption, 52, *54*, 56–60, *58*, *59*, *60*, *61*, 144, *145*
numeric variables, 18

ordinal variables, 156
ordinary least squares (OLS) regression, 28–9, 97
outcome variables
  defined, 10, 18, 21
  logarithmic transformation of, *81*, *82*
outliers and influential observations, 45–6, *45*, 53, 64–70, **66**, *68*, *69*, *145*, 146–7, **146**

parsimony, 135, 139, 140
Pearson correlation, 5, 20, 29, 33
Poisson regression, 157
power pose example, 6–14, *8*, **11**
prediction intervals, 42–4, *43*
predictor variables
  defined, 10, 18, 21
  logarithmic transformations of, 81–2, *81*
  quadratic transformations of, *81*, 83
proportional reduction of error, 31–2

q–q plots (normal quantile–quantile plots), 58–60, *60*, *61*, 144, *145*, 146
quadratic transformations, *81*, 83
quantile regression, 158

R²-statistic, 29–33, *31*, 97
  adjusted, 139–41
randomness of errors assumption, 53
reference categories for dummy variables, 118, 119, 121, 122
regression diagnostics, 54–6
  Cook's distance, 67–8, *68*, *69*, 70, 146–7
  histograms, 58, *58*, *59*
  homoscedasticity assumption, 61–4, *63*, 144–6, *145*
  independence assumption, 70
  influential observations and outliers, 64–70, **66**, *68*, *69*, *145*, 146–7, **146**
  linearity assumption, 61–4, *63*, 144–6, *145*
  for multiple linear regression, 144–8, *145*, **146**
  normal quantile–quantile plots, 58–60, *60*, *61*, 144, *145*, 146
  normality assumption, 56–60, *58*, *59*, *60*, *61*, 144, *145*
  spread-level plots, 61–4, *62*, *63*, 144–6, *145*
  uncertainty and, 59
regression sum of squares, 30, *30*
regression to the mean, 35, 37, 38
residual standard error, 33, 97
residual sum of squares, 30, *30*, 138, 139
residuals, 26–7, *27*, 28, 54–5
  see also standardised residuals
response *see* outcome variables
Richter scale, 74

Saito, K., 105
signal and noise, 14–15
simple linear regression, 18–49
  confidence intervals, 38–9, **38**
  confidence range for regression line, 39–41, *40*, 42
  data subgroup selection, 46–7, *46*
  errors of prediction and random variation, 24–5
  extrapolation dangers, 47–9, *48*
  fitting a model, 25–6, *27*–9

influential observations, 45–6, *45*
intercept and slope, 22, 23–4, *23*, 28–9
interpretation of results, 33–5, *34*
model fit, 29–33, *31*
origins of, 18–20, **19**, *19*, 33–5, *34*
prediction and prediction intervals, 42–4, *43*
proportional reduction of error, 31–2
R^2-statistic, 29–33, *31*
regression line, 21–4, *22*, *23*, 26, *27*–9
residual standard error, 33
residuals, 26–7, *27*, 28
standard error, 35–6, 40–1
sums of squares, 29–30, *30*
t-test, 35–9, **38**
true and estimated models, 25–6
slope *see* intercept and slope
spread-level plots, 61–4, *62*, *63*, 144–6, *145*
spurious relationships, 90, *90*
square root transformations, 83, 84
square transformations, 80, *81*, 83
standard errors, 13, 35–6, 40–1, 126–8, **127**
residual standard error, 33, 97
standard normal distribution, 56–7, *57*, 64–5, *65*
standardisation of coefficients, 148–53, **148–9, 150–1**
standardised residuals, 55–6
histograms, 58, *58*, *59*
homoscedasticity assumption, 61–4, *63*, 144–6, *145*
influential observations and outliers, 64–70, **66**, *68*, *69*, *145*, 146–7, **146**
linearity assumption, 61–4, *63*, 144–6, *145*
normal quantile–quantile plots, 58–60, *60*, *61*, 144, *145*, 146
normality assumption, 56–60, *58*, *59*, *60*, *61*, 144, *145*
spread-level plots, 61–4, *62*, *63*, 144–6, *145*
uncertainty and, 59
statistical models, 2–3
linear and non-linear relationships, 4–5, *4*, *6*
signal and noise, 14–15
uses of, 3–4
structural equation models, 53, 161
sums of squares, 29–30, *30*, 132, **132**, **134**, 137–8, **138**, 139, 140, **140**
suppressor variables, 91–2, *91*
Sure Start programme, 92

t-test
assumptions, 13
inheritance of height example, 36–9, **38**
mental wellbeing example, 129–30, **130**
multiple linear regression, 128–31, **130**
power pose example, 6–14, *8*, **11**
simple linear regression, 36–9, **38**
total sum of squares, 29–30, *30*
transformations *see* variable transformations

UNICEF index of child wellbeing, 4–5, *4*

variable transformations, 52, 71, 79–85
choosing, 83–5
cubic, 83
fractional polynomials and, 158
identifying suitable, 80, 158
inverse, 80, 83, 84
logarithmic, 80–2, *81*, 83, 84
quadratic, *81*, 83
reflected, 84–5
square, 80, *81*, 83
square root, 83, 84
see also logarithmic transformation of GDP example
variables
confounding, 88–90, *89*, *90*
continuous, 18, 157
count, 157
dichotomous, 25, 156
discrete, 18
dummy, 94, 117–22, **118**, *119*, **120**, **122**, 151
mean-centred, 83
nominal, 156
numeric, 18
ordinal, 156
suppressor, 91–2, *91*
see also categorical variables; outcome variables; predictor variables
variance inflation factor (VIF), 142–4, **143**

x-standardisation of coefficients, 150–1, **150–1**, 152
xy-standardisation of coefficients, 150–1, **150–1**, 152, 153

y-standardisation of coefficients, 150–1, **150–1**

z-standardisation of coefficients, 150